A Safe Place

A Safe Place

Place

THE STORY OF A FATHER, A SON, A MURDER

Lorenzo Carcaterra

VILLARD BOOKS   NEW YORK   1993

ISBN 0-679-40282-9

Book design by Susan Hood

THIS IS FOR MY MOTHER AND FATHER

AND FOR SUSAN

ACKNOWLEDGMENTS

There are several dozen people whose help enabled me to finish my father's story, their memories providing pieces of the family puzzle. For their separate reasons, they have asked to remain anonymous.

I am grateful for the storytelling abilities of both my parents, thankful for the small details they added to each tale and for the time they gave to my many questions.

Thanks to David Hirshey for first planting the idea; to Jay Lovinger and Peter Bonventre for nourishing it as a *Life* magazine article; and to Jim Gaines for publishing it.

Thanks also to Loretta Fidel for seeing beyond the story, and to the dynamic duo of Adam Berkowitz and Amy Schiffman for their intelligence and care. Thanks to Irene Webb for her words of cheer and keen insights.

Thanks to Peter Gethers for being the dream editor all writers look for, and to Stephanie Long, who never tired of answering every one of my questions, even the dumb ones.

There are many others, from Pete Hamill, who took the time long ago to encourage a New York *Daily News* copyboy, to Dick Burgheim, who taught his Time, Inc., writers to keep it short and sharp, and to Jack Sanders, who told me to always write, no matter how painful.

Acknowledgments

A big thank-you to William Diehl, a friend from the heart, and to my blood brother Eugene Izzi.

Another big thank-you to Sonny Grosso and the crew at *Top Cops*—especially Liz Wagner and Johnny Garage—who helped in more ways than they know.

Thanks to Mr. G for a heart as big as the Hudson, to Laurie Prencipe for taking care of business, and to Hank Gallo for always being there.

Thanks to my daughter, Kate, for putting up with me during the months I worked on this book and to my son, Nick, for the smiles he gave when the going was less than easy. Thanks to my wife just for understanding.

Also, thanks, Cicco, Bam-Bam, Big Dan, Bobby, Paolo and Little T. Don't have to tell you why. See you at the feast.

PROLOGUE

I was fourteen, walking on a beach in Ischia, a Mediterranean island forty miles off the coast of Naples, when I found out about my father. A white cotton towel hung around my neck, the morning sun warmed my back and soft waves rolled against a pea-green fishing boat. A cluster of children were building sand castles by the shore while three German tourists nodded in approval. It was mid-July 1969, my first summer away from home and the most peaceful time in my life.

My mother, slumped and weary, stood at my side, staring out to sea. She hardly noticed the Moroccan merchant who was offering good buys on cheap goods or the beach bum selling cool slices of fresh coconut. She reached for my hand, her brown eyes softened by the passing years.

"It's time you knew the truth," she said. "About your father."

"What about him?"

"His first wife," she said. "She didn't die of cancer."

"How did she die?"

"He murdered her."

*   *   *

My mother's words struck with the force of an ax. I stared at her, making sure that what she said was real, that the sudden anger and confusion inside me was justified. With tears streaming down her tanned face, she kissed me on the cheek and walked away. I sat at the water's edge, shivering in the sun, the towel wrapped tight around my shoulders. I stayed there well into the evening, looking out at quiet waters, thinking about my father.

I imagined his face before me and tried to picture him during his moment of violence. Through the years, I had learned to live with my father's vicious rage, choosing the easier route of acceptance, never once believing he would ever take his ugly side further than a certain number of hard slaps and painful punches. Ever take it past the limit of murder. Not with me. Not with my mother. Not with someone he loved.

I loved my father. We were inseparable, united by both friendship and blood. Now, in the small space of a few hours, those feelings had been forever altered, all because my father murdered a woman I had never met. For the first time in my memory, the thought of my father frightened me.

The sea was calm most of that day, low waves beating against soft edges of the beach. I dug my feet into the wet sand and turned my face toward the water's spray, my mind armed with dozens of unanswered questions. Why did my father kill his wife? What could she have said or done that would have sped his rage to its blindest point? How did he do it? When? Where? What happened after he killed her? If he did it, why wasn't he still in jail? Why was he free, with a wife, a son and a job, passing time as if nothing sinister had ever happened?

I knew I would have to learn all I could about the murder and its aftermath, though I didn't know then how difficult that would be. I didn't know about all the relatives and neighbors I would have to confront, or all the lies and deceptions I would have to overcome.

I didn't know when the eventual showdown with my father would take place, or even if I would survive it.

During that long day on that bright beach more than four thousand miles from home, I had no idea that my father's crime was destined to reach into every part of my life. How could I have known that one day I would have to tell the woman I wanted to marry that there was a terrible stain on my family—then look into her eyes for signs of fear? I had no way of knowing then how the murder would affect me as a father, or how it would touch the lives of my own children.

I didn't know back then how very much like my father I was and what a burden that knowledge, and the fear behind it, would carry. Most of all, I didn't know if I could ever answer the question I feared everyone would always be asking: Was I as capable as my father was of murdering someone close to me?

All I knew was that my father was a murderer and that I needed somehow to find the truth behind the man and the murder.

It would take nineteen years. What began on a warm day on a beach in Ischia would end on the cold, cloudy morning of November 8, 1988, with my father's death. He was seventy-one years old, and the last five months of his life had been painful to watch. The spreading bone cancer had taken away the use of his legs. A mild form of dementia had set in, making lucid conversation difficult and brief. The muscles around his face sagged, his eyes were sunken, and his voice had wilted to a harsh whisper. His weight had dropped, his arms were brittle to the touch, and his entire body was smeared with droplets of cold sweat. His was now the body of a tired and dying old man who bore no resemblance to the father I had feared for so long.

My father had left me with a number of final requests.

"I don't want to be buried," he said. "No rats are gonna eat off of me. Burn me. Understand? Burn me. It's fast and easy. Don't put me in any vault either. I hate feelin' closed in."

He wanted my mother to be told how sorry he was for the troubled decades he had given her.

"You're better with the words than I am," he said. "She listens to you. She doesn't believe me anymore. I try telling her myself, but I cry when I see her."

Some days I would visit his hospital room and stare at him for hours, sadly watching his once-powerful body give up the fight. The lower half of his face would droop against his right shoulder, spittle forming at the corners of his lips. He would look at me and smile.

"This is what you wanted, isn't it, fucko?" he would say. "This is what you stayed up nights prayin' over. At least your prayers were answered."

Other days, I could stand to stay near him for only a few minutes, dropping off the tabloids that would remain unread on his night table and the fruit that would remain uneaten near his dinner tray, then walking away.

"Can't stomach it, can you, fucko?" he would shout then. "Can't watch me die, can you?"

I would rush for the elevator banks, head down, hoping to avoid the concerned gaze of the nurses who cared for my father.

He was right. I couldn't stand to watch him die. I had prayed for his death on so many nights over so many years, and yet, when it came close, I wanted death to leave him alone. There was no victory in his suffering, no satisfaction in his end. My anger at him remained, perhaps stronger than it had ever been, but so, too, did a sadness, for with the death of this old man, I would not only lose my most bitter enemy, but a trusted friend. It was what the bookies in the old neighborhood called a push.

One morning, close to the end, my father, chewing on half a grapefruit, signaled me to come closer.

"You always wanted to know about my life," he said. "Why?"

"It's important to me."

"Why?"

"I can't really explain it. It's important, that's all."

"Gonna write about it?"

"Maybe. I never thought about it."

"Will they pay you if you write about me?"

"Someone might."

He looked away, out the window of his tenth-floor room, thinking back to hundreds of scams, dozens of cons, all planned against the fear of work. His biggest regret, which had gone unspoken between us, was that he would die and not have any money to leave me or, more important, my two children. In fact, there was still more than four thousand dollars in debts that needed to be paid.

"How much?" he asked. "How much would someone give you to write about me?"

"Dad, please."

"How much?"

"I don't know."

"A million?"

"What?"

"Would someone pay a million for my story?"

I looked in his eyes, saw them alert and alive for the first time in months, saw his breathing come easier, his hands tense with excitement and realized that, to my father, having someone get paid to tell his story could only be the ultimate scam. Especially if that someone was his son.

"Would someone pay a million for my story?"

"It's possible."

He reached out his hand for me to shake. I took it.

"I'll never lie to you again," he said.

"About anything?"

"I swear on your mother."

"Even about the murder."

He took a deep breath. I could hear the rasping in his chest, the cancer having weaved its way to his lungs.

"Yeah," he said. "Even about the murder."

He held my hand tighter, the grip a stranger to what it once was. We were inches apart, dead man's breath leaving his open mouth.

"Take your best shot, fucko," he said. "Give it all you got. Just do what I didn't do."

"What's that?"

"Tell the truth. I don't care who gets hurt. You hear me, fucko? Tell the truth."

On my next visit I brought my father two slices of watermelon, a Hershey bar with almonds and the *Daily Racing Form*. I walked quietly down the hospital corridor toward his room. I stopped at the door, waiting as a nurse finished changing his sheets, fluffing his pillows and adjusting his bed. She was short, pudgy, a middle-aged Jamaican woman with a sing-song voice and a cheerful manner. She saw me standing by the half-open door, reading my father's medical chart.

"Come in, young fellow," she said. "I'm about finished."

She reached for my father's hand and stroked it.

"I'm going to leave you, Mario," she said. "You don't need me anymore. Your son is here."

"What time's dinner?" my father asked.

"Soon," she said.

She looked at me.

"He barely finishes one meal before he asks about the next," she said. "I tell you."

"He's too old to change," I said.

The nurse turned toward my father and winked.

"See you later, handsome," she said.

She walked toward me and reached for my arm, a wide smile across her face.

"I'm so happy for you," she said in a whisper.

"Why?"

"Your father told me," she said. "About leaving you the million dollars. I think it's wonderful. You are so lucky to have a father like him."

I looked over her shoulder at my father, sitting in bed and smiling at both of us.

"Such a good man," she said, walking out of the room. "Such a good man."

My father's body was cremated on November 11, and a memorial Mass was held two days later. Following the service and the customary cookies, coffee and small talk with friends and family, I bundled up my children and took them for a walk in the park. We headed for a playground, the same one my parents had taken me to when I was a child. I put my son, Nick, then two, in a swing and watched as his sister, Kate, then six, gave him a few strong pushes. I leaned against a pole and watched them both.

Kate looked at me, stopped pushing her brother and came by my side.

"I need a tissue, Dad," she said.

I pulled one out of my coat pocket and bent down to rub her nose. She reached out and hugged me.

"Sorry about Grandpa," she said.

The remark caught me off guard.

"I'm sorry, too," I said.

"What did he die of?"

"Cancer."

She went back to pushing her brother.

"Is that bad?" she asked.

"Yes, very bad."

"Did you send him flowers?"

"No. No I didn't."

"Why not?"

"He didn't like flowers."

"Oh."

She pushed her brother as high as the swing would take him, his legs stretched out against the cold wind, a smile locked across his face. I watched them, grateful for the inner warmth they provided.

Nick tired of the swing about the same time Kate tired of pushing him. I reached for my son's outstretched arms, and together the three of us continued our walk.

We made our way past the near-empty carousel, the music from its shell resonating through the park.

"Grandpa used to bring me here every weekend," I said to my daughter. "Once gave me a five-dollar bill and told me to ride until the money ran out."

"How long it take?" Kate asked.

"Long time," I said. "Most of the afternoon."

"Did you like it?"

"Almost threw up, I was so dizzy," I said. "But I liked it. Liked being with him even more."

"Mom says you and Grandpa look alike," Kate said.

"A lot of people say that."

A soccer game was in full swing on a hard dirt field to our left, played in front of a scattering of homeless men and women sitting on park benches, their eyes staring blanks, their lower lips mumbling words. Nick was asleep inside his stroller, his head leaning to one side, a half-empty bottle of apple juice still clutched in one hand.

"Did I ever meet Grandpa?" Kate asked.

"A long time ago," I said. "When you were Nick's age."

"Did he like me?"

"Very much," I said. "He used to call you Doll-face. He loved to hear you laugh. Always talked about it."

"What was he like?" she asked.

I bent down and scooped Kate into one arm, pushing Nick and the stroller with my free hand.

"You ask a lot of questions," I said, kissing her on one cheek.

"Please tell me," she said. "What was Grandpa like?"

"He was just a dad," I said. "Better than most, maybe, but just a dad."

"Like you," Kate said.

"What?"

"A dad just like you," she said.

"That's right," I said. "Grandpa was a dad. Just like me."

I walked out of the park and onto Central Park West, heading for home, my daughter still clutched to my side.

Book One

I TOLD YOU ONCE, RYAN, IF ONLY ONE GETS OUT
IT'S A VICTORY.

—Trevor Howard to Frank Sinatra in
Von Ryan's Express.

I

The first closed fist landed just below my mother's jaw. The second hit flush against her upper lip. The blow's force bounced her head off the bedroom wall. My father raised his right arm, ready to strike again. His left arm was stretched out, his hand clutching chunks of my mother's apron and housedress. His eyes were wide open and filled with rage, his face the color of chalk.

My mother stood helpless, waiting for the next painful shot. Her legs were buckled, both knees rubbing each other, as one black slipper hung off her foot. A thin stream of red blood moved from her nose to her chin, and tears flowed from both her eyes.

The right side of her face was already starting to swell. Her dark-tinted glasses, opened and shattered, rested between her chest and my father's left arm. The next blow landed over her right eye, raising an immediate welt. My father was all that kept my mother from falling to the floor.

He stared hard at her face, the anger starting to dissipate from his body. His muscles began to relax, a natural redness returning to his fleshy cheeks.

"Don't fuck with me, *puttana*," he said to my mother. "If I see you talking to him again, I'll cripple you. Nobody is gonna talk about me behind my back."

"He just stopped to say hello," my mother said to him in Italian. "His sister and I were close friends. His ship is in port for a few days and he knew I lived close by. He was bringing news from home. That's all. I swear. That's all."

"Did you go with him?" he said, still holding a strong grip to her dress and apron. "Did you, you fuckin' bitch?"

My mother, her English still weak, shook her head, confused by the question.

"No," she said. "No. I didn't go anywhere with him."

My father looked down at his wife, took a deep breath and spit in her eyes. He turned and tossed her face down on the bed behind him.

"I'm gonna go see my mother," he said. "Have dinner ready when I get back."

My father walked past me, rubbed my head, kissed me on the forehead and headed out the front door of our three-room cold-water tenement apartment.

It was four-thirty on the afternoon of January 9, 1956. My mother's thirty-fourth birthday. I was two years and three months old, sitting atop an old steamer trunk that doubled as both playpen and bed, holding a discarded box of Ronzoni No. 9 spaghetti. Watching my father beat my mother is the earliest memory I have of my parents together.

My parents first met on the island of Ischia in the summer of 1938.

Italy was then in the sixteenth year of Benito Mussolini's dictatorial rule and enjoying an economic revival. Overall, prices were low, the lira strong and work available in abundance. Resort islands such as Ischia and Capri were thriving, with hotels filled to capacity and beaches packed with sun-hungry tourists.

Though talk of a possible world war made many of the islanders nervous, the sight of so many visitors eager to spend vacation money on their shores helped ease the tension.

"Ischia was such a safe place to be then," my grandmother Maria once told me. "The thought of war was in the distance, something for politicians in Rome to fight over. In Ischia, as in all of Italy, it was a time for peace."

My parents were first cousins. They were introduced to each other by their aunt Nanella, oldest sister to my father's mother, Raffaela, and my mother's father, Gabriel.

My mother, also named Raffaela, was sixteen at the time. She was of short-to-medium height, with thick and curly dark hair, full red lips and a shy smile.

My father, Mario, was twenty-one and visiting Italy for the first time. His face was expressive and handsome, his body boxer hard and his dark brown hair beginning a slide toward baldness. He had been on the island less than a week and was already boasting to strangers and friends of having "ruined three girls."

My mother wiped her hand nervously on the side of her light blue skirt and shook my father's extended hand. My father leaned down and awkwardly kissed my mother on both sides of her face. He smiled when he saw her blush.

"Relax, honey. I'll never hurt you" were the first words he said to her. He spoke a poor version of Italian as he made an attempt to ask my mother to a movie. She looked to her aunt for help and said "no" once she understood the request.

"Okay," my father said. "Maybe tomorrow."

He stared at her as she and Nanella walked away, heading toward the deli the Carcaterra family owned and operated.

"He's a good-looking young man," Nanella said, holding on to my mother's arm. "He's wild, but name someone who isn't at that age."

They walked quietly for a few moments, the older woman careful not to trip on the slippery cobblestone street. Nanella stopped a few feet from the deli entrance and turned to her young niece.

"So, bella," she said, "what do you think of our wild boy? Do you like him?"

"He scares me," my mother said.

After that initial meeting my parents would not see each other again for fifteen years. Much would happen to both during that time, most of it tragic. My mother was, by the fall of 1953, a thirty-one-year-old widow, raising a sullen eleven-year-old son with help from

5

her family. A six-month-old son and a policeman husband lay buried in the soft soil of the Northern Italian province of Udine, two silent World War II victims.

That war and those deaths had altered my mother's physical appearance considerably—her hair and body had thinned out, her eyes were sunken and sad, her walk slowed and her once-sharp sense of humor all but vanquished.

She wore only the widow's black, having handed over the multi-colored skirts and dresses she once favored to her youngest sister, Nancy. She ate little, spoke even less and attended church on a daily basis.

"*Casa e ciesa,*" my mother's sister Anna said. "Home and church. That's all she cared about. It was the only life she knew. As far as anyone was concerned, Raffaela had no plans of ever getting married again, especially not to a man like your father."

My father arrived in Ischia on a lemon boat. He had $175 rolled up in the zippered pocket of a dark brown windbreaker and kept another $50 tucked inside a shoe. He was thirty-six years old, slightly overweight, bald and less than six months removed from the maximum security facility at Comstock in upstate New York. He had with him one piece of luggage, a small, blue hand-held valise. Inside were two black sport shirts, a gray sweater, two pairs of brown slacks, three large Hershey's chocolate bars and a blue dress with a small white floral design. The dress was a gift for my mother, the woman my father had come to Ischia to marry.

On his second night on the island, my father sat next to my mother in the white-walled dining room of her parents' home, working his way through a second large bowl of pasta. He had wasted little time in stating his intentions, announcing to all who would listen that he had been in love with my mother for quite some time. It was not until now, he explained, that he felt he was in a strong enough financial position to give her the kind of life she would feel comfortable with in America.

He spoke to them about large apartments and large cars, big salaries and long vacations. He told them about trips he'd taken to faraway places, places they had never heard of nor even knew existed. He promised my mother the world and her son the universe and not one of those trusting people, sitting around a table crammed with food and drink, ever once doubted him. My father was family to them. There was never a reason to think he was telling anything but the truth.

His timing was perfect. My grandfather Gabriel lay in a Naples hospital dying of stomach cancer. The growing medical bills were a drain on family finances, and my mother felt she and her son would further deplete what few funds existed. She was also a lonely woman who longed for a change, who was desperate to get away from what had become tedious day-to-day rituals. She had enjoyed her six married years in Salerno and Udine, miles away from the locked-in mentality of Ischia, and was excited by the thought of living in America.

My mother was also well aware of what the change would mean for her son, Antonio. The boy was shy and withdrawn, seldom spoke and never smiled. While he was surrounded by doting aunts and uncles, it was clear the boy needed a father, someone he could look to for guidance. She knew he wasn't suited, either physically or mentally, for the careers often selected by Ischia's young men.

She didn't quite see her son behind the wheel of a tourist bus, nor did she feel he would find happiness as a merchant seaman. Like most mothers she wanted better. She thought she would find better in America.

My parents were married on January 18, 1954, in a quiet ceremony, one devoid of flowers, music, photos and any outward displays of emotion. My mother wore a navy blue suit over a cream silk blouse. My father wore a borrowed tie, and fidgeted during the fourteen minutes it took to become a married man for the second time. He had on one of his black sport shirts, the short sleeves covered by a jacket on loan from a family friend. He appeared angry and distracted.

My mother cried and held on to a railing, barely listening to the monotone words of a sickly priest performing the ceremony. My father hardly knew his best man, while my mother's maid of honor had spent the previous evening trying to get the wedding postponed.

Off in a corner, his head bowed in silence, Antonio fought back tears, afraid for his mother and for his own future.

"I never understood it," he said years later. "No one did, really. The marriage just seemed to happen. They weren't in love, you could see that just by looking at them. I don't know why either one of them ever did it. I don't even think they knew why either."

In place of a reception, there was a quiet dinner cooked by my grandmother and attended by a somber group of family members. The mood was tense, hardly conducive to a festive occasion. My father ate little of his meal and drank more than his normal share of red wine. He left the table at one point, walked out the front door, stood on the top step, bowed his head and sobbed openly.

My mother stared out at him from the open kitchen window. She was pouring olive oil onto a large tomato, basil and red onion salad and was herself holding back tears. She did not go out to comfort my father nor did she even act curious as to why he was crying.

"I knew right then and there that I had just made the biggest mistake of my life," she said. "I tried to think of all the reasons why I married him and none of them made any sense. I didn't love him. I barely liked him. Yet, I was married to him. I looked down at my new wedding band and somehow knew I had done something horrible."

The marriage was less than one hour old.

They left late that afternoon for a one-week honeymoon stay in Pompeii. Their wedding night was spent on the third floor of the Siracusa Hotel in a large airy room furnished with a four-poster bed in the center, two brown antique end tables, a brown lounge chair and a clear view of the St. Giovann Guiseppe orphanage.

It was there in that room that the marriage between my parents was consummated and I was conceived.

Minutes after they had made love for the first time, my father, holding my mother in his arms, told her he had been previously married and had a thirteen-year-old daughter living in New York.

My mother sat up in the bed.

"Who does she live with?" she asked.

"My wife's family," my father said.

My mother's stomach felt queasy.

"Where's your wife?"

My father leaned closer to my mother.

"She's dead," he said. "I killed her."

My father then reached out and began to make love to my mother for a second time.

On their third night together my parents had dinner in a small restaurant next to the hotel. They were halfway through a main course of spaghetti and squid cooked in a hot red sauce when a waiter came over carrying a chilled bottle of champagne.

"With the compliments of the gentleman in the corner," the waiter said, pointing toward a short, dark-haired man sitting by himself, sipping an espresso.

My father looked at the man and waved his thanks. The man nodded his head and waved back.

The waiter put down two champagne glasses, uncorked the bottle and poured, the overflow spilling onto the thick white table cloth. The waiter looked at my father and flicked his head toward the man at the corner table.

"Luciano," he said in a near whisper.

"I know," my father said.

"Who is he?" my mother asked.

"He's a great man," my father said. "He's the head of the Mafia."

On the morning of their planned return to Ischia, my mother packed their two bags and straightened up the hotel room. When she finished, my mother went into the bathroom to get dressed for the trip.

My father had gone out to buy an American newspaper and confirm the boat's time of departure. He came back into the room while she was standing in front of the bathroom mirror, brushing her hair.

"What are you doing?" he said.

My mother jumped.

"You scared me," she said. "I didn't hear you come in."

"What are you doing?" he said, pointing at her hair.

"What do you mean?" she said. "I'm getting ready. Doesn't the boat leave soon?"

"Never comb your hair over the sink," my father said.

"Why?"

"I don't like to see hair in the sink," he said. "Makes me sick. I shared a cell with a guy who always brushed his hair in the sink. It was awful. Never do it again."

My mother gave her hair one final stroke. My father grabbed the brush from her hand.

"What the fuck did I just say?" he said. "What!"

My mother put both her hands across her mouth, holding back a scream.

"I'm sorry" was all she could manage.

My father swung the wood base of the brush against my mother's face. It landed just below her left eye. He swung it a second time, hitting her forehead. The third blow struck the bridge of her nose, breaking the skin and drawing blood.

My father then threw the brush against the white tiles. He walked out, closing the bathroom door behind him.

"I'll wait for you downstairs," he said over his shoulder. "The boat leaves in fifteen minutes. Don't be late."

My parents stayed in Ischia until April 1, when my father decided it was time for him to get back to New York. My mother was, by this time, three months pregnant. They were living off my grandmother Maria's food and my mother's small police-widow's pension.

My father had sold a sailor on leave his windbreaker for fifteen dollars and borrowed four hundred dollars from a cousin. He told my mother he needed the money to send to America to pay for four months back rent and a new couch he ordered for their West Side apartment.

"Wait till you see where you'll be living," he told her. "The rooms are so big, you'll be able to dance in them. You can see the river from our bedroom. You will be so happy."

My mother was not happy. Most nights she cried herself to sleep, frightened she would do something to anger her new husband and concerned over the life she would soon face in a country so different from anything she knew or understood.

Until this point, she had lived in a simple manner, warmed by the circle of family and friends that surrounded her. Her first husband's relatives had taken her in, welcomed her as a daughter and loved her as one of their own. She wasn't sure that her new husband's family would do the same.

My father's mother was not well liked on Ischia, while his father was considered little more than a buffoon. Except for his youngest brother, Albert, not much was known about my father's siblings.

"Albert had been here during the war," my mother's sister Nancy said. "He was a soldier, thin and very handsome. He spent some time with my father and they got along well. The rest of them were a mystery to us. None of us knew how they would react to Raffaela."

My mother spent her mornings helping care for her father. Gabriel Carcaterra was a tall man, with a full smile and an open heart. The cancer spreading through his body had weakened him, causing his once constant smile to all but disappear. The disease and the pain had sapped his desire to live as much as his strength.

"What is it, little one?" he asked my mother one day. "You look as sad as I do."

"Nothing, Papa," my mother said. "Nothing's wrong."

They both fell silent for a while, my mother dusting the sparse bedroom furniture, my grandfather, his head back against the pillow, his eyes closed, trying to take a pain-free breath.

"I'm sorry," he said.

"It's not your fault, Papa. I'm the one who married him."

"I just thought, my sister's boy, he would take good care of you," he said. "One family. Same blood."

"I guess I felt the same."

"Then we both bet on a bad card."

My mother looked at her father, his eyes bulging from his sallow face, then turned away. My grandfather pushed aside the white quilt covering what was left of his body and slowly moved his legs to the side of the bed. He stood up, on bare feet, holding on to the headrest. He was wearing a long white sleeping gown, the top half wet through with sweat.

"Listen to me," he said, his frail voice reaching for an edge. "If he gives you any trouble, if he doesn't treat you like a man should treat a wife, then you come home. Whether I'm dead or alive, you come home."

My mother's eyes welled with tears. "I will, Papa."

"You take the baby and come home to your family."

"Yes, Papa."

My grandfather sat back down on the bed. "I let you down, little one," he said. "I got you into something and I won't be around long enough to get you out of it."

My mother walked over to him, a cold towel in her hand. She sat in a chair next to the bed. She wiped her father's forehead and held his hand. "It will work out, Papa. Don't you worry. Just be well, that's all that matters."

My grandfather patted his daughter's growing stomach and smiled. "Getting big," he said. "What's it feel like, boy or girl?"

"Everyone says it's going to be a boy. A big boy."

"A boy, that's good," my grandfather said. "So long as . . ."

"Don't worry, Papa," my mother said. "He won't be like his father. I'll see to that."

On September 6, 1954, my mother boarded the ocean liner *Christofero Colombo* in the port of Naples for the eight-day trip to New York City. She left behind a widowed mother, three mournful sisters, two young brothers and her soon to be twelve-year-old son. She was in the eighth month of her pregnancy and was placed directly in the ship's medical ward, under the care of round-the-clock nurses.

She had packed only her most useful possessions and mementos, leaving the rest of her belongings with her mother. By her bedside my mother placed a picture of her son and her father and wrapped a purple set of rosary beads around them. She put on a white cotton nightgown and a pair of short white socks and was helped into bed by an elderly nurse who then left to tend to other duties.

When she heard the ship's horn blow, signaling their departure, my mother lifted her head from her pillow and gazed out the open porthole, taking a last look at Naples. As she did, my mother felt a sharp spasm across her stomach. She lowered her head and threw up into a urine-stained bedpan.

Five days into her voyage, my mother was given a hot cup of chicken broth by the day watch nurse. She took two small sips and handed the cup back. "Please, Signora," the nurse said. "You must eat. It's not good for the baby if you don't."

"I'm not hungry," my mother said.

The nurse placed the cup on a tray next to the bed. "Maybe later," she said. "After it cools."

My mother wiped drops of sweat from her upper lip with a crumpled tissue. The oppressive heat in the room mixed uncomfortably with the stench of sickness.

"How many more days?" my mother asked.

"Soon, Signora," the nurse said. "Very soon."

"Have you ever been to America?"

"Many times."

"Do you like it?"

"There are many things I like about it," the nurse said. "The different restaurants, the big buildings, the faster way of life. Still, Italy will always be Italy."

The nurse handed my mother a clean tissue. "Where will you be living, Signora?" she asked.

"New York City," my mother said. "West 65th Street."

"That's Manhattan," the nurse told her. "The center of the city. You are very lucky."

"Why lucky?"

"My family lives in Brooklyn," the nurse said. "Most of the Italians do. Not many can afford to live where you live. What does your husband do?"

"He's a butcher," my mother said.

"And you don't have to worry about food, either," the nurse said with a smile. "You're a very lucky lady. The baby, too. Everything will be fine, you'll see."

My mother put her head back against the pillow and nodded.

"I hope so," she sighed.

The nurse reached for the soup and fed some to my mother. "I have a good feeling about you," the nurse said. "And I'm never wrong."

My mother froze in the middle of the tenement hallway. Cooking fumes that seeped through the cracked apartment doors mingled with stale cigarette and cigar smoke from the bathrooms on each landing. Conversations could clearly be heard from apartments as far as two floors away. My mother put a tissue to her mouth and swallowed back the need to vomit.

"C'mon, baby," my father said, "we're on the third floor. Can you make it all right?"

"I'll be okay," my mother said. "I just need to take my time."

"No rush, baby," my father said. "We got all day."

My father went first, holding my mother's handbag in one hand and her withered brown valise in the other.

"This place is only temporary," he said over his shoulder. "Our real apartment is around the corner, being painted and fixed up. Just for you. Should be ready in a coupla months."

He turned to face his wife at the top step of the second floor. He reached out to hug her.

"I'm so glad you're here," he said. "Home, with me, where you belong."

The furnished room was cramped, a large bed with a box spring and mattress taking up the bulk of the space. There were two windows, both closed and dirty, a tiny walk-in closet and a warped three-shelf bureau. The walls were grayish white and the ceiling was peeling and chipped. A white lamp with a low-watt bulb and a hot plate were on a creaky table next to the bed.

"Where will we put the baby?" my mother asked.

"Wherever you want," my father said. "There's plenty of room."

Three weeks to the night after they had moved into that furnished room on West 65th Street off Tenth Avenue, my mother asked my father to take her to the hospital. During the short cab ride down to St. Claire's Hospital on West 50th Street she ignored the pain, ignored my father holding her hand and thought only of those first three weeks in America.

My father was working in a 14th Street slaughterhouse, clearing twenty-six dollars a week, more than enough to cover the twenty-five-a-month rent on the furnished room. He had been loving and affectionate toward her and had exhibited none of the physical flashes of anger she'd seen on their honeymoon. Each night on his return from work he would bring her a prepared steak, baked potato and salad for dinner. "Gotta keep that baby strong," he would say to her. "Big and strong."

He would be home by five, they would eat dinner no later than six and be in bed by eight. He would leave for work in the middle of the night, kissing her on the cheek, patting her stomach and quietly locking the door.

She hated living in the furnished room and was uncomfortable sharing a corner bathroom with three other couples. The steady noise and the strong hallway odors gave her headaches and made her grateful for the chilly autumn breeze that blew in through the half-open windows.

She spent the bulk of her days alone or at her mother-in-law's apartment, located across from the three-room flat she would soon inhabit. Initially her mother-in-law and the rest of my father's family had greeted her warmly, but the warmth seemed tinged with suspicion.

Her two sisters-in-law spoke choppy Italian at best and reverted to English when they wanted to talk privately. Her father-in-law, Lorenzo, remained as remote a figure in America as he had been in Ischia. My mother's main source of comfort and friendship was my paternal grandmother, Raffaela.

My father's mother was a hefty woman with a deep voice, thin curly hair and a large-jowled face, all crunched atop a squat brick-oven body. She was quick to laugh, doted to excess on her children, especially her three sons, and thrived on repeating or generating neighborhood gossip.

Raffaela was disliked by many in the area and seemed threatening to others. She kept an active mental file on the personal life of everyone she knew. My mother enjoyed her company, but was troubled by the older woman's hold on my father. He was a different man in her presence, timid and childlike, afraid to disagree with anything she said or did.

"He was an affectionate man," my mother said. "Always hugging or kissing me or holding my hand. Except around his mother. He never touched me then. If I brushed against him, he would avoid my touch. He would only do or say things that he knew would be sure to please her."

It was late on a Friday night when my mother was wheeled into the delivery room on the second floor of St. Claire's Hospital. The baby was a large one, and the doctors at first thought they would have to perform a Caesarean. My father kissed his wife as she was taken away, told her he loved her and wiped tears from his eyes. He skimmed a few magazines in the waiting-room vestibule, checked his watch, found a pay phone, made a thirty-second call and left the hospital.

"I couldn't stand the wait," he said. "Never could. I called this broad I knew on West 63rd. Went over there and spent a few hours. It didn't mean anything, just somebody to be with. Someone must have seen me either going there or leaving to go back to the hospital and told your mother. She didn't say too much about it, but I knew she was angry."

I was born at three P.M., Saturday afternoon, the sixteenth of October, almost exactly nine months from the date of my parents' marriage. I weighed in at slightly over ten pounds and, despite my mother's fierce objections, was named after my paternal grandfather. Other than my father, my mother had no visitors, spending her four recovery days either alone in her room or sitting in a pew in the hospital chapel. There were no flowers, no candy, and despite my father's display of happiness, her overall mood was one of sadness. The hopeless reality of her situation had, by now, made itself all too clear to my mother.

"I lay in that hospital bed," she said, "and wished you had been born dead. I prayed that God take you. It was the only way out."

My father left his job the day after my birth, borrowed some money from his mother and spent two nights with an old girlfriend in an apartment less than one block from the hospital. The rent on the furnished room was one month past due and he owed fifty-four dollars to a local bookie. To balance out his lack of incoming funds, my father pawned the few pieces of jewelry my mother owned and borrowed seventy-five dollars from a neighborhood loan shark. To show his gratitude, my father gave the dress my mother wore on their wedding day to the loan shark's wife.

My father held me in his arms on the walk home from the hospital, my mother by his side. A cold wind off the Hudson River hit at them as they crossed Ninth Avenue and headed toward Tenth. My mother was wearing a thin cloth coat, a black scarf covering her head. Her walk was stilted and slow, while my father forged ahead at his usual fast pace. A short, stubby middle-aged man with a cane walked up behind my parents while they waited out a red light at the corner of 63rd Street and Tenth Avenue. He tapped my father on the shoulder and smiled.

"Hello, Mario," he said. "That the new kid?"

"Hey, hello, Carmine," my father said, off guard and wary. "How's it goin'?"

"Good. Things are good," the man said, nodding and smiling in my mother's direction. "I tell you though, buddy, things would be a whole lot better if you came across with the money."

The light changed and the three made their way to the next corner. My father leaned closer to the man.

"C'mon, Carmine," my father said. "Go easy, will ya. I'm with my wife and my kid. I'll get the money, no problem."

"Fuck 'no problem,' " the man said.

He turned toward my mother, who was weak and shivering in the cold. He stopped in the middle of the block and faced her as she stood in front of a crowded greengrocery. The man reached down and yanked the straps of the black snap handbag my mother was holding across her chest. The snap broke and the bag fell to the ground. The man bent over, picked up the bag and opened it.

"Carmine," my father said, his hands gripping me even tighter than before. "What the fuck you doin'?"

The man pulled out the six singles my mother had in her bag, crumpled them in his fist and jammed them into his trouser pocket. He handed the broken bag back to my mother.

"Make your payments, Mario," he said to my father. "Don't be a jerk about it."

The man lifted the collar of his jacket and pressed it to his neck.

"I'll see you next week, Mario," he said. "Don't keep me waitin'."

He tipped his hat to my mother.

"Good luck with the kid," he said.

II

My parents moved to 226 W. 67th Street three months after my birth. The dark red brick building was in the center of an Italian neighborhood known as Little Naples. The area tenements all looked the same, each four stories tall with black- or red-painted fire escapes lining their fronts. The halls and stairwells were as meticulously kept as the rent-controlled apartments. Garbage cans, scrubbed clean and odorless, were lined three-deep in front of the superintendent's basement rooms. More than eight thousand people lined the six streets of Little Naples, and few, if any, spoke English. The majority were from the poorer sections of Salerno, Ischia, Capri, Margellina and Naples. The men were laborers, working on union construction crews, building midtown high-rises or renovating Greenwich Village brownstones. The weekly paychecks, with stacked-in overtime hours, were handed over to the trusting wives—most of whom had met their husbands on country roads back in their home ports—who would spend all the days of their lives caring for restless children and patiently cooking elaborate peasant meals.

Little Naples had nothing in common with the rest of 1950s Manhattan. The supermarkets were small and compact, modeled after their Southern Italian counterparts, their aisles filled with imported oils, pastas, cheeses, doughs and spices. The only prominent American brand names were Kellogg's and Nestlé's, while items such as Skippy peanut butter and Wonder enriched white bread were treated as new and exotic discoveries. There were no restaurants in the area, only one three-table Neapolitan pizzeria and a small brown-bricked barber shop that the neighborhood men used to get away from their wives and children and solve the problems of the world.

Salvatore the butcher sold live rabbits, killing and skinning them at no extra cost. During the forty days of Lent leading up to Easter Sunday, Salvatore had a special on lamb's head, which my parents would roast, leaving only the eyes for my grandmother's headache cure. Alphonso the tailor would sew suits from Italian fabric, the sounds of his opera records blasting out of the front door of his West 69th Street shop.

The fruit stands were where my mother and the women of the neighborhood shopped and gossiped. The fruit and vegetables were fresh, the basil and parsley were free, and the talk was vicious and usually on the money. It was in Umberto's Fruit Parlor, standing on wooden floors sprinkled with sawdust, that my mother learned that her friend Louisa was moving back to Ischia. It was there she first heard of Frank Sinatra, Dean Martin, Jerry Lewis, Perry Como and other locally respected entertainers. It was there that she first became aware of how much my father was distrusted and disliked and, to a lesser extent, feared.

It was also there, on a sunny Thursday morning in April, while juggling me and a handful of lemons in her arms, that she found out my father was having an affair with a married woman my mother considered a friend.

"The fruit store was like a courtroom," one of my mother's friends, Rosalie, now eighty-four, remembers. "There, rumors were fact. A lot of marriages were made down those aisles. A lot of them were unmade. People shopped there every day, whether they needed anything or not."

The fish store gave away a half-pound of shrimp for every mackerel purchased. They also made a thick orange sauce filled with snails and mussels, selling it for a dollar a pound. The delis sold provolone and proscuitto heros on crusty brick-oven bread for seventy-five cents each. Daniello's Pastry Shop made their own cannolis and éclairs and had a regular half-price deal on birthday cakes.

It was a neighborhood where no one spoke any English and no one had to. The church, St. Matthew's, was crowded on Sundays and holy days; the streets were crowded the rest of the time. For the people of Little Naples, there were no vacations on Caribbean islands, no summer homes to drive to on weekends, no air conditioners to ward off the heat and only a handful of TV sets to fill out empty nights.

Few read the American newspapers, fewer still read books of any language and no one went to the theater. Movies were an occasional diversion from the summer heat or the winter cold. In Little Naples, entertainment meant little. Work, and the paycheck that resulted from that work, was all that mattered, for as much as the people of

Little Naples loved the area they had carved out as their own, they were well aware that life in America could offer them much more than a bed and a hot plate in a cold-water walk-up. For most, it was only a matter of time before a move to the suburbs. Once there, they would be free to build a larger version of Little Naples, one with grass lawns, barbecue pits and above-ground pools.

My mother left my father for the first time three days before my second birthday. Her motive for leaving had nothing to do with the physical beatings that my father handed out regularly with little provocation. Nor was it over another woman, though my father openly pursued several neighborhood wives, including one who lived directly below our apartment. Instead, my mother left over an unpaid Con Ed bill.

"They cut our lights," my father said. "It was our third or fourth bill, I forget which one. Your mother never saw them, anyway. I took care of all that. I needed the money for something else. I never thought they would turn off my fuckin' lights. When that happened, your mother really lost it."

My mother spent two nights with a cousin on West 70th Street and then returned to my father. It was the start of a pattern that would exist throughout their thirty-five years of marriage. The frequent separations never lasted longer than a month and were quickly followed by a benign form of reconciliation.

"They had troubles, more than their share," a family friend said. "Despite that, you could see that there was genuine affection between the two. They had a lot to overcome—he was lazy and always looking for the fast buck, she didn't trust anyone, kept to herself and never allowed people enough room to really like her. But their biggest mistake was living that close to his family. From the get-go, his family caused nothing but trouble."

The Carcaterra family on my father's side was, at best, tolerated by the people in Little Naples. The women, especially the older ones, did little to hide their disdain for my father. To them he was nothing more than a small-time con man, a windbag whose delusions of grandeur were played out with other people's money. They viewed his crime not as one of passion, but as a well-planned, totally thought-out murder committed against a naïve neighborhood girl too innocent to know the type of man she was up against. The rest of the family was viewed suspiciously. "You fell in with that group," one neighborhood resident said, "and it would cost you."

The apartment was filled with the odor of a thick, fresh red sauce crammed with shrimp, snails, squid and spices. My mother sat with her back against a creaky old wooden chair, two pounds of string beans resting on her apron-covered lap. I was up to my chest in the iron-plated bathtub, surrounded by a black rubber duck and thick white bubbles. A large wooden slab rested across the tub.

My mother had made zucchini-and-egg sandwiches for both of us and placed the two plates on the wood along with her cup of tea and my glass of juice. She broke the ends off the string beans and began telling me a story about the place in Italy where she was born. I was four years old and enjoyed the afternoons I got to spend with her. It was our special time, which my mother set aside for the telling of tales.

Within the structure of a closed world, my parents were at its anointed center. My formative years were spent in their company, with little if any privacy existing between us. Italian was the only spoken language, and since my parents didn't own a television or even a radio, it was difficult to learn any other words. Neither of my parents ever read to me, and there were no play dates and no nursery schools to attend. My early education was based on the stories my mother told me about Italy, the war and the people who survived it, and those my father told me about the great fighters of the twenties and thirties, lightweights and welterweights mostly, men with rocks for hands and hearts as big as ballrooms.

During the telling of those tales, as I was held tightly by one of my parents, or left soaking away in a tub as my mother dramatically reenacted the crucial points in a story, was the time when we most resembled a family, when we were as close together as any three people could be.

That afternoon, just as my mother got to the part in her story where a German soldier held a gun to my grandmother Maria's throat, my father walked into the apartment. His long white butcher's coat was streaked with dried blood, and his hands were nicked with cuts and bruises. He held a large bundle under his arm, a small rack of baby ribs wrapped in brown freezer paper, and had a copy of the *Daily News* folded up in his back pocket. He had on a Yankee cap, droplets of cow blood laced across the peak. My mother seemed surprised to see him and sensed trouble. He didn't usually come home from work until four, sometimes five. "Why are you home?" she asked him. "Is there something wrong?"

"Relax," my father said. "Nothin's wrong. It's just slow. That's all. Just slow."

He leaned down toward me and kissed my cheek. "How you doin' boss?" he said. He sat next to the tub, reached for a plastic cup and began to pour warm water down my back. He looked up at my mother. "Got anything to eat?"

"There's sauce cooking," she said. "Fish sauce. Won't be ready for another twenty minutes."

"I'll wait," he said.

My mother went into the kitchen to put the water on for pasta. My father soaked his hands in the tub, watching me as I ate the rest of my sandwich. His youthful face looked heavy and sad. His dark brown eyes were moist, and he seemed unable to speak. My mother walked up behind him and handed him a small plate filled with hot squid and Italian bread. My father took the plate and put it on the wooden board next to mine. He held my mother's hand. She knelt down next to him. "What's wrong?" she said.

"I got laid off," he said. He bent down and washed his face with the tub's water and then reached his hands out for me. "C'mon," he said, "you've been in long enough."

My mother handed him a white towel off the rack. My father stood me up in the tub, double-wrapped the towel around my body and lifted me up. "It's gonna be okay," he said to my mother. "We'll be all right. We just gotta catch a little luck."

My father took my mother into his arms, and the three of us stood in the center of the room, finding comfort in each other's warmth. The only sounds in the apartment came from a radio playing Italian love songs two floors below.

*　　*　　*

The next night, we were invited to dinner at my grandmother's apartment next door. We sat around the kitchen table and waited for the hot bowls of lentils and sausage to cool down. My grandmother was agitated, my grandfather quiet; my mother braced herself, anticipating another confrontation. My parents faced numerous disadvantages living next to my grandmother, none as destructive as the lack of privacy.

My grandmother knew all that could be known about my parents' finances and their arguments. She knew if the rent was late or if my mother overspent on weekly groceries. She knew who my mother spoke with, who she shopped with and how much she paid for a new housedress. She knew details of my parents' sex life. She knew all these things because my father told her.

My grandmother chewed on a spoonful of lentils and looked at my mother. Her ruddy face was covered by a thin layer of facial hair, and her dark eyes shone with anger. She nudged herself closer to my mother. "Be good to him," she said.

My mother didn't respond.

"Don't be all over him about work," my grandmother said in a louder voice. "He'll find a job. He always has."

"Come down the docks," my grandfather said to my father. "Plenty of work there."

"Fuck that shit, Pop. I'll stick with the meat."

"You do what you think is best," my grandmother said. "You are the man and the man always knows."

My father pushed his lentil bowl aside and started on a plate filled with sliced steak, salad and fried mushrooms. "You know," he said, "I've been thinkin' about startin' my own business. Why the hell should I break my ass for other people when I can work just as hard for myself?"

"Bravo," my grandmother said. "Wonderful idea."

"But you don't know anything about running your own business," my mother said.

"There's nothing to know," my grandmother said. "You work hard, you make money and you keep it all."

"That's right," my father said, breaking off a piece of bread. "You keep all the money."

"What about the money to start it?" my mother asked. "Where are we going to get that?"

"*We* ain't gonna get shit," my father said. "That's my worry. You just do what you gotta do. Let me figure out the rest."

"But we're already in debt," my mother said.

"Hey, whatta you gotta tell everybody our business," my father said. "We'll get the money. Okay? Now shut the fuck up before I rap you right in the fuckin' mouth."

My grandmother sat back and sipped her wine, a smile across her face. She poured her son a glass of ice water and gently patted his hand. "You'll do fine," she said. "All you need is a chance."

"Bet your ass I'm gonna do fine," my father said. "Just do me a favor would ya? Keep this bitch away from me. She's no fuckin' good."

He stood up, the large glass of water in his hand, the explosive temper fully lit. He stared at my mother as he spoke. "You hear me, you're no fuckin' good to me," he said. "No good to me in here when I need you to back me up, no good to me in bed when I need you to be a woman and not some fuckin' nun. You're no good to me any fuckin' place I go. No good."

My father moved closer to my mother, one hand clenched into a fist. He paused and then threw the glass of water into my mother's face. He pulled his windbreaker from the back of his chair, tossed his mother a kiss, patted my head and walked out of the apartment.

My grandmother watched silently as my mother cleaned the water from her face and eyeglasses. The glass my father had thrown had caught her just above the right eyebrow, leaving a red mark. My grandmother handed my mother a fresh napkin and then bent over to pick up the now empty glass. She sat back down and set the glass on the table next to the wine decanter. She smiled at my mother.

"You want me to make you a cup of tea?" she said.

In the spring of 1960, the State of New York, under the orders of then-governor Nelson A. Rockefeller, issued a condemnation order for the neighborhood that had come to be known as Little Naples. On April 1 of that year, the paperwork was completed and the tenements of Little Naples were scheduled for destruction in order to make way for the building of Lincoln Center.

Each family was given $250 in moving expenses by the Housing Authority of the city of New York and allotted ninety days in which to move to a new location. The majority of the people of Little Naples opted for the outer boroughs or the suburbs and the opportunity to live in a home of their own. The bulk of my father's family settled in houses or apartments in the borough of Queens. My grandparents led the way, choosing a two-bedroom, rent-controlled apartment in an Astoria housing complex.

Since my parents had less money than the others and my father had no intention of commuting to any job, their options were limited. Following a three-week search, my mother found a five-room, forty-two-dollar-a-month apartment at 532 West 51st Street, in the middle of a Manhattan neighborhood known as Hell's Kitchen.

"A lot of people cried when those buildings went down," my mother said. "Not me. You'd think we were living on Park Avenue, the way people reacted. I knew we needed to get away. That building, that area, was like a prison without bars. If the buildings had stayed and we didn't have to move, then I knew, eventually, another year, maybe two, I would kill myself."

My parents took me to a Central Park playground on the Saturday afternoon of our last weekend in Little Naples. My mother sat on a cracked wooden bench, eating a vanilla ice-cream cone, watching my father push me on a swing. It was the middle of summer, and the 67th Street playground was overcrowded with parents and children. My father slowed the swing, pulled me out and led me toward the sandbox. My mother followed us, my pail and shovel in hand.

While I played in the sand, my parents moved to a small bench by a leaky water fountain. My father had gotten up to take a sip of water when he saw a tall man in a white shirt standing off to the left of the playground. The man was smoking a cigarette and staring at my father. He had an open six-finger knife in his right hand. My father drank some water, wiped his mouth and watched as the man came closer. The man looked familiar, someone my father had seen before; he just couldn't place where.

The man stopped less than five feet from my father. The two stared at one another, my father glancing down at the hand gripped around the knife handle.

"You lose somethin'?" my father asked.

"My wife," the man said. His voice was frail, cracked, his lower lip shaking as he spoke. "You know my wife, butcher?"

"Why would I know your wife?" my father said, aware now of people listening to the conversation.

"You know where she was this morning, butcher?" the man said. "Do you know where my wife was?"

"Hey, whatta I give a fuck where your wife was this morning? She's your wife."

"She was with Filomena, the midwife," the man said. "They did her bad. She lost a lot of blood."

"Listen, enough with this shit," my father said. "Your wife's pregnant, she's having a hard time. I'm sorry to hear it. But what the fuck does it have to do with me?"

"My wife's name is Claudia," the man said. "The child she carried was yours."

My father backed up two steps and clenched both fists, waiting for the tall man to make a move with the knife. The playground parents, sensing what was about to happen, rushed to scoop up their children and retreat to a safe distance. My mother sat in silence on the bench where my father had left her and stared at her husband. I still sat in the sandbox, content to have the entire area to myself.

"You killed one woman already," the man said. "Isn't that enough?" The tall man flicked the knife to eye level and lunged for my father. The tip of the blade nicked my father's T-shirt, a red circle forming around the tear.

My father moved to his left, planted his feet and landed a hard right cross to the tall man's chin. The crunch of the blow knocked the man back. The knife fell out of his hand, landing blade up on the concrete. My father moved in.

"Okay, prick," he said. "Time to dance."

My father kicked the man in the chest and groin. He reached down and grabbed the back of the man's head and began to slam it against the base of the water fountain. "Who you gonna stab, fuck?" my father said. "Who you gonna stab?"

My father lifted the man to his feet and put three hard lefts to his stomach. A woman screamed just as my father landed a right to the man's nose, blood squirting onto his face and shirt. My father leaned into the tall man, put his lips to his ears and wiped the blood from his face. "You're right, I do know your wife," my father said. "I fucked her. I fucked her a lot. And now she's no good to nobody."

My father backed up again and hit the tall man one last time across the face. As the man fell to the ground, my father kicked him twice in the back of the head. "Die, prick," my father said.

He walked over to the sandbox and picked me up. To my mother, he said, "What the fuck you staring at?" My mother gathered her purse and my toys and walked toward him. When we reached the top of the hill leading out of the playground, my father stopped and turned to look at the crowd surrounding the tall man. Police sirens could be heard in the distance.

"I tell you one thing," he said. "I can't wait until we're the fuck out of this neighborhood."

III

Vito the Limp's body rested against the black chimney wall. His plaid hunting shirt was open to the waist, thin blood streams still flowing from the three quarter-size bullet holes in his chest. His stained brown slacks were also open, pulled down around his paste-white thighs. The word "junkie" was scrawled across his belly in black felt-tip, and his penis had been sliced off and tossed into a nearby pigeon coop.

Vito's flea-infested dog, Blackie, was next to him, strung up from the chimney, a barbed-wire loop tight around his neck. The dog had been shot twice in the head, and its belly was cut open, blood still dripping onto the roof's tar floor. It was the middle of summer, 1963, and the two-day-old bodies were beginning to smell.

The next afternoon, during a hard July rain, the bodies were discovered by a boy named Gomer, who was up on the roof to check on his pigeons. The boy stared at the bodies for a few minutes, at the blood and the rain running together into puddles. He then leaned over toward Vito's body, standing mere inches from the man who dealt heroin in Hell's Kitchen, and spit in his face.

Gomer then went back inside the building, calmly walked down the three flights of stairs to where he lived, told his parents what he had found and watched as his father phoned the police. Three hours later, my father, just returning from work and still in his blood-stained butcher whites, was brought into the Sixteenth Precinct and questioned about Vito the Limp's murder.

A heavyset Irish detective sat across a wooden desk from my father, blowing filterless cigarette smoke in his direction. My father sat motionless in a dirty brown chair and stared down at the dried blood spots on his hands.

"What the hell you guys want from me?" he finally said, brushing aside the foul smoke. "There must be at least fifty guys in the neighborhood could have killed that scumbag. Why you bringin' me in?"

"'Cause you're the only one I know about threatened to murder him," the detective said. "In front of a dozen witnesses."

"Yeah, I said I would kill him," my father said. "If the prick went near my kid again. So far as I know, he didn't. And I didn't."

"What *do* you know, Mario? Let's start there."

"I know shit, is what I know."

"C'mon, tough guy, cut the horseshit," the detective said in a weary voice. "A guy kills his wife, wouldn't think twice about killin' a fuckin' dope dealer. Would he, Mario?"

My father swallowed his anger and stared at the detective. "You got it wrong, cop, All wrong. You can look it up. I'm not a gun guy. I'm the wrong guy."

The police released my father later that night. While he had been in the station house, my mother paced our five-room West 51st Street apartment, crying and cursing aloud.

"It's all your fault," she said to me. "Why were you talking to that bum? Tell me, why?"

"I didn't," I said. "He talked to me."

"And you let your father see you do it? Stupid, that's what you are—stupid. You know the kind of man your father is. You know."

"Mom, please stop," I said, starting to cry and feeling as afraid for my father as my mother was, knowing in my seven-year-old heart that he had nothing to do with Vito the Limp's murder and thinking I would never see my father again.

Seconds later, we heard my father's key begin to unlock the door. My mother went to him first, hugging and kissing him as he came in. They held each other for a few moments, and then my father turned from my mother to me. I leaned against the living room wall, too nervous to move, not knowing what my father's reaction would be.

He stared down at me, the brim of his pigeon-gray fedora tilted up, his face whiter than usual.

"Hey One-punch," he said. "Do me a favor, would you?"

"Sure," I said.

"Get us two 7UPs and go out on the fire escape," he said. "You and I need to talk."

My father and I sat on the fire escape sipping from cold sodas, my legs dangling through the bars. He was wearing blue jockey shorts and torn brown slippers. I had on black shorts and a white Police Athletic League T-shirt.

"Sorry about today," my father said. "Fuckin' cops got nothing better to do than bust my balls."

"Why did they arrest you?"

"Who the fuck knows," he said. "They got to arrest somebody. It's over. Forget about it."

We drank our sodas in silence and stared at a couple kissing and petting on a rooftop four buildings away, a large radio at their feet blasting out a Beach Boys single.

"I want you to stay away from shit like Vito," my father said, wiping his lips with the back of his right hand, looking away from the couple to me. "Understand?"

"He just asked me if I was feeling okay," I said. "He heard I was sick and wanted to know if I was better. I said I was. That's all, Dad. That's all I said."

"Guys like Vito deal shit to kids like you," my father said. "That's how they live. That's how they make money. He hooks you on that shit and then he owns you."

"You mean like Ralphie from downstairs," I said.

"Yeah," my father said, "like Ralphie. He's a fuckin' dead man only he don't know it."

"He stole his mother's color television last week," I said. "Took it right out her bedroom window."

"Steals from his own mother," my father said. "That's the shit in him. She's not careful, he's gonna kill her in that bedroom." My father handed me his empty bottle. I put it in an open slot in the wooden soda crate to my left.

"You want another one?" I asked.

"No," he said. "I'm okay."

My father stretched his strong arms and shoulders and yawned. He gazed out at the black rooftops, the rust-red fire escapes and the blue and white lights coming out of dozens of half-opened apartment windows. He reached over, gripped me with both hands and lifted me up onto his lap. The top of my head rested against his thick-haired chest.

"I love you, One-punch," he said, stroking the top of my head as he spoke. "I'll never do anything that hurts you. Ever. But . . ." He stopped and lifted my head toward his. "If you ever take that shit and end up a scumbag like Vito, I'll kill you myself and then bury you. Understand?"

"Yes, Dad," I said.

"C'mon," he said, kissing me on both cheeks, "it's late. Let's you and me get us some sleep."

Hell's Kitchen was, during my childhood years there, a unique New York neighborhood. Its crammed redbrick tenements were home to an uneasy alliance of working-class Irish, Italians, Puerto Ricans and Eastern Europeans. The men worked the docks or drove trucks, they cut and hauled loins of beef or wore construction hard hats, the fruits of their daily physical labor headlined by a steady union paycheck. Many of the men left for work in the hours before dawn, leaving behind crowded apartments filled with sleeping wives and children huddled in rooms that were too hot in summer and too cold in winter.

The women had a hard edge to them, withered but not beaten by the strain of their struggles. Their lives were measured against the clothes they washed, the meals they prepared, the children they bore and raised. Early in married life they learned not to question but to silently accept the wayward ways of their husbands as well as the occasional hard slap or closed fist doled out when wine or whiskey flowed too freely.

They were devoted wives, religious women who wanted little more than hot coffee and toast for breakfast every day and enough end-of-the-month table money to pay the family bills on time. They loved gossip, yet trusted no one they had not known for at least two decades.

Hell's Kitchen was their universe, a private twenty-one-block inner sanctum immune to all but the most basic outside laws. What began on West 35th Street and ended on West 56th, bounded on one side by the Hudson River and on the other by the sharp lights and tailored crowds of the Broadway stage, was a world few New Yorkers knew existed. Even if a general awareness of the area and its harsh customs and rituals were to materialize, no stranger would ever be allowed to penetrate the depths of its concrete borders.

A neighborhood with a sinister history, it began honest enough, with a mixed breed of German and Irish laborers, dock workers who emptied and loaded the ships that lined the West Side piers. Mom-and-pop diners and luncheonettes sprang up along Eleventh and Twelfth avenues, serving as a safe place for the longshoremen to sip coffee and talk about the families and the countries they left behind. One such diner was run by a devoted old German couple named Heil who, if West Side legend and a sketchy history can be believed, are credited with naming the area. "The diner had no name on the outside, but everybody knew it as the Kitchen," one of the locals told me years ago. "Heil soon enough became Hell and that's how the place got coined. Who knows? It could all be total bullshit, but it makes for a nice story."

In those turn-of-the-century years, the Ninth Avenue El shook and rattled tenement windows every hour of every day, while the Hudson River Railroad moved its live cattle freight under the often scornful gaze of local residents, who even then despised outsiders. The New York piers were on one side, shipping and receiving goods from all ends of the world. The elevated railroads were on the other side,

31

hauling food and products on the tracks just above the near-empty ice boxes in the kitchens of the working poor. For the restless young of Hell's Kitchen, the two sites became easy marks, a place to turn stolen produce into profit. By 1905, "gang member" had become the area's profession of choice.

Gangs controlled the neighborhood, and none were more prominent or powerful than the five-hundred-strong Gophers, who were led by the Kitchen's deadliest man, Monk Eastman. By the time World War I began, Eastman was the prime suspect in a number of unsolved murders and the police were ready to move in. Eastman, low on options, enlisted in the Army and was sent to the European front. There he worked at what he had mastered in Hell's Kitchen, killing two dozen German soldiers in fields of battle. He came home with a chestful of medals and was given a parade down Tenth Avenue. "By the time he got back, the cops couldn't touch him," my father used to tell me, always with a laugh. "He was a war hero. You can't put a fuckin' war hero in jail. The cops, the politicians, none of them could lay a hand on him. They just turned their heads and let Monk go about his business."

The Gophers remained a neighborhood presence until the early 1920s, though dwindling numerically with each passing year. The remaining street gangs, however, were all but eliminated as early as the summer of 1910 when they were badly beaten by a security force organized by the owners of the New York Central Railroad. Any suspected gang member was clubbed into a coma, often in broad daylight, in a show of power designed to keep the tracks free of their rule. "Those railroad guys left you for dead," one former Gopher, now in his late eighties, told me. He was short and shriveled, long dirty hair hanging over the back of his blue parka, an unfiltered cigarette at his lips. "They beat you till their arms got tired. They tried to run us right out of our own neighborhood. For a few years there, that's what they pretty much did. Then Prohibition came around and brought Owney with it and the Kitchen was ours again."

Owney "Killer" Madden was the first major league gangster to come out of Hell's Kitchen and the first one my father talked about with any sense of pride and respect. Madden was a bootlegger with a banker's eye for investments. He held partnerships in a number of profitable dance halls, including the Cotton Club, as well as a piece of the eventual heavyweight champion of the world, Primo Carnera. Some say he even owned a church. "There wasn't a till in town he didn't collect from," my father would tell me, usually at night, in what passed as a Hell's Kitchen version of a bedtime story. "Booze, cabs, laundries. Name it and Owney got money from it. He was a smart man. A class act, and he wasn't even Irish. He was born in England. Shows you what a tough bastard he was, just to survive in this neighborhood."

The stories my father began to tell me about Owney Madden always ended with the shooting deaths of Dutch Schultz and Vincent "Mad Dog" Coll. The two gangsters had declared war on one another, a war that would eventually claim the life of a five-year-old boy as well as cause the near-fatal shooting of four other children. "Coll would drive up and down Tenth Avenue and shoot his machine gun," my father said. "He was as fuckin' crazy as you can get. Owney Madden called in every gun he could find and brought them into Hell's Kitchen. He had to get rid of that crazy bastard."

Madden got his man on the night of February 8, 1932, at a local drugstore on West 23rd Street off the corner of Eighth Avenue. Four men in a car pulled to a stop by the drugstore entrance. Three of the men blocked the entrance, while the fourth moved inside. All four carried Thompson submachine guns. Inside the store, Coll was on the phone, in a heated discussion with Owney Madden. "Owney kept him occupied, while the shooter moved in," my father would say to me. "It was the perfect setup."

The main hit man, the one assigned the task of murdering Coll, was tall and thin and wore a dark brown fedora over a gravy-colored suit. Coll, still arguing with Madden, had his back to him when the first spray of bullets blew through the phone booth door. In all, 123 bullets were fired at Coll, a high percentage of them on target. "They put so many into him that the damn phone booth almost collapsed on top of his body," my father said. "They did the job and put an end to that no-good bastard."

By the time my parents moved into Frank and Kate Antonelli's building at 532 West 51st Street in the summer of 1961, the exploits of Monk Eastman, Owney Madden and Mad Dog Coll had taken on legendary proportions. Through time, the trio had grown into legitimate Hell's Kitchen heroes, earning equal stature alongside middleweight boxing contender Joey Archer and then Ivy League professor Daniel Patrick Moynihan. All five were often lumped together and used as prime examples of how a graduate of the Kitchen could manipulate his way to success. "They were our best," some of the longshoremen would say. "The fuckin' best. You gotta be smart, you gotta be good and you gotta be lucky to be included in a group like that."

Physically, the Kitchen had not changed much despite the passing decades. The tenements were still redbrick and well kept, and the Twelfth Avenue piers and 14th Street meat market remained the prime source of local working income. While the railroad tracks were no longer elevated, they still moved live cattle through, on the way to a midwestern slaughterhouse. Domestic car dealerships and used auto dumps had replaced the dozens of diners that previously dotted the area. Warehouses, once used to store bootleg liquor during Prohibition, were now converted into garages and used as depots for the flatbed, multiwheeled trucks filled with the "swag," or stolen goods, that was bartered on the open market to neighborhood residents. "Anything I needed I got from the back of those trucks," my mother told me. "Shirts, pants, coats, belts, even your communion suit came from there. If the trucks didn't have what I wanted, all I had to do was ask. In a few days' time, whatever it was I wanted would be there."

The orders were always given to a tall, angular-faced man named John who dressed in the same clothes each day—a long-sleeved checkerboard shirt, jeans and construction boots. Over his right ear he slid a short-nubbed pencil, and in the right rear pocket of his jeans there was an open notebook crammed with orders. If the order was large enough and the anticipated tip worth it, John would even include a to-the-door delivery.

Every night, never later than six-thirty, John's trucks would roll into Hell's Kitchen. Two men, in clothing similar to what John wore, would hold open the large wooden doors leading into the two-story warehouse at the Eleventh Avenue end of 51st Street. The three lead trucks would cruise in, cabin first and lights out. John's truck was always last. He would roll past the garage doors, crank the gears in reverse and half-moon into his allotted space. The doors were then closed and locked.

At six forty-five, the mothers of Hell's Kitchen, some of them still in aprons and house slippers, came out to shop. They carried large brown grocery bags under their arms and change purses stuffed with singles in their hands. They entered the garage through a side door manned by a light-skinned dock worker named Red, who never smiled, never spoke and carried a fully loaded .38 in his waistband. Inside, two men were assigned to work the back of each truck, showcasing the merchandise and bargaining with the women over prices. John sat inside his truck's cabin, chain-smoking Camels and collecting the money handed him by the women. By nine-fifteen, it was over, and the garage doors were once again bolted shut.

"For us it was like shopping at Macy's or at Alexander's," Mrs. Antonelli, our landlady, told me. "Only it was a lot cheaper and there were no refunds. The salesmen were a lot nicer, too."

The trucks and the goods they offered were only a part of the thriving underground economy that existed in Hell's Kitchen. Contraband fruit, wheat, grains, cheese and liquor came courtesy of the ships in port, while the 14th Street meat market supplied everything from ground round to lamb ribs to live baby rabbits prime for slaughter. Lobsters, clams and large ocean squid were brought in fresh every week from the Fulton Fish Market. "Nobody ever got wise to it," my father said. "That's because nobody ever skimmed from the top. We always took from the bottom and nobody got greedy. It was good business not to get greedy. Everybody got a taste. It was beautiful watching those trucks come in loaded end-to-end with food and clothes. Or to watch your mother come up from the piers, her arms filled with fresh bananas or a twenty-pound sack of sugar. I tell you, who the fuck needed Park Avenue? We had everything anybody could ever want right there, right on our fuckin' block. Nobody was better than us. We had it all."

Hell's Kitchen was a neighborhood grounded in the traditions of its violent and isolationist past. Strangers were never encouraged to walk its streets, while residents roamed outside its borders only to attend weddings, funerals or baptisms. Street fights were the most acceptable way to solve a dispute, and they were never allowed to end until there was a clear victor. The children of the neighborhood were openly encouraged to fight, regardless of their age or size. Many nights, a boy would be caught in the middle of a street brawl, barely fending off a barrage of body blows, his face and hands soaked with his own spit and blood. There, in the middle of the gathered crowd, the boy would look up and see his father staring back at him, a look of sheer disgust etched across his face. I know. On many such nights, I would be that boy.

My father hated the way I fought. He thought I was too soft, too close to my mother, that I didn't carry the anger that was needed to survive on the street. He had heard stories about me that he didn't like, stories that ended with me walking away from a fight. "Here's the rule," he told me one night. "If you're smart, you'll remember the rule as long as you live. If you come home with a black eye, I'll give you two. If you come home with a broken arm, I'll break the other. That's it. Simple. If you let these punks push you around now, then you're going to let people push you around the rest of your life. When I hear about you, about your fights, I want to be proud of you. I want to hear you stood up. I want to hear that you nearly killed a guy."

On Friday nights during the summers, local street gangs gathered in the middle of a 50th Street parking lot, next to the stickball field. The neighborhood men, my father among them, would lay down their bets, lean against the red brick wall and cheer on their gang of choice. The fights usually lasted until the police arrived to take the wounded to the hospital and the survivors to the Sixteenth Precinct holding pens. Afterwards, our fathers would take us for a nightcap of Puerto Rican ices drenched with fruit juice.

The Italian and Irish gangs often fought as one, their sharp knives and open animosity reserved for the blacks who came down, heavily armed, from the uptown neighborhood of Inwood. The Puerto Ricans encouraged any gang to take them on, arriving at the lot with an entourage of women and children, all of them toting garden chairs and coolers. The Eastern European residents of Hell's Kitchen did their best to avoid confrontations both verbal and physical. They stayed to themselves, observed the rules of the neighborhood and walked away whenever a situation became tense.

"Nobody fucked with them," my father told me. "Just because they *didn't* fight didn't mean they *couldn't* fight. They were sons of bitches with a knife. Especially if they had a couple of shots of liquor in their belly."

*   *   *

I fought in my first gang fight two months shy of my ninth birthday.

"There isn't anybody's ass you can't kick," my father told me. "This is your chance to prove it. To me and to you."

My father brushed aside my mother's objections. "What, you want him to be a fag?" my father said after listening to her complain at length. "He's my son and he's going to fight. Case closed."

"He's just a boy," my mother said. "A little boy. What's wrong with you? How can you do this?"

"What the fuck you talking about?" my father said. "It's good for him. Make him feel like a man."

"He's not good with his hands. He's not like you. He's scared."

My father whirled in my direction. "Are you scared?" he shouted at me. "Are you?"

"No, Dad," I said. "I'm not scared."

"Are you gonna make me proud of you?"

"Yes, Dad," I said.

" 'Yes, Dad' what?"

"Yes, I'll make you proud."

My father turned back to my mother. "You see, as usual, you don't know what the fuck you're talking about. He's not scared. Now, you comin' with us or you just gonna sit here and say your fuckin' prayers?"

My father and I left the apartment together, leaving my mother behind, crying. We walked the half block to the parking lot, my father's right arm hanging over my shoulder, a huge smile across his face. I was wearing a new pair of blue jeans, low cut P.F. Flyers and a starched white T-shirt, tight around the collar. Except for the sneakers, my father was dressed in the same outfit. He also wore his favorite hat, the lid up both front and back.

A Puerto Rican gang led by a small, heavy-muscled teenager had already arrived at the lot, the six members each checking out the surroundings, exchanging low fives and drinking cold beers half-hidden inside brown paper bags.

An eight-member Irish gang waited by two open doors of a Chevy convertible, their arms crossed, the pockets of their jeans stuffed with makeshift weapons.

Three members of the Uptown Hawks, a gun-dealing gang from the East Side, stood next to an open fire hydrant, silent and still.

The Italian gang waited by Moncho's candy store, the five of them hand-checking the zip guns nestled under their belts, next to their spines.

My father waved to the Italians. Then he turned to me.

"Remember to do what Joey tells you to do," he said, in a voice high with excitement. "They don't come any better than him. He won't let anything happen to you."

My father stopped by the dark red stoop next to the parking lot and bent down closer to me.

"I love you, One-punch," he said. "Now go out there and make me proud. Make the whole fuckin' block proud. I'll be watching, rootin' you on."

He gave me a kiss and a hug, then pushed me the few feet toward the lot.

"Go on," he said. "I'll pick you up after it's over."

Joey introduced me to his crew. I wasn't given a name. To them, I was "Mario the butcher's boy."

I was given a black-and-silver-handled four-finger knife. It had a narrow point and had been razor-nicked along the edges.

"Use this when you have to," Joey told me. "Don't always wait for someone else to pull one first. Might be too late then. The Ricans will be the ones to cut you. Stick you in close. Watch for that. The spooks will pipe you out, and those Irish bastards over there, they'll put a bullet in you just as easy as they would fuck your mother."

Joey stopped talking long enough to spit, wiping the loose spittle from his lower lip. "Those fucks are in for a big surprise," he said, nodding toward the other gangs. "We got enough ammo on us tonight to take them all out. Especially that prick Ryan. He belongs to me."

He turned around and took a long gulp from a five-gallon jug of homemade Italian wine. He put the jug back near his right leg and reached one hand into the front left pocket of his blue jeans. He pulled out a crushed pack of Pall Malls, squeezed a cigarette out and bummed a light from an overweight teenager to his left.

Joey took a long drag and, clenching the cigarette with his teeth, let the smoke flow through his nose and mouth.

He looked at me and shrugged. "So, you ready or what?" he said.

"Yeah, I guess," I said.

"Don't fuckin' guess," the chubby kid said. "Either you ready or you ain't. We got no time to baby-sit."

"I'm ready," I said.

"That's good," Joey said. "That's very good."

Joey reached again for the jug of wine, took an even longer swig than the first one and passed it back to the overweight teenager. The chubby kid, whose name was Paulie, took large swallows, letting tiny rivers of wine flow down the front of his powder-blue T-shirt.

Paulie then passed the jug to me. I struggled to raise the heavy bottle to my lips, managed a short sip and passed it to my right. The strong taste of the wine stung my throat and warmed my chest.

"Okay," Joey said after everyone had a taste. "Let's dance."

The parking lot was ethnically divided.

The black gang members and their families gathered in the farthest corner of the lot, their garden chairs placed in a semicircle, their sweaty red coolers resting against the fence, their backs kept to the West Side Highway traffic.

The Puerto Ricans sat with poker chairs resting on a white line in the middle of a stickball strike zone that was painted on the side of a red brick wall. They came equipped with three cases of cold beer and a large radio blasting out Danny Rivera tunes.

The Irish stayed near the stoop at 538 West 51st, the building across from the lot. Friends and families sat catty-corner on old kitchen chairs, a steady beer supply coming out of an open first-floor window.

All bets for the night were also placed through that first-floor window. White-haired, toothless Irish Mike took the cash and set the odds. Winnings were always paid out on the same night.

The Italians also kept to themselves. They sat facing the outside of the fence, their backs to the fading sun. They drank wine out of plastic cups, smoked heavily and talked in murmurs. The men all sat the same way, open-legged, arms resting over the backs of wooden chairs that they had carried down from their living rooms and kitchens. The wives mingled among themselves, talking more about feuds and family squabbles than the fight about to happen in the parking lot.

The fights always began on time. Eight P.M. in July, eight-thirty during the month of August. The anointed leaders from the assembled gangs would make their way to the center of the split-gravel parking lot, eye their opponents and square off, the first round of a bout destined to end in bloodshed.

"Those first minutes were a bitch," a friend from the neighborhood told me. "Everybody checkin' out everybody. If they even *thought* you were scared it was over. It was all a game, like Cowboys and Indians. Except, instead of us havin' bows and arrows, we had knives, pipes and guns."

I stood in the center of the parking lot, my fists clenched, the back of my shirt soaked with sweat. The knife Joey had given me was open, hanging between two belt loops on my jeans.

I squared off against a fourteen-year-old black kid with a shiny forehead and a set of brass knuckles wrapped around his right hand. My mouth was dry, and the veins on either side of my neck pounded at an accelerated pace. I had trouble focusing my eyes. The black kid swung first, his brass-knuckled fist brushing against the top of my arm. The punch, short and hard, stung, forcing me to take two steps backward.

"I'm gonna kill your ass," the black kid said. "You dead meat."

The pipe seemed to come out of nowhere, a six-inch piece of steel, packed hard with gravel. I ducked as Joey, cursing and sweating, swung the pipe past my head, landing a strong blow right above the black kid's nose. A thick spray of blood showered my face and shirt. The black kid crumpled down to his knees.

Joey pulled me by the shirt and dragged me closer to the black kid.

"Stick him," he said. "Take your knife. Stick the motherfucker. Don't wait. Stick him now."

Blood flowed from the black kid's mouth as he rocked back and forth on his knees. I stared at him, the taste from his blood still running down my face. My shirt was sticky and red.

"Stick him!" Joey screamed. "Stick him. Make him dead. Make him dead."

I reached for the knife hanging from the loop in my jeans. I closed my hand around the handle and freed it from the loop. I held the knife, point down, by my side, ready to kill the bleeding boy before me.

I stared into his glazed eyes, saw the growing puffiness on his face and head, saw the blood flowing from his wound. Joey was standing behind him now, his eyes wide with anticipation, his face flushed and angry. He had his hands by the boy's neck, lifting his head toward the sky.

"Slice him here," he said to me, pointing at the boy's throat. "Ear to ear. Like a fuckin' pig."

I looked away from Joey and tried to catch a glimpse of my father. The parking lot was filled now with swinging pipes, slashing knives and blood. Blood everywhere.

On all sides, our parents, by now half-drunk and rowdy, cheered us on, crying for us to bring down our opponent. They screamed and applauded when one of their own landed a solid blow. They moaned and grimaced when the reverse happened.

I froze as I watched, not wanting to move, not caring if a pipe or knife landed in my direction. A Puerto Rican holding a zip gun fell against me, his face and arms a blanket of red. The weight of his body pushed us both to the ground. An open gash in the young man's chest poured blood out of him and onto me. The man balled one hand around my T-shirt and shifted his face closer to mine.

"I'm dying, man," he said. "Do something."

I rolled away from him, scrambled to my feet and saw my father standing less than fifty feet from me, both hands spread out against the fence. I wiped blood from my eyes, turned from my father and back toward Joey. He had, by now, tossed the bleeding boy to the ground, his attention focused instead on a large black kid with two pipes in his hands.

I threw my knife to the ground and walked to my father, my body caked with blood.

My father met me by the hole in the fence. He held his arms out and hugged me.

"You did good, One-punch," he said. "Real good. I'm proud of you."

We separated and began to walk up the street, away from the fighting. As we walked, my father winked and waved at the people we passed.

"His first fight," he said to them. "The little fuck did good, didn't he?"

We continued walking, past our building and up toward Ninth Avenue.

"Tell the truth," my father asked me, "you have a good time tonight or not?"

"It was okay," I said.

"I told you you'd like it."

We kept on walking, the blood drying on my skin and shirt.

"Where we going, Dad?" I asked him.

"Let's top it off," my father said. "Pizza and an Italian ice. That sound good to you or what?"

That same summer, my father began a love affair with a married woman from 52nd Street named Irene.

Irene was tall and thin, with long auburn hair ribbon-tied in a ponytail. She had a pale white complexion that was partly covered by a set of moles and freckles dotting her back and arms. She wore flowered dresses and light-colored shoes, loved to bet on horses and was said to be an excellent cook. She smoked heavily and drank beer and whiskey the same way.

She worked part-time as a waitress in a diner down by the piers and lived in a six-room third-floor walk-up with her mother and two small sons.

Irene was also married.

Her husband was in prison, in Attica, serving out the first year of a six-year sentence for robbery and assault. Irene would make the drive up to Attica once a month, borrowing her brother's Chevy Impala, and spend an afternoon with the father of her children.

"He was a real prick," my father said. "The kind of guy you could never really trust. He liked bossin' people around, always telling them what to do, what not to do. Those kind of guys always have a tough time in jail. He was no different."

Everyone knew about my father's affair with Irene. Even my mother. It was a given in Hell's Kitchen that married men cheated on their wives, but few conducted their affairs as openly as my father. He and Irene took walks through the neighborhood together, usually with her two sons—one in a stroller, one alongside.

They ate pizza at Mimi's on 52nd Street, sharing a back table, kissing and holding hands between bites. They saw first-run features at the Beacon and the Loew's 83rd, sitting in the balcony, drinking wine and making out. They had Chinese food at Ho Ho's, usually sharing a large bowl of chicken chow mein.

They acted like newlyweds, while everyone around them pointed fingers in their direction or whispered behind their backs.

"I was mad in love with her," my father told me. "Forgot all about your mother, made like she was invisible. I couldn't spend enough time with Irene, didn't give a shit about anything or anybody else. Even quit a good job for her. She was the closest I came to leaving your mother."

My father took me on a number of his dates with Irene. He would tell my mother to dress me in my best outfit—navy blue jacket, white-on-white button-down shirt, gray slacks with quarter-inch cuffs, black loafers—and have me ready no later than five. He never told her anything more than that, and she, for her part, never asked.

On those days, my father would walk through the door between three and four in the afternoon, holding a huge bouquet of flowers in his hand. He carried the flowers to the bedroom, left them on the bureau by an open window, stripped out of his clothes and headed down the hall for a quick bath. He would be cleaned, shaved and dressed in fifteen minutes.

During those minutes, my mother never moved off her kitchen chair, rosary beads in hand, eyes staring out past the fire escape and tenement rooftops. She didn't bother looking up when my father swooped past her, flowers back in hand, his favorite hat atop his head, heading for the door.

"Let's go, One-punch," he would say to me. "We're gonna be late."

He slammed the door behind us and headed for the street.

Irene always waited by the corner pharmacy, chain-smoking Marlboros, a nervous smile, which seemed more like a sneer, on her face.

She waved when she saw us and hugged my father when he handed her the flowers. She then always turned to me.

"Hi, honey," she'd say. "You sure look handsome tonight. Almost as handsome as your dad."

"I don't feel handsome," I'd reply, the jacket tight around my shoulders.

"Good-lookers never do," she'd say, taking my father by the arm and beginning our twenty-block walk to the Beacon Theater.

When I was with them, their routine was almost always the same. A movie, dinner at the Market Diner and then a slow walk back to Irene's apartment building. There I would sit, on the top step of the stoop, a chocolate ice-cream cone in one hand, my jacket folded neatly on my lap, and wait for my father, who was upstairs with Irene. On quiet nights, I could hear them, laughing and moaning, in the bedroom that faced out on the dark street.

On many of those nights, I wanted to get up and run back to my home, afraid for my mother, ashamed of my father. I never did. Instead, I waited until he opened the hallway door, scooped me in his arms and carried me, my head resting on his shoulder.

I always held him tight, listening to him whistle, feeling the strength in his arms and in his step.

On all of those nights, I cried.

I was walking home from school, having just finished my second day in fourth grade at Sacred Heart Grammar School. I liked my school, felt comfortable with the Christian Brothers and nuns who taught there, grateful for the help they had given me with English when all I could speak was Italian. They encouraged me to read, and to try to think beyond the confines of Hell's Kitchen. Most important, the school functioned as a safe haven for me, away from the turmoil that always existed in my home.

I carried my books slung in an old belt over my right shoulder. I was dressed in my school uniform—maroon corduroy pants with matching tie and loafers, a white-on-white, button-down shirt and red socks. The weather was New York steamy, and the air carried a hint of rain.

I had stopped on the corner of 50th and Tenth Avenue to roll my shirt sleeves up to the elbows when I saw my father. He had his hands on his hips and seemed agitated. He was leaning against the side of the pizza shop, his eyes fighting off the sun's glare, searching me out among the pack of children.

I waved and ran across the street to meet him.

"Hey, Dad," I said. "What are you doing here?"

A SAFE PLACE

He grabbed me by the arm and pulled me closer to him.

"Let's go to the docks," he said. "We need to talk."

We ran across the avenue, barely missing the oncoming traffic. As we walked, my father mumbled and cursed.

"I can't fuckin' believe this happened," he said. "It must be a fuckin' dream. It can't be real."

"What's wrong, Dad?" I asked him. "Did someone die?"

"I wish," he said. "I wish someone would drop dead. Make things easy for me *and* her."

"Who you talking about? Mom?"

"No, not Mom," he said. "Mom don't have nothin' to do with this. It's that bitch Irene."

"What did she do?"

"She got pregnant, that's what the fuck she did," he said. "Can you fuckin' believe it? The bitch is pregnant."

It was hard to speak, let alone grasp the impact of what my father had just confessed.

"What does that mean?" I finally said.

He looked at me as if I were insane. "What does that mean? What the fuck you think that means? She's gonna have a kid. My kid. At least that's what she says."

We walked past the back fence of De Witt Clinton Park and made our way toward the empty piers of Twelfth Avenue.

"Does Mom know?" I asked him, afraid of what the answer might be.

"No," he said. "As usual, she don't know shit."

We reached the edge of the pier, both of us wet with sweat from the brisk walk. My father sat on one of the rusty iron moorings and faced the ocean, his back to the city. I sat to his left, my feet dangling over the side, feeling the spray of the oil-slicked waves as they beat against the cement.

A massive Dutch oil tanker lay anchored to our left, a stream of water pouring out a large hole in the lower galleys.

"There's a ship that's had better days," my father said. "Probably older than me. They'll dry-dock her now, melt her down, build another, and she'll come back new."

My father reached into his pants pocket and pulled out a pack of gum. He unwrapped it, tossed the foil into the water, handed me a

45

piece and took two for himself. He reached down for me, lifted me up and sat me between his legs. He put his arms around my neck and chest and kissed me on both cheeks.

"I need your help, One-punch," he said, the gum stuffed to the side of his mouth. "You can't say no."

"I won't."

"I'm gonna work it out with Irene," he said. "Talk to her about a doctor, someone who can help her, understand?"

"I think so."

"I want you to go to the doctor with her," he said, his voice starting to choke. "I'll give you money to pay him."

"Will you be there?"

"No," he said. "I can't. Try to believe me, One-punch. I just can't."

"When?"

"Soon as me and Irene work it out. Couple of days, tops."

My father spit his gum into the ocean, took me off his lap and stood up.

"So," he said, "we got a deal?"

He put out his hand. I reached for it.

"Yeah," I said. "We got a deal."

The doctor's office was airless. On four sides, the gray walls were chipped and stained. Single beads of water dripped steadily from the ceiling. A dirty plastic partition separated a tiny waiting room from the doctor's area. The entire office smelled of stale cigarette smoke.

Irene sat in a torn red leather chair, turning the pages of a newspaper. I sat next to her, feeling as nervous as she looked, my right hand holding the six twenty-dollar bills my father had given me. Every so often, Irene would look at me and force a smile.

After a half-hour wait, a short woman in a blue skirt and white blouse came out from behind the partition and called out Irene's name. The woman held a clipboard in one hand and a burning cigarette in the other. On one of her eyes, the deep purple makeup was smeared.

"C'mon, honey," she said to Irene. "Doctor's waiting for you."

Irene looked at me, tears coming from both her eyes. Her hands shook, and it looked as if it would be difficult for her to stand. She reached out and grabbed me by the arm.

"Come with me," she said. "Please. Don't let me go in there alone."

Before I could answer, the woman with the clipboard spoke.

"Boy can't come in," she said. "Not allowed. Not by the doctor. Not by me."

The woman moved closer to Irene. "It's gonna be fine. You'll see. You won't even feel it."

Irene held my arm tighter.

"Please," she said to me. "Please."

"I can't, Irene," I said. "They won't let me."

I bent down and hugged her as tight as I could, tighter than I had ever hugged my own mother. I didn't think I would ever see her alive again and had only the slightest idea as to what they were going to do once she went inside that room.

The woman walked Irene past the partition.

"I'll wait here for you," I said.

Irene never looked back.

I could see figures through the partition and watched as the woman helped Irene out of her clothes. I heard the low voice of the doctor asking Irene to relax. Then, I saw the woman with the clipboard again, this time walking toward me.

"She says you have the money," she said. "That true?"

"Yes," I said. I opened my hand and watched as she took the crumpled bills.

"How is she?" I asked.

The woman turned away and never bothered with an answer.

IV

The bill, from Macy's department store, arrived with the morning mail, sandwiched between the Con Edison bill and a late notice from the Household Finance Corporation. My mother had placed it face up in the center of the kitchen table, resting it against a wooden napkin holder. She had her back to me, scrubbing soap onto a saucepan, when I walked in, sweaty from an afternoon of stickball. "Your father left us another surprise," she said, not bothering to turn her back. "On the table. Look for yourself."

I reached for the Macy's bill and tore it open. "How much?" my mother said. "How much this time?"

"One thousand, two hundred dollars," I told her. "A refrigerator and two washing machines."

I saw my mother's shoulders sag and watched as she closed the faucet, wiped her hands against her apron front and walked toward me. She took the bill from my hands, brushed past me and moved toward the small living room. I followed quietly behind her. She sat on the arm of our worn couch, the bill resting on her lap, her brown eyes vacant and moist.

"He's a sick man, your father," she said, looking at me, the anger now beyond her control. "We have no money, nothing. You understand, we have nothing. And he goes out and buys and spends as if we were millionaires."

She stood up, crumpling the Macy's bill in one hand. "Look at this," she said. "Look at this." She moved closer toward me. "I have no new refrigerator," she said. "I have no washing machines. These, these are my washing machines." She held up her two hands, one of them still clutching the Macy's bill. Tears rolled down behind her glasses and past the sides of her cheeks. "He buys gifts," she said. "Mr. Big Shot. Gifts for the union boss. Gifts for his girlfriends. Instead of working and worrying about his family, he hands out gifts." My mother began to rip the Macy's bill into little pieces and threw them on the floor. "I'm not paying it," she said. "I'm not paying it anymore."

"Nobody asked you to pay shit," my father said.

We hadn't heard him come in. He stood in the living room doorway, fresh from work, still wearing his long white butcher's coat, thick blotches of dried blood smeared on the right sleeve and chest. As usual, he held a newspaper in one hand and a bundled-up package of meat under his arm. He walked toward me, tossing the package of meat onto the couch as he moved.

"How ya doin', One-punch?" he said, bending down to kiss me.

"Okay, Daddy," I said. "Okay."

"How was school today?"

"Good," I said. "Brother Vaughn said I did an excellent job on my homework."

"Good kid," my father said. "That's what I like to hear."

He stood up and turned to my mother. She hadn't moved since she heard his voice, her face and hands shaking visibly. "What's the matter, baby?" he said to her. "Nervous about something?"

"No," she said, barely able to speak. "Do you want your dinner now?"

"No," he said. "Not now. Later."

He took his white butcher's coat off and tossed it on the floor. My mother moved to pick it up. "Leave it where it is," he said. My father removed his white T-shirt and threw it on top of the coat. He bent down, untied his heavy work boots, took them off and dropped them on the pile. He did the same with his ankle-high white socks. He undid the buckle of his thick black belt and whipped it out of its loops. He wrapped the belt around his right hand, unbuttoned his pants and stepped out of them once they fell to the floor. He stood in the middle of the living room, in his underwear, running a hand across the top of his head. He asked me to go into the kitchen and bring him a cold glass of seltzer with lots of ice. I left as soon as he spoke. He and my mother waited until I returned. No one said a word. No one moved.

I came running in and handed my father his drink. He took the glass, downed its contents in one long gulp and handed it back to me. "How old are you now, One-punch?" he said to me.

"Nine, Daddy," I said.

My father smiled, reaching over to stroke my face. "Before you know, you'll be out of the house, married, with a family of your own to raise," he said. "It's very important for you to know how to take care of your family. Especially your wife. When she loves you, when she respects you, it's beautiful. But when she doesn't, you have to take care of it. Understand?"

"Yes, Daddy," I said.

"Good," he said. "Now sit down on the couch, watch and learn."

As I walked the three steps to the couch, I saw my father grab the back of my mother's hair and throw her against a wall. He undid the belt around his hand and began swinging it, hitting her numerous times across her shoulders and back.

"You fuckin' bitch," he said. "You fuckin' bitch. You talk about me like that in front of my son. I'll kill you. I swear to Christ, I'm gonna kill you."

My father tossed the belt aside and began to punch my mother. Red spots began to appear on her neck and legs, her head hitting the wall from the force of each blow. My father then lifted my mother to her feet, slapped her glasses off and spit in her face. He ripped her apron off and began to rip at her dress.

He lifted her off her feet, his hands gripped tight around her throat. He tossed her onto the linoleum floor as easily as he would a dish towel. My mother now lay face down on the floor, her legs and thighs exposed. My father walked over and straddled my mother. As he did, he looked over at me, smiled and winked. He bent down, ripped my mother's underwear off and slapped her hard across the rear. He then reached over, grabbed the back of my mother's head and lifted her face to his.

"I know what you need," he said to her. "You need something to get your mind off the bills. Am I right?"

He tossed her head down hard against the floor and turned to me. "Hey, One-punch, do me a favor," he said. "Go out and play, okay. I'll call you after I finish taking your mother here for a short ride."

I ran out of the apartment and down the two flights of steps to the street, running to the sounds of my mother's cries and screams.

V

My father loved sports, boxing and baseball in particular. He preferred middleweights over heavyweights and would root for *any* team to beat the one he hated the most, the New York Yankees.

We would take the subway out to Yankee Stadium at least once a month, and *always* when the Minnesota Twins and Harmon Killebrew, my father's favorite ballplayer, were in town.

We sat in box seats along the third base line, close to Tom Tresh, Clete Boyer and Hector Lopez, the three Yankees I most admired. My mother had packed zucchini and egg sandwiches for us, and my father bought all the soda, pretzels and hot dogs a twenty-dollar bill could get.

My father and I regarded Yankee Stadium as our own private refuge from the heat and crowded streets of our neighborhood. We took the subway to the game and, if there was any money left over, would often hail a cab home. Twi-night doubleheaders played against teams with losing records were our favorites.

At those games, the best seats were available, the ballpark was near empty and the stadium felt as comfortable to us as a suburban backyard. My father and I would sit together, both rooting on the other team, our mouths full of food, our shirts off, exposing ourselves to the remaining warmth of the late-afternoon sunlight.

Those games, those warm days and long nights of baseball, are among my fondest childhood memories, the images as real today as they were back then—fresh-cut grass, watered-down red infield dirt, a Yankee in the batting cage, stand hawkers selling yearbooks, pennants and cold beer. My father by my side.

Nothing else mattered to me in that ballpark. My father's violent mood swings, his affairs, his problems with my mother were all remnants of another place, one that did not come equipped with dugouts or bats or umpires.

It was a place of peace, for my father as well as for me. We laughed a lot in that ballpark, and the only arguments we ever had were silly ones about the merits of one ballplayer or one team over another. Those arguments were always the easiest to lose.

The Yankees and Twins were tied 2–2 going into the top of the ninth. Steve Hamilton was on the mound for the Yankees, a tall, thin left-handed relief pitcher who would low-pump his fist and yank it back whenever he recorded the final out of a game. He called it "pulling the chain." My father was not impressed.

"Look at this clown," my father said. "C'mon, will you please. Where they find these losers?"

"He's not bad," I said. "He beat the Angels last week."

"Who the fuck can't beat the Angels?"

"Give him a chance."

The first batter Hamilton faced was Twins outfielder Bobby Allison. Hamilton played with the corners, throwing the power-hitting Allison nothing but breaking balls. The strategy proved effective when Allison went down swinging after six pitches.

"See," I said. "He's good."

"Good my ass," my father said. "Got lucky. Let's see what he does with the Killer."

Harmon Killebrew stepped into the batter's box. He was the muscleman of the Twins, a slow-moving, home run–hitting machine with large arms, a bald head and a farm boy's demeanor. My father liked him as much for his appearance as for his ability.

"The Killer doesn't have time to fuck around," my father said. "Watch what he does with this skinny cocksucker."

Hamilton's first pitch to Killebrew was a called strike, a sharp curve over the plate. The second pitch was just as nasty, hitting the corner for an 0–2 count. I nudged my father.

"Looking good, Dad," I said.

"Fuck you," he said.

Killebrew swung at Hamilton's third pitch, a curveball that didn't. The crack from the bat echoed through the stadium. My father stood, hands on hips, and watched the ball's short flight, clapping when it landed somewhere in the upper deck of left field. My father sat back down and laughed as he saw Hamilton pound his glove against his thigh in disgust.

"Where's that chain of his now?" my father said. "I'll tell you where. Killer shoved it right up his fuckin' ass."

My father leaned over and kissed me. "When you gonna learn, One-punch," he said. "The Yankees are losers. You only waste your time goin' with losers. Be like me. Go with winners. It's the only play."

Baseball was a chance for me to be a little boy around my father. Boxing was different. In that arena, I was treated like a man. The weekly bouts were held at either Sunnyside Gardens in Queens or in the old Madison Square Garden two blocks from home, on 50th Street and Eighth Avenue. Both places allowed me entry into a club that was the private playground of the middle-aged men of Hell's Kitchen.

I was eight when I saw my first boxing match. I don't recall much about it other than the fact that a fighter named Florentino Fernandez won a boring ten-round decision. Afterward, my father took me to Nathan's for two hot dogs and a papaya drink.

I was twelve when I saw the bout I most remember.

It was a winter Friday night, the day after a crisp four-inch snow-fall. There were seven bouts on the Madison Square Garden card, topped by the main event, a ten-rounder between top-ranked mid-dleweight contenders "Gentleman" Joey Archer and Rubin "Hurri-cane" Carter.

Two dozen men from Hell's Kitchen walked toward the Garden in groups of six, my father somewhere in the middle of the pack. They wore dark coats and hats and had pockets full of betting slips. A number of them stopped at a Ninth Avenue liquor store to pick up a few pints of Cutty Sark. Three other men stopped at the candy store next door to load up on cigars and cigarettes.

Walking up toward Eighth Avenue, one of the men asked me who I liked in the fight.

"Carter," I said. "I like Carter."

The ones who heard the answer laughed out loud.

"What's the matter, Mario," one of them said to my father. "Don't the kid know the rules?"

My father grabbed my arm and slowed his walk.

"Carter *can't* win," my father told me. "They won't let him."

"He's better," I said, still not convinced. "You said so yourself."

"I'm not sayin' he ain't better," my father said. "Alls I'm sayin' is he ain't gonna win."

"Why?"

"Because the Garden owns Archer," my father said. "He's the guy. So be smart and wise up. Don't make me look like a jerk."

The Carter-Archer bout was a Garden sellout. The bookie action both inside the arena and on the 50th Street side of Eighth Avenue was intense, with most of the street money heading Carter's way. At the time, Carter was the number-one ranked contender and Archer number two. The winner would be assured of a title shot against division champion Emile Griffith.

My father and I sat in the fourth row ringside. The minimum age to attend a boxing match was then sixteen, but that didn't stop any of the Hell's Kitchen men from bringing their sons to the fights. They simply slapped a five dollar bill into the palm of a more-than-willing Garden attendant and headed for their seats.

It meant a lot to my father and his friends to have their sons at the fights. It was a coming-of-age ritual, a special way of bonding man to boy. We ate whatever it was we wanted, were occasionally offered a sip from a passing tin flask and were asked to hug and kiss the women our fathers would sometimes pick up at ringside. Most of all, we were there to watch the spectacle of boxing, the wonders of which had been told to us by our fathers since we were old enough to make a fist.

I always noticed the smoke. Half the men smoked unfiltered cigarettes, crushing out the old under their shoes and lighting fresh ones in a near-rhythmic pattern. The other half puffed down on El Producto cigars that, lit or unlit, never left their lips. They used matches instead of cigarette lighters and kept their faces in a squint, eyes ducking the thin line of smoke flowing up.

They dressed the same, slacks and a short-sleeve sports shirt buttoned to the top. They shot their pants when they sat, so there was always a few inches of skin showing from the bottom of their cuffs to the top of their white socks. They carried no bill larger than a ten and kept a pocket full of change in a jacket fold-out. They never took their hats off during the fights.

My father seemed nervous as the preliminary bouts went on. Every few minutes he would leave his seat, either to make a phone call, go to the bathroom or get something to eat. I knew by now that my father's restlessness was never a good sign. .

"Dad, you want to go home?" I asked him.

"Why the fuck would I want that?"

"I just thought you weren't feeling well."

"I'm okay," he said. "It's just my stomach. Must have been that shit I ate for lunch. Don't worry about it."

At ten P.M., the introductions for the main event began. A couple of ex-champions and a few minor celebrities were introduced before ring announcer Johnny Addie got to the matters at hand. There were murmurs of anticipation from the ten thousand fans in attendance as Addie worked his way through the New York State Athletic Commission requirements.

While Addie's voice resonated through the Garden, I looked over at my father, who was sitting forward in his seat, his hands balled in two fists, his forehead glistened with sweat.

"Dad?"

"Shut up," he said without taking his eyes from the ring.

Hurricane Carter was wearing dark trunks, his mouthpiece already in place. He shifted from one leg to the other as a corner man laced on his padded gloves. Carter was head-to-toe muscle, a tough house fighter from New Jersey who could put down any opponent with either hand.

In the other corner, Joey Archer stood silent. He had a young pug's face, scar tissue already forming around the eyes. He had rattled off several impressive victories in a row, boxing and finessing his way to success, and was now one raised hand away from a title shot.

"Carter looks good, don't he?" my father said, sipping a soda and wiping sweat from his brow.

"Looks better than Archer," I said.

"My mother looks better than Archer," a longshoreman to my right said. "Don't mean shit."

"All it takes is one punch," my father said. "One fucking shot and Archer's down."

"Save your breath, pal," the longshoreman said. "It ain't gonna happen."

55

"I ain't your fuckin' pal," my father said.

The first four rounds were even, as Archer peppered Carter's head with soft jabs and hard hooks, while the Hurricane worked the body and waited for an opportunity to land a more telling blow. Both fighters looked sharp and did little to hide the animosity they held for one another. The crowd, heavily in Archer's favor, screamed its approval at every landed punch.

By the end of the fourth round my father had his jacket and hat off and was halfway through his fifth beer. I had never seen my father drink before and was surprised to see him drinking now. He was animated only when the fight was in progress, throwing punches in the air, mumbling words of encouragement, breathing heavily.

"What do you think, Dad?" I asked before the start of round five.

"We're fucked if Archer don't win this fight," he said.

"Everybody says he will."

"That's just talk," my father said. "Don't mean shit to those guys up there. In the ring is where you gotta win it."

"So he gets his chance at the title."

"I give a fuck about his chance at the title," my father said. "I bet two thousand dollars on the fuck. Put it down with a bookie in the Bronx. Two thousand I ain't got to give if he loses."

"Why'd you bet what you don't have?"

"Shut up and watch the fight," my father said.

By the eighth round it was clear that Archer's stick-and-move approach was more effective than Carter's free throws. The word around ringside was that the Irishman was comfortably ahead and only a knockout could spoil his chance at victory.

"It's in the bag, pal," the longshoreman next to me said to my father. "Just like I told you before it started."

"I'm not your fuckin' pal," my father said. "Just like I told *you* before it started."

There were two minutes left in the tenth round. By now, the crowd was on its feet cheering their man Archer on. My father stood up, grabbed me into his arms and kissed me.

"I'm gonna buy you something nice when I get my money," he said. "Maybe a suit."

"I don't want a suit," I said.

"How about a bike?" my father said. "Bike sound good?"

"You mean it? I can get a bike?"

"Why not?" my father said.

The loud roar of the crowd brought our conversation to an end. My father and I turned our attention back to the ring. There we saw Joey Archer slumped against the middle strand of the ropes, his legs wobbly, his eyes glassy, the victim of a powerful Hurricane Carter right hand.

There was less than a minute left in the fight.

"I don't fuckin' believe this," my father said. "He's gonna go down. The fuck is gonna go down."

Carter drove a left hook to Archer's midsection. Another right hand grazed his temple. One of Archer's knees appeared limp.

The seconds on the official clock ticked down to the teens.

My father put me down, stood back up and wiped a hand over the top of his head.

"C'mon, kid," he prayed. "Stay up. Stay the fuck up."

One more Carter right snapped Archer's head back. Hurricane repositioned his feet, weighed his opponent and threw one last punch, a from-the-waist left hook that landed just above Archer's right cheekbone. Carter then lunged for Archer as the final bell sounded, ending the fight and any hopes of an upset.

"Jesus Christ," my father said. "The fuck almost blew it for me."

The longshoreman next to me tapped my father on the shoulder. My father turned just as Joey Archer's victorious and unanimous decision was being announced.

"What is it?" he said to the longshoreman.

"I told you, didn't I, pal," the longshoreman gloated. "Nothing to worry about."

My father reached over me and grabbed the man by the shirt collar and threw him back down to his seat. He then landed two successive right-hands on top of the man's head and another just above his nose. My father then tossed his jacket over the man's head and hit him with a half-dozen solid blows. The crowd around us parted, giving my father room to fight.

My father finally removed the jacket from the dazed and bleeding man's head. He leaned closer to him, holding the man's face in one hand.

"I told you before, fucko," my father said to him. "I ain't your fuckin' pal."

I have never gone to either Yankee Stadium or Madison Square Garden with anyone other than my father. I want the memories that exist in those places to remain as fresh and intact for me as they have been all these years. Neither the stadium nor the new Garden could possibly have the same hold for my children as they do for me. The far happier circumstances of their lives just wouldn't allow it to be true.

The afternoons and nights I spent with my father at Yankee Stadium and Madison Square Garden solidified the bond that existed between us. We were much more than a father and his son. I was my father's best friend, and he was mine. He spoke to me as he would speak to any adult in his circle. He also afforded me responsibilities far greater than any that would normally be given to a child of my age.

At night, after work, after he had his bath and dinner, my father would sit with me in our living room, talking about whatever he felt needed to be discussed. He would bring home as many as five newspapers a day and would sometimes ask me to read the sports sections aloud to him.

While I read, my father would lay on the floor, a pillow mashed against a side of the couch, in his underwear, trying hard not to fall asleep. For my father, it was a relaxing way to keep up with the scores and highlights of the sports he followed. For me, the reading served as a nice introduction to the voices of Jimmy Cannon, Dick Young, Bill Gallo and, on those occasions when I read straight through to the front of the paper, Pete Hamill and Jimmy Breslin.

On the nights we didn't read the papers together, I would sit and listen to my father tell stories. He talked to me about the summer he spent in the Northwest woods working in a logger camp. He talked about his days as a fighter, boxing under an assortment of pseudonyms and handing over as much as a hundred dollars in winnings to his father.

He talked about how hard his father worked and how difficult it was to be Italian and *not* get into fights with the Irish kids who taunted him for that very reason.

He told stories about some of his girlfriends and about how he almost killed a man in a Connecticut diner for spilling ketchup on his shirt. He talked about his brothers and the arguments they had, the great fighters he saw do battle and how he rode the rails cross-country at an age when other kids were still in school. Behind every story told, there was a lesson. My father made sure of that.

"I used to think kids who went to school were jerks," he would tell me. "Sittin' in a classroom all day, listening to some guy talk about all kinds of boring shit. Not for me, kid. I was too smart for that. I wanted to see the country. Well, I did see the country and look where it got me. No-fuckin'-where, that's where. Be *really* smart, One-punch, stay where you are. Stay in school. Let someone *pay* for you to go cross-country."

My father was a man who cursed through every sentence he spoke but would never allow anyone to use the words *nigger, kike* or *spic* in his presence. He beat my mother for no reason and cheated his friends and family out of money, yet he prayed daily and attended Mass on Sunday. Once a month, whether we had it to give or not, he would mail out a cash donation to the Maryknoll Sisters.

He would sit through any movie that starred James Cagney or Humphrey Bogart, cry at the corniest melodramas and smile whenever he heard my mother in the kitchen singing old Neapolitan love songs as she washed his work clothes in cold water.

He would take me to Italian summer feasts in upstate New York twice every summer and to Aqueduct racetrack on Long Island once a month.

He knew that my mother, like many other Italian immigrants, loved wrestling, finding as much fun in the spectacle as she did in the sport. One Monday night a month, my father would take us both to Madison Square Garden to watch World Wide Wrestling Federation champion Bruno Sammartino take on the newest villain in town. The Garden was always packed on wrestling night, a theater for the working poor in full operation.

We also attended the six-day bike races, though neither one of us quite understood the rules or the scoring. We simply went to see the legendary Nando Terruzzi furiously pedal his way to yet another impressive victory. We went to the Ringling Brothers Circus every spring and the Ice Capades every winter. If there was an event in town that I knew about and wanted to see, my father made every effort to get us tickets.

"He spoils you," my mother would say to me. "Treats you like a rich kid. There isn't anything he wouldn't do if you asked him. Name it. He'd go out and get it. Steal if he had to. You must never forget that. You're all your father lives for now, and when you're older, he's gonna want to live through you. Through what you do."

In the summer of 1962, my father sent my mother on a charter flight to Italy to spend a few months with her family. While my mother was away, I was expected to live with my aunt Mary, my father's sister, on Long Island. I was opposed to the move, not wanting to leave either the neighborhood or my father.

"Don't be crazy," my father said. "You'll love it out there. It's like going to camp."

"Why can't I stay here, with you?"

"Who's gonna watch you? I'll be at work all day. What you gonna do with yourself?"

"I'll stay with my friends. There's plenty to do. I'll be all right."

"Forget it," my father said. "You're going to Mary's house. Case closed."

I didn't cry as I watched my mother leave on her Alitalia flight, heading for Rome's Fumicino Airport. I stiffly hugged her by the customs gate area, and watched as she just as stiffly kissed my father goodbye. In many ways, I was as distant from my mother as I was close to my father. Until I was nine I called her Raffaela instead of Mom. My father saw no harm in the practice, and my mother never said a word about it to either one of us.

The night she left, my father and I ate in an airport diner, sharing a hamburger and french-fries platter. He didn't speak much, staring out the terminal windows, watching planes from various airlines arrive and depart.

"I'm really gonna miss her," he said, tears forming in his eyes.

"It's only a few months," I said.

"I can't be alone," he said. "Not cut out for it."

"Why am I going to Aunt Mary's then? I can stay with you. This way you won't be alone."

"Don't start that shit again, will you please? You're goin' and I don't wanna hear another fuckin' word about it."

My father reached into his pocket and pulled out enough money to cover both the check and the tip.

"C'mon, One-punch," he said. "Let's get home. It's getting late."

VI

I was at my aunt's house a little more than a week when my father came back for me. I wasn't happy there and he knew it. My aunt Mary had done all she could to make me feel welcome—day camp, nightly cookouts and weekend visits to the beach. None of it mattered. I wanted to be home. In my neighborhood. With my father.

My father arrived at his sister's on a rainy Tuesday night. We had just returned from watching my cousin Joey and his team play through a two-hour soggy and sloppy version of Little League baseball. I had just finished a chocolate ice-cream cone when I saw a rusty, four-door taxi sedan pull up near the front hedges. My father got out the back, a brand-new brown suitcase in his right hand. He waved when he saw me looking at him from the window.

"Hey, One-punch," he said. "Pack your clothes, we're takin' a trip."

I ran down the front steps of the house, my arms extended, eager to hug and kiss my father. My aunt and uncle followed behind me, as surprised as I was at my father's unannounced arrival.

"What are you doing here?" Aunt Mary asked him. "Is there anything wrong?"

"Nothin's wrong," my father said. "I'm just here to pick up the kid."

"Why?"

"We're goin' on a trip."

"A trip where, Mario?" my aunt asked, curiosity and suspicion mixed in her voice.

"Chicago," my father said. "I got a deal workin' out there and I want to take my kid along. All right with you?"

"I'll get his things together," she said. "I figure you'll want to leave right away."

"That's right," my father said. "I want us to be ready to leave for Chicago in the morning."

My father and I sat in the rear car of the Long Island Rail Road commuter train, heading into Manhattan. We ate roast-beef sandwiches, held uneasily across our laps. Two cans of A&W Cream soda rested against the window ledge, next to our seats.

"How was it back there?" my father said, wiping mustard from his lower lip. "You have a good time?"

"It was okay," I said.

"Cheap bastards," my father said. "Didn't even offer us a ride home."

"How long we going to be in Chicago?" I asked.

My father took the last bite from his sandwich and drank down the remains of the cream soda. He looked out the window for a few moments and then turned back to me.

"There ain't no Chicago," he said.

"But you told Aunt Mary we were going there."

"Fuck what I told Mary," he said. "That's not important. What's important is what I tell you."

My father looked down at what was left of my roast-beef sandwich.

"You gonna leave that?" he asked.

"Here," I said, handing the sandwich over to him, "you can finish it."

He spoke as he ate.

"What you and me need to do is none of Mary's business, understand?" he said. "That's why I made up the bullshit about Chicago."

"What do we need to do?"

My father crumpled up the sandwich wrapper and tossed it on the seat next to him. He reached over toward me, picked me up and put me on his lap. He kissed my face and held me tight.

"When we get to New York, we're going to take a cab straight to the police station," he said.

"Why?"

"We gotta fill out a report," he said.

"What kind of report?"

"A report that says Mom left us," he said. "A report that says she left her family."

"But she didn't leave us," I said. "We sent her to Italy to visit her family. You sent her."

My father threw me off his lap and back onto my seat, across from him. His face was red with anger, and both his fists were clenched.

"Listen to me, you little prick," he said. "You're gonna tell the cops that Mom left you and me. That we begged her to stay, but she wouldn't listen. You got the picture?"

I began to cry, which angered my father even more. He reached over and grabbed my cheeks with his hands, squeezing them hard as he did.

"Listen to me, fucko," he said. "You fuck this up and I swear I won't let you out of the police station alive."

My father released his grip and sat back in his seat. He took several deep breaths before he looked in my direction again.

When he did, I saw the tears in his eyes.

"I miss my baby," he said. "I miss her bad. You gotta help me on this, One-punch. I don't know what to do without her."

"Why'd you let her go?"

"I had to let her go," my father said. "She wanted to see her family, spend time with those humps. You see how she gets, otherwise, walkin' all over the fuckin' house with a puss a mile long on her face. Those people mean more to her than you and me do, that's for fuckin' sure. You and me don't stand a chance next to her family."

The train pulled into Penn Station on time. We made our way past the late-night commuters, my father carrying his new suitcase in one hand and my battered one in the other. Outside, under a light drizzle, he whistled for a Checker cab.

Minutes later, we were both standing in front of a Sixteenth Precinct desk sergeant filling out a report charging my mother with the crime of abandonment of family.

The next morning, my father began a series of threatening phone calls to my mother. He accused her of cheating on him, of stealing his money, of marrying him just so her son could come to America. He insulted her and her family, and claimed to have personal knowledge about the number of lovers my mother had during her eight years as a widow.

"You're a whore," he screamed into the phone. "Everybody knows I married a whore. I'm gonna kill them all, bitch. All those men, I'm gonna find 'em and kill 'em. Then, I'm gonna come kill you. You hear me, whore? You hear? Answer me, you fuckin' bitch. Answer me."

My mother never did answer. She would listen to the tirade and not speak a word, afraid that anything she might say would rouse my father's anger even more.

"What could I say?" my mother told me later. "There was someone in the room with me whenever he called. My mother, one of my sisters, someone. I couldn't say anything. I didn't want them knowing what a hell my life with your father had become. I swear to you, if you were with me instead of with him I would never have come back to America. Never."

After ten days, my father finally gave up and stopped calling my mother. He had come to the frustrating realization that both the phone calls and the police report were useless attempts to get his wife back home.

Within that ten-day period, my father had also stopped working, quitting a steady job over what he perceived to be a lack of respect from his boss.

"That prick thinks I'm a fuckin' machine," my father said on his second day out of work. "Money-hungry bastard, don't give a shit about me. What do I need him for? I got plenty of money in my pocket and there's plenty of people out there who want me to work for them. I told him to shove the job up his ass. Fuckin' bum."

The day my mother left for Italy, she handed me a passbook from the Central Savings Bank on West 73rd Street. Despite the bad loans and heavy debts incurred by my father, she had managed to save $12,200 in a joint account.

I scanned the numbers, saw the weekly deposits of thirty, sometimes fifty dollars, and handed the book back to my mother. She shoved it back inside her apron pocket.

"I wonder how much will be there when I return," she said.

Less than one month after she left, the passbook total was down to zero, and my father had borrowed an additional $2,400 to handle his day-to-day living expenses.

"Your father was a weak man," a close relative of his once told me. "He had a weakness for the horses and another for his family. Didn't have it in him to ignore either of them. They ganged up and stripped him naked as a baby. Without those demons around, your father might have ended up a comfortable man. Not rich. Comfortable."

I was passed from one relative to another as my father figured out ways to get my mother back sooner than planned. I spent a pleasant week with my father's other sister, Anna, and her family, and a miserable one with his younger brother, Albert, and his wife and children.

Aunt Mary didn't want me back, more or less holding me responsible for the Chicago fiasco. My father's parents would only take me for a weekend, which was just as well since I felt they cared as little for me as I did for them.

Truth was, I hated being shunted around and was happiest when in Hell's Kitchen. I felt safe on its streets and comfortable with the people who lived there. If the weather became too warm, I would escape inside the darkness of Sacred Heart Church, sit in a back pew and watch the old women of the neighborhood go through the Stations of the Cross. If I was short on money and needed to eat, Tony, the counter man at Mimi's Pizzeria, would always spot me a slice.

Hell's Kitchen was my home, and I resented anyone who tried to change that. I took comfort in the fact that I lived in a neighborhood that maintained a code of conduct, a series of rules set up to keep outsiders out and insiders safe. Hell's Kitchen was never a haven for civil libertarians. It was, however, a great neighborhood in which to be a child.

I was two months shy of my ninth birthday.

"Kids could stay out and play till midnight if they were allowed," Dick, the local deli man, remembered. "I kept the store open till eleven most nights, sometimes later during the summer. Never got held up. Reason for that was simple enough. We kept to ourselves. Didn't bother anybody else. Didn't expect to be bothered. A stranger walks into the Kitchen, he knows soon enough there are eyes on him, watching his every move. He gets out of line, he gets straight—fast."

Eventually, my father gave up on the relative shuttle system and, for the two weeks prior to my mother's return, let me stay by myself during the day, allowing the neighborhood, in effect, to function as my baby-sitter.

On Wednesday and Thursday afternoons, my friends and I would head over to the Metropole Café, a go-go bar on 48th and Seventh. The bouncer at the door knew our faces, if not our names, and would let us in. There in the back room, keeping time to the dancer's shimmies, was Gene Krupa, the man our fathers called the greatest big-band drummer who ever lived.

We would make our way down the dark bar, sneaking a glimpse up at the dancing girls, and find a table in the back, inches from Krupa and his magic drums. By this time, Krupa was years past his prime, the abuse of drugs and drink visible on his face and hands.

At one point in the afternoon, the house lights would come all the way down. Krupa switched to the glow sticks and began to pound away on "Sing, Sing, Sing." It didn't sound as good without Benny Goodman, Teddy Wilson and Lionel Hampton, but it was still Krupa, and it was still special.

I sat there, in the dark, watching Krupa's sticks swing through the air, and imagined what it would have been like to have seen him twenty years earlier, as my father did, in a packed dance hall, his tie undone, sweat flowing down his forehead, the music he was playing fresh and new.

Those warm afternoons spent with my Hell's Kitchen friends inside that near-empty go-go club, sipping ginger ales in sweaty glasses and listening to Gene Krupa, were, by far, the happiest moments of my summer.

Three days before my mother's expected arrival, my father told me I was going to meet a sister I didn't know I had. It was early on Labor Day morning, the apartment quiet and dark, my father shaking me out of a somber sleep.

"Hey, One-punch," he said, "get up. I got great news."

I lifted my head from the pillow, barely awake, my father's face and body shaded in shadow.

"What's wrong?" I said.

"I got a surprise for you," he said. "Something I know will make you happy."

I sat up in my bed, an iron-based junior that closed into a lounge chair.

"What, Dad?" I said. "What is it?"

"Your mother comes home Friday, right?"

"Right," I said, still not fully awake.

"Well, guess who'll be coming over on Sunday?" he said, his voice rising with excitement, his face flushed. "For dinner?"

"I don't know, Dad."

"You not gonna guess?"

"I can't think who it would be."

"Forget it then, I'll tell you," he said. "Your sister's comin'. About two o'clock. Bringing her husband, maybe her kids."

I got out of bed and looked in his face to see if what he had just said was all a joke.

The smile on his face told me it wasn't.

I knew both my parents had previously been married. My mother frequently spoke about her first husband, detailing how they met, where they lived, the region of Italy he came from, how stern he was with my brother and how happy they all were putting together a life in the small town of Salerno.

My father, on the other hand, never spoke about his first wife. I knew from my mother her name was Grace and she died young. I did not know how she died or what she looked like or what kind of life my father had with her. I did not know if he had loved her more than he loved my mother or if he treated her in any way different.

I also did not know my father had another child until he mentioned it on that Labor Day morning.

My sister, Phyllis, sat across the table from me and smiled. My mother had prepared a roast beef and baked potato dinner and set the table with what passed for our best silverware. My sister's husband, a thin, fidgety man quick to laugh and slow to talk, sat to my right. At first, my father looked and acted nervous, his hands shaky as he sliced the roast, his voice soft and distant when he spoke. But he seemed to relax as he ate and, by the second serving, was himself again.

Throughout the meal, my mother, home from Italy less than two days, concentrated on her food and spoke to no one.

My mother had arrived late Friday night, her flight from Rome delayed more than three hours. At the arrival gate, she did not smile or wave when she saw my father and me signal to her. We rushed up to welcome her back. She was stiff and sullen when we hugged, and the kisses she gave us were cold and distant.

The cab ride into Manhattan was a quiet and uneasy one. My mother sat in the front, trying to ward off the effects of motion sickness, while my father and I spread out in the rear of the Checker, guessing makes and models of the cars that passed us on the highway.

The first thing my mother did when we got to the apartment, even before unpacking her bags or changing her clothes, was to ask my father for the savings-account passbook.

"There's plenty of time for that later, baby," my father said. "How's about a cup of tea before bed?"

"I don't want anything," my mother said. "I just want to see our bank book."

"C'mon, baby," my father said, reaching his arms out for my mother. "Sit down. Relax a little bit. You just got home."

"Yes, I'm home," my mother said, pushing my father's arms away from her. "And I want to see our bank book."

"Hey, enough with the fuckin' bank book," my father said. "That's all you give a fuck about, money. I give you enough. Enough to support you and that whole fuckin' family of yours. And you still want more. Well, guess what, bitch. There ain't no fuckin' more. Understand? Fuckin' ride's over."

"You spent it all?"

"Yeah, that's right," my father said. "I spent it all. It was my money and I spent every fuckin' nickel. You got a problem with that, take your bags here and head right back to where you came from. I sure as shit don't need ya and my kid here don't need ya."

My mother brushed past my father and headed toward me.

"I trusted you," she said to me. "I asked you to make sure this wouldn't happen. Instead, you went around and had yourself a good time. You don't care. Just like your father. You don't care."

"What did you want me to do?" I said.

"Stop him," she said. "That's why I left you behind."

My father reached over and grabbed my mother by her shoulders, spinning her around to face him.

"He got nothin' to do with this, bitch," he said, shaking her. "This stays where it is, between me and you."

"I was only gone eight weeks," my mother said, starting to cry. "Only eight weeks."

"That's a long time, baby," my father said. "A long fuckin' time to be away from your family."

"You told me to go."

"I got tired of listenin' to you piss and moan about your family," he said. "It was all you could talk about."

"I'd been away for eight years," my mother hissed. "I wanted to see my mother again before she died."

"So whatta you bitchin' about?" he said. "You got your fuckin' vacation. You got to see your mother. You should be happy."

"You spent all our money."

"What the fuck you mean, *our* money," my father said. "*My* money, baby. Mine. I worked for it. I'm the one got up at three every morning to go lug beef on my back all fuckin' day. You were here, nice and warm under the fuckin' blankets. You didn't do shit except put money where I told you to put it."

"When did you lose your job?" my mother asked, both her hands slowly pulling at her hair. "And why?"

"I didn't lose shit," my father said. "I quit."

"To do what?"

"Hey, baby, you ain't the only one here needs a vacation," my father said. "I took a break. Don't go makin' a federal case out of it."

My father moved away from my mother and walked over to the refrigerator. He opened the freezer top and stared at its near-empty contents. He nudged at the top of my mother's shoulder with the back of his hand.

"I'm hungry," he said. "Give me some money. We'll go get some Chinese."

The next morning, my parents argued again, this time over Phyllis. My mother sat with her back against the kitchen wall, sipping from a cup of tea, looking out a half-open window at dozens of crossing clotheslines burdened by the weight of linen left out to dry.

To me, my mother looked much older than when she had left. Her deep tan failed to hide the worry and anxiety that masked her eyes. She seemed frail, frightened and tired. She was angry at my father and disappointed in me. It was difficult for her to speak without starting to cry. I looked down at her lap and noticed how her hands shook as they held the cup.

My father seemed not to notice or care about my mother's depressive state, though he appeared genuinely happy to have her back. There was an almost childlike excitement to him as he hurriedly prepared for his daughter's arrival the next day.

"I called Louie downtown," he said. "He's puttin' aside a roast beef for me. Said I could pay him later. A couple of baked potatoes, some string beans, a salad. What do you think? We need cake, somethin' like that?"

My mother's face and eyes never moved from the open window.

"Why did you ask her here?" she said. "Why now?"

The smile left my father's face.

"I'll tell you why," he said. "Because she's my fuckin' kid. That's why."

My father walked over to where I was standing, sorting out a pack of baseball cards, and put his arm around me.

"Besides," he said, looking at me, "I think it's time my kids got to know each other."

The dinner was awkward. My father did most of the talking, telling everyone about his summer, his lineup of jobs and the various deals he had in the works. Phyllis paid close attention, nodding or laughing at the conclusion of each story.

"That's great, Daddy," she said. "It sounds like you're doing really well."

It was strange to hear someone else call my father Daddy. I also found it especially strange to sit across from someone who looked so very much like my father. Phyllis was in her mid-twenties and had already started on a family of her own. She had smooth skin, an open face and a contagious smile. Her voice was as soft and mild as her manner, her hair was brown, and her eyes were dark as night. There was no mistaking the obvious fact that we were blood-related.

Phyllis lived in Brooklyn, in a neighborhood that sounded similar to ours. She talked about relatives I had never heard of, but whose names struck a receptive chord with my father. She told me how she met her husband, where she went to school and what flavor ice cream she liked. She was an easy person to warm up to, and by the start of dessert, I began to feel comfortable around her.

My sister and her husband left minutes after dinner ended. My father appeared sad that the short visit was over, but had to be glad that it had all gone well. For her part, my mother was just glad her latest ordeal was finally at an end.

Everyone hugged and kissed by the door. Both my father and his daughter did their best not to cry. Promises were made from both sides to make the visits more frequent, to spend a lot more time together, especially around holidays.

"It was really nice to see you," my sister said to me, my hand held in hers. "Make sure Dad brings you out to Brooklyn, anytime you want."

"I will," I said.

My sister leaned down and kissed me on both the cheek and forehead.

"We'll see each other soon," she said. "I just know it."

I waved to her as she headed down the two flights of tenement steps, beginning the four-block walk to the subway.

"See you soon," I said. "Real soon."

My father closed the wooden front door of the apartment. He looked over at me and smiled.

"Nice kid," he said, his voice choked. "I got myself two really nice kids."

My father wiped at his eyes with the back of his hand. My mother stood near the kitchen entrance, holding a dish towel, an angry look on her face. While my father and I were saying our goodbyes to Phyllis, my mother busied herself clearing off and washing the last of the cups and dishes. The best she could muster for either Phyllis or her husband was a lukewarm handshake.

My father walked over to where my mother was standing, wiping his hands against the sides of his pants as he moved. My mother stood up straight as my father approached.

"I warned you, you bitch," he said, stopping only inches from her face. "I warned you about fuckin' with me today, didn't I?"

"I did everything you asked me to do," my mother said.

"I asked you to be nice," my father said. "And you weren't nice. You were a fuckin' bitch."

"I didn't say anything," my mother said. "I didn't do anything. What do you want from me?"

My father took a deep breath and hit my mother in the face, his closed fist landing just below her right eye. My mother's eyeglasses flew from her face and her legs gave way.

My father threw another punch, this one shorter than the first, as he watched my mother sink down in front of him. The blow landed just above her forehead.

My mother lay on the kitchen floor, knocked cold from the two punches.

"Nothin'," my father said as he walked away from her. "That's what I want from you. Not a fuckin' thing at all."

My mother had a number of health problems during the years we lived in Hell's Kitchen. She had a hysterectomy when I was four and painful cysts removed from her stomach and arms when I was six. She had corrective oral surgery when I was seven, and again a year later. It always seemed she was either on her way to or coming home from a doctor.

It was during her recuperative periods that my mother and I grew to know each other. We never had the normal mother and son relationship that existed in more traditional environments. My father would not allow that to happen.

For many years, I kept a distance from my mother. Her nonconfrontational personality made it easy to do so. She and I never talked about school or my friends or what existed in the world beyond our front door. She never attended a P.T.A. meeting or a school function of any type, using her language barrier as an all-encompassing excuse.

She was friendly with my first-grade teacher, a warm, intelligent young nun named Sister Josephine Maria. My mother envied Sister Josephine, longing for the quiet, reflective life she seemed to lead. To my mother, Sister Josephine lived in an ideal world, free from the burdens of husbands, children, in-laws and abuse.

I spent many hours alone with my mother during the time she was recuperating from her various illnesses and surgeries. My father, except for brief periods during the late afternoon, would disappear during those weeks. There was no telephone to interrupt us or television set to distract us. There was nothing to do but talk.

During those hours, my mother would tell me stories about Ischia, the Italian island where she was born and raised. She would talk about the war and how difficult it was for the Italians to live under a dictator's fascist rule. She would remember the American and British bombs landing on her island and on Salerno, the town she lived in with her first husband and where her second son died.

On many afternoons, she spoke about her brothers and sisters, of the fights and fun they had growing up in a large family with little money. She told me funny stories about her father and described how courageous her mother was to go into the then Nazi-occupied city of Naples and bring back food for them to eat.

I would always sit next to her on the bed, occasionally wiping her head with a damp cloth. She left her glasses off and kept her dark curly hair combed back. She held rosary beads in one hand and a soiled linen handkerchief in the other. She looked very sad and seemed to be in a great deal of pain.

"How many brothers do you have?" I asked, initiating the stories with a question.

"Three," she said, dabbing at her upper lip with her hankie. "Giovann Guisseppe, Mario and Johnny."

"Johnny was the one that was adopted, right?"

"Yes," my mother said. "Grandma brought him home when he was only a day old."

"Did he ever find out he was adopted?"

"We never told him," my mother said. "He found out for himself when he was about nine years old."

"Who told him?"

"Kids from school," my mother said. "Someone wrote his real last name, Murano, across a blackboard. Johnny came home and asked Grandma if it was true what the kids were saying, if he was really adopted. She said it was true, but that it didn't matter what others were saying because he was her son and that's all there was to it. But, Grandma told him, if he wanted to meet his real mother she would try her best to arrange it."

"What did he say?"

"He said he was looking at his real mother."

I poured her a strong cup of Lipton tea, Irish style, with milk and sugar. My mother took two deep slurps and propped her pillow up higher. She put the cup down and looked at me for a few silent moments, her wrists and arms still bruised from the recent surgery.

"He had magic hands," she said, once again talking about her brother. "He could build anything—a table, a cabinet, a car engine. He had a natural talent. He used to tell Grandma that someday he would build her a giant house on the biggest mountain in Ischia.

"Grandma would tease him and say, 'Why would I want to live on a mountain? I'm afraid of heights.'

"Johnny would laugh and tell her he would build the house without windows so she would never know how high up she was. Johnny really loved my mother, but the one he was closest to was Grandpa. They were crazy about each other. The only time I saw my father cry was the day Johnny went off to fight in the war."

My uncle John was stationed on an Italian submarine, where he worked in the engine room. He was barely twenty years old, with thick dark hair, olive eyes and a handsome face.

"He wrote to us every week," my mother said, starting to cry. "He told us how much he missed everyone and how soon he would be back home. His last letter arrived on the day they said he died."

The British destroyer spotted the Italian submarine three hundred miles off the Adriatic coastline. The sub was moving due north, heading home to port after having completed its reconaissance mission. The first British depth charge exploded less than 150 feet from the sub's front end. The second and third charges landed, forcing the sub to take on water. The fourth explosion blew out the engine. The fifth and sixth shattered the submarine, killing everyone aboard.

The members of the British destroyer cheered and whistled when they saw the bubbles and foam from the deadly explosion rise to the top of the sea. The alarm clanged victorious and the sounds of the happy crew singing songs of conquest rang through the otherwise silent night.

"Two men in uniform knocked on our door," my mother said. "We were eating lunch. Grandpa had just poured himself a glass of red wine. We all knew what it meant. Grandpa held the letter in his hand, crumpled, and walked off toward the fishing boats. Grandma took the folded flag the men gave her and went to her bedroom. The two men bowed their heads and left. Johnny was gone. That's how simple life and death is when you're poor and send sons off to fight in wars you don't understand."

My mother wiped the tears from her eyes and drank some more of her tea.

"Grandpa was never the same after that day. None of us were. How could you be?"

My mother looked at me and ran her hand down my cheek. "Do me a favor, would you?" she asked. "Get me my pocketbook. It should be on the kitchen table."

I came back holding a black handbag, tattered at the edges, and handed it to my mother. She opened it and rummaged through it for a few minutes before she found what she wanted. It was an old photo, covered in plastic, a short Italian prayer written on the back.

My mother sat up in bed and handed me the photo. It was a picture of my uncle John.

"Here," she said. "Keep this. You spend too much time with your father, his friends and his family to really know. This might help you."

"Help me with what?" I said.

My mother held her teacup in her hand and smiled for the first time all day.

"Help you to know what an honorable man looks like," she said. "Since you won't see any here."

My father never held a job longer than two years. He borrowed money constantly, either from loan sharks or the equally exorbitant Household Finance Corporation. The money was used to pay off gambling debts or to purchase appliances for corrupt union officials, enabling my father to buy into his next job.

"It takes money to make money," he would say to me. "Your mother doesn't understand that. That's why she'll never have shit. That's why she'll always be poor."

He was a man of extravagance, eager to buy people's affections with large packets of meat, fish and poultry, usually paid for with freshly borrowed money. My father would help unpack the food, pointing out how expensive each item was, insulted if anyone offered to help with the costs.

"People never had to ask him for anything," my mother said. "He did it all on his own. He loved to show off, brag about himself and the work he did. He never let on that he paid for the food. He always acted as if it were his to give. Everyone he gave food to knew the truth. They didn't care. So long as it was for free, they didn't care."

The same held true with money. If my father had it, he gave it. If he didn't have it to give, he borrowed it. No one exploited this character flaw in my father more than did the members of his own family. Whatever the need, money or food, ours was the first door they always came to knock on.

"They used us as a bank," my mother said. "We were as bad off as they were, but that didn't matter to them. They knew your father. They knew he would do anything for them, especially if his mother asked him to do it. Your father would kill if his family asked him."

The pattern of one-way loans and packages of meat leaving our apartment came to a temporary halt on November 14, 1964, with the death of my father's mother. She died of a massive stroke brought on by blood pressure that was too high and a diet that was too rich.

The funeral was a long, drawn-out three-day affair, punctuated by the hysterical wails of anguish from my father and his brothers and sisters. Everyone cried at the wake except for my mother and my uncle Danny. Despite the bad blood that existed between the family, my mother and uncle maintained a mutual respect.

"They conned your mother into coming here and marrying your father," he once told me. "She had no idea what this family was all about. Who would? They came at her like vultures, ate her up, a little bit at a time."

"Whatever your uncle did, whatever scams he pulled, he did them for the benefit of his wife and children," my mother said. "Your father was just the opposite. His scams never helped us. They only helped others. Sometimes, he gave money to people he barely knew."

At the wake, my father insisted on paying for his mother's tombstone and told his sisters to make all the necessary arrangements and that he would have the money with him when he came by the next day.

VII

"We don't have it," my mother said.

"Then get it," my father said. "I told my sister I'd get it to her today."

"Where?" my mother asked. "Where am I going to get that kind of money? We've borrowed from everyone we can borrow from, there's no one left. No one that stupid."

"Look, I told my sister I'd give her the money today," my father said. "And I'm gonna give her the fuckin' money today. You understand?"

"Why did you have to be the one to buy the headstone?" my mother said. "Why you? Why not one of your brothers? Your sisters? Or all of you together? No, no, it's got to be you. Always you. Mr. Big Shot, with no money. You don't have two nickels in your pocket, but you got three hundred dollars for a tombstone. They know, your family knows you have no money. But they don't care. As long as they don't have to pay for it."

"It's for my mother, bitch," my father said. "I'm doing it for my mother."

"Be like everybody else," my mother said. "Don't worry about your mother. Worry about yourself. About your own family. You're buying a tombstone and your sisters are back there cutting up the money your mother left behind."

"There ain't no money to cut up," my father said. "Believe me, I would know if there was."

"You'll see," my mother said. "Wait a few months. Then see how everybody starts to get strong. While you're still trying to figure out how to pay back the shylocks."

My father stood up, pushing his chair back against the far wall, away from the kitchen table.

"Forget that shit," he said. "Let me worry about that. All you gotta figure out is where to get me my three hundred dollars."

My father leaned over, grabbed the back of my mother's hair and pulled down on it.

"Because if you don't, I'll come back here and kill ya. I swear to God, I'll fuckin' kill ya."

He pushed my mother down to her knees and slammed her head three times against the base of the porcelain sink. He let her slip to the floor, standing over her, both fists cocked.

"Now, cut the bullshit," he said. "We're runnin' out of time. Go get the money. Get the money now."

One hour later, my mother returned with the three hundred dollars, borrowed from a neighbor half a block away. My father had spent the time pacing, cursing my mother and the life he was forced to have with her.

"Every time I ask that bitch for a favor, she gives me an argument," my father said. "Every fuckin' time. I've had enough of this shit. Believe you me, I've had enough to last me a fuckin' lifetime."

My mother chain-locked the door to the apartment, turned to my father and handed him the money, all of it in bundled-up groups of tens and twenties.

"I have to pay it back the end of next week," my mother said, her voice stripped of all emotion.

"You'll get it when you get it," my father said, folding the crisp bills and shoving them in the front pocket of his pants.

"I gave my word," my mother said. "They need it back by the end of the week. It's important."

"I give a fuck about your word," my father said. "Who gave it to you? Who the hell is in such a rush to get money from me? Huh? Tell me. Who?"

"It's not important," my mother said. "Just get the money back."

"Not important," my father said. "I'll decide if it's not important. Who gave it to you? Huh, bitch? Who? One of your boyfriends?"

My mother turned away from my farther, heading toward the living room.

"Don't turn your back on me, you fuckin' bitch," my father said. "Don't ever turn your back on me."

My father grabbed my mother by the neck and whirled her back toward the kitchen. As she scurried past him, he kicked her in the stomach, knocking her to the floor.

"What you do for this money?" he said, holding her face in his hands. "Whose cock did you suck? Tell me, bitch, before I kill you."

I was standing against the kitchen wall, unable to move.

"Dad, stop, please" was all I could manage to say.

My father looked up, startled at the sound of my voice.

"Stay the fuck out of this," he said to me. "Before I beat you all over this fuckin' house."

My father picked up one of the wooden kitchen chairs and began slamming it against the floral-patterned linoleum floor, not stopping until one of the legs came loose in his hand. He turned back toward my mother and began beating her with the base of the leg.

"I'll teach you how to behave, you fuckin' cunt," he said, hitting my mother repeatedly about the head, shoulders and back. One slicing blow cut my mother just below her right ear; blood began to flow in single strands onto her dress.

"Dad, stop it," I said. "Please stop it."

My father looked at me, his face flushed with rage. His eyes were wide open and the veins above his temples seemed swollen with blood. His right arm, the closed fist wrapped tight around the chair leg, was raised high above his head, ready to land another blow.

"What'd I tell you?" my father said to me. "Did I tell you to stay the fuck out of this? Didn't I, you little prick?"

"You're gonna kill her," I said.

"What's it to you if I do?" he said, moving away from my mother and toward me. "What, you a tough guy now? Gonna take me on. Well, let's see it, fucko. Let's see it."

My father swung the chair leg at me, the force of the blow catching me just above the forehead. He then tossed the chair leg aside and grabbed onto my shirt with his left hand. He leveled two punches from a closed right fist against my chin, the blows sending me flat down to the floor. A short kick to the chest snapped the air out of my lungs.

He stalked around the room, his temper still hot, his fists closed shut. He kicked a kitchen chair out of his way and threw a vicious punch against the back of the apartment door. My mother lay about ten feet from me, groaning in pain. I held both my arms against my chest and prayed it would all soon be over.

My father walked to a back room and returned within minutes wearing a windbreaker zippered to the top and a hat tilted forward. He walked right up to my mother's prone body, the tips of his black shoes touching the back of her dress. He looked down at her and then over at me.

"The wake starts in two hours," he said. "You better both fuckin' be there, if you know what's good for you."

He stared at my mother for the longest time, his hands shoved deep inside the pockets of his breaker. He took a deep breath, smirked and spit down at her.

"Bitch," he said, more to himself than to anyone else. "One fuckin' no-good bitch."

He slammed the apartment door shut, heading out toward the subway and a night spent in prayer, sitting by his mother's open coffin.

The beatings my father handed out grew in frequency in the period following his mother's death. He seemed in a constant state of anger, as if something had been unjustly taken from him. He'd always been quick to hit, needing little to light his short fuse, often beating my mother just for overcooking the pasta. It was just that now the beatings were intensified, growing more severe by the week.

He broke a glass bottle over my mother's hand, took her to the hospital and told the resident who stitched her that it happened while she was washing dishes. On another occasion, he rushed my mother to the emergency room, two of her lower ribs cracked and broken, the result, he said, of a fall down a flight of stairs. On still another occasion, my mother needed four stitches to close a wound on the top of her head, the victim, my father said, of a rock thrown by a fleeing teenager.

My mother wasn't the only victim. By the time I was eight years old, I had received thirty-five stitches, more than half of them courtesy of my father's fists.

One night, for reasons now long forgotten, my father came after me on the streets of Hell's Kitchen. I saw him coming, and headed up toward Printing High School on West 49th Street, running as fast as I could. I was looking to make the corner before the light changed to red. I turned to see if my father was still chasing me—and ran full speed into an alternate-side-of-the-street parking sign, knocking myself unconscious.

My father saw me fall and left me there, bleeding from the face and mouth.

A woman from the neighborhood helped me up and took me to St. Clare's Hospital. Once there, I woke to see an elderly nun sponging down my wounds. In truth, I wasn't totally relieved at the sight of her, visibly upset that I was still alive, that my ordeal of endless beatings was still nowhere near an end.

My father's behavior fell right into what was an acceptable norm in Hell's Kitchen. The area was populated by physical men and their obedient women and children. Acts of violence were as open and common as a Sunday afternoon stroll through the fresh-cut grounds of nearby De Witt Clinton Park.

All my friends suffered regular beatings at their fathers' hands, and no one complained. The only children spared the rod were the ones with fathers away serving prison time. Over the span of countless summer nights, cracked tenement windows opened wide, the slaps and screams resulting from a father beating his son or a husband beating his wife were clearly heard.

On other nights, when tensions gave way to passion, children were heard laughing and giggling, and couples could be heard, and sometimes seen, making love.

Most of the fathers I knew had long police records and were constantly being dragged in for questioning over one crime or another. Nearly all of them gambled and cheated openly on their wives. The majority owed money to loan sharks. It was, simply enough, the only way they knew how to live.

In this respect, my father was no different from any other man in the neighborhood, and what he expected of me seemed no more than natural.

When I turned nine, my father told me I was allowed to fight back, to hit him whenever he hit me. "You're a man now," he said, "so start fighting like one. I hit you. You hit me. Simple as that."

I grew determined to beat my father. I began taking daily boxing lessons at the Police Athletic League gym across the street from our new apartment, my afternoon hours spent pounding away at a heavy bag, working on a speed bag, looking to perfect whatever boxing abilities I possessed. An old gym rat named Whitey kept an eye on me, offering verbal encouragement in between long puffs on unfiltered Camels.

"You throw a punch, make sure it hurts," he said. "Ain't no sense goin' to all that trouble without causin' someone some harm."

"I'm tryin', Whitey," I said. "I'm tryin' my best."

"Don't know if your best is good enough," he said. "It all depends, you see."

"On what?"

"On who you goin' up against," he said. "On who you thinkin' of takin' down."

I threw one more right hand into the heavy bag, a solid overhead blow I felt way into my shoulderblades. I hugged the bag and looked over at Whitey.

"My father," I said. "I'm gonna take down my father."

Two afternoons a week, Mondays and Thursdays, I would ride the subway downtown, heading for the 14th Street gym to watch the professional boxers train. I sat on a wooden stool, facing the center ring, and watched how men who were paid to fight moved away from an opponent, how they attacked an opening and, most important, how they fended off the heavy blows headed their way. I watched and I learned, determined not to lose to my father anymore.

It was all a waste of time.

A week after my first boxing lesson, my mother and I each spent the night at St. Clare's Hospital, in separate rooms, on separate floors, mending from the latest wounds inflicted by my father.

My left eye was closed shut, my lower lip cut and puffy and the left side of my chest bruised. I sat in my hospital bed, a discarded food tray off to my left, and stared out a half-open window, listening for familiar city sounds.

My head rested on a bloody pillow; tears flowed with ease down my face. I was having a difficult time swallowing or breathing normally. I was angry and helpless, filled with a rage I had never felt before, never knew existed in me.

In my right hand were several stitches I had pulled from the back of my head, my small knuckles streaked with blood.

I was a poor student, lazy about both my work and duties. I did all that was possible to hide the poor grades and shoddy performance record from my father. I begged each of my teachers not to tell my father and, more often than not, the Christian Brothers who worked at Sacred Heart were tolerant and understanding of the situation.

"Eventually, he's going to find out," one of my teachers said to me. "He'll know something's going on. Be honest with him. It's the only thing you can do."

"You don't know," I said. "He really wants me to do well in school."

"So," my teacher said. "What's so wrong about that?"

"There's nothin' wrong with it," I said. "Except I'm not doin' all that well and I can't let him know that."

"Why?" he asked. "Why can't you just tell him? Tell him the truth."

"I don't want to let him down," I said. "It would hurt him and I don't want to hurt him."

My father walked through the door, threw his hat and jacket over the side of a chair and dropped my report card onto the kitchen table. He undid the belt around his pants, whipped it off with a tug of his hand and laid it on the table next to the report card. He took off his watch and put it in his shirt pocket.

"Get me a cold glass of seltzer," he said to my mother. "Fill it up with ice, would ya please."

I watched my mother move quickly into the kitchen and return moments later with a large glass filled to the rim. She handed the glass to my father, who drank down half its contents, wiped his mouth with the four fingers of his right hand and placed it down on the table.

"Why don't you leave us alone," my father said to my mother. "Go for a walk. Visit a friend. Do any fuckin' thing you want, just go."

"Mario, please," my mother said. "He's just a boy."

"Get out," my father ordered. "Now."

Then he looked over at me, standing, my hands by my side, by the edge of the table. His eyes glanced down at the report card.

"I don't have to tell you how bad your grades are, do I?" he said, his voice tight, controlled.

"No," I said. "I know."

"Your teacher says you keep this up and he won't be able to promote you," my father said. "Is that what you want?"

"No."

My father pulled a chair back, sat down on it and reached for his glass of seltzer.

"C'm here," he said when he finished drinking. "Stand next to me."

I didn't move, frightened about what my father might do.

"C'm here, I said. Next to me."

I still didn't move.

"What, you afraid?" my father said. "You think I'm gonna beat the shit outta you? If that's what I was gonna do, it woulda been done by now."

I walked toward my father, arms at my side, stopping a short distance away.

"You're scared of gettin' hit," my father said. "But you ain't scared of gettin' left back. Why's that?"

He paused, knowing I had no answer. My father reached over and, with one arm, brought me closer to his side.

"What? You wanna be like me?" he said. "Is that what you want? 'Cause if that's what you want, tell me now. Save everybody a shit-load of time. Easiest thing in the world to be like me. But I was hopin' that my son would want more out of life than to be a bum."

"You're not a bum," I said.

"I'm not?" he said. "And what do you call it? Half the time, I got no job. I'm always short of money. And I owe everybody. There isn't anybody I can think of I don't owe money to. I got no friends, take no vacations and my own wife probably wishes I was dead. That sound good to you? Does it?"

"No," I said.

"You bet your ass it don't sound good," he said. "But that's exactly what you're gonna be lookin' at unless you shape up. Can you understand that?"

"Yes," I said.

"You gotta do well in school, kid," my father said. "And not just for me. In fact, fuck me. I don't mean shit. You. You're the one that counts. What you're doin' to yourself right now is gonna fuck you years from now."

I had moved closer to my father, holding back my tears as he spoke, realizing, probably for the first time, how important it was to him to have me do well.

My father reached out his arms and hugged and kissed me. He picked me up and placed me on his knee.

"My time is over, One-punch," he said. "You're my last shot. Shit, you're my only shot. Don't think I don't know what people say about me behind my back. I know. Believe me, I know. And you know what? They're right. I'm everything they say I am. But I don't give a fuck 'cause I got you and you're gonna make me proud. And you're gonna make them eat shit. Am I right?"

"Yes, Daddy," I said.

"Okay," my father said. "I'm through talkin'. Get me a pen, would ya, and let me sign this fuckin' report card."

I jumped from his lap, looking to get a pen from one of the kitchen cabinet drawers.

"Hold on a second," my father said, grabbing me by the elbow. "There's one more thing I forgot to tell you."

"What?"

"Don't ever bring home another report card like this one," he said. "If you do, forget about comin' home, 'cause I'll kill you myself. Do we understand each other?"

"Yes, Daddy," I said. "It won't happen again. I swear."

"That's good to hear," my father said. "Now, c'mon, let me sign this and then we'll go try and find your mother. She's probably in the park bullshittin' with those old-lady friends of hers."

One month later, in a move that pleased both my parents, I became a Sacred Heart altar boy.

I studied Latin daily, helped by my mother, who encouraged me in my lessons. I learned all about the seven sacraments and how to administer a proper religious blessing, and read, in detail, about every form of sin, original or otherwise.

I enjoyed that time spent after school learning how to serve Mass in the quiet darkness of an empty church. For me, there was a great deal of comfort in the ritual of religion, which functioned as an escape valve from the corrupt madness that existed on the streets and in the apartments beyond those church doors.

On the second Sunday of the month, two full weeks before Christmas, I was assigned to serve my first Mass, the five o'clock, the last one of a busy day. I didn't bother telling my parents about it, figuring it would be best to serve this one alone, without an audience. As it was, few people came to the five o'clock, rummies mostly, on occasion a family that had overslept and missed the noon Mass. It was a perfect place to make a mistake and not have anyone notice.

I was on my knees, hands folded in prayer, halfway through Mass, ready to ring the bells for the preparation of the host and the wine, when I looked back and saw my father sitting in the back row of the church, his black shirt buttoned to the collar, his arms hanging over the pew in front of him. Except for my father and three Italian sailors huddled in the third row and an elderly couple praying and lighting candles next to a statue of the Blessed Mother, the church was empty.

I got up to help the priest pour the water and the wine into his large chalice when I heard one of the back doors to the church open and then, quietly, close. I looked and recognized a neighborhood woman standing there, facing the altar, blessing herself with a few drops of holy water from the fountain.

She walked down the center aisle of the church, the clicks of her high heels causing a loud echo. She was wearing a dark wool coat, white gloves and a hand-knit white shawl that covered the top of her head. She had flame-red hair and wore wrap-around dark glasses. She moved slowly down the middle of a long pew, knelt down and hung her head in prayer.

My father saw her the same time I did. He inched his head forward, watching her motion as she made her way down the aisle. My father and the woman knew each other. On many occasions, I had seen them talking and laughing on the front steps of her building. There had been neighborhood talk linking the two of them together. She was a part-time nurse with a disabled husband living at home. Some of the women of Hell's Kitchen, my mother among them, often told stories of how she would entertain male guests in her bedroom while her husband sat in the living room, his wheelchair placed in front of a turned-on television set.

I walked down the three steps of the altar, moving to the center rail, ready to help with the distribution of communion. The priest, old and frail, was behind me, his tiny hands shaking as he held on to the base of the chalice. I turned and helped him down the small, red-carpeted steps.

When I looked back up, I saw my father sitting next to the woman, whispering in her ear. They both giggled.

My father grabbed the woman's hand as she brushed past him, heading for the main altar to receive communion. She knelt down next to one of the Italian sailors and winked at me when I approached, standing next to the priest.

"The body of Christ," the priest said, lowering the host onto her tongue.

"Amen," she said, looking at me, not bothering to hide her smile.

She got up, turned and walked down the center aisle, going past my father and out the church door, never bothering to look back.

I looked over at my father, watched him stand up, zipper his jacket and grab his hat. He threw me a kiss and a wave, knelt beside the pew and walked out of the church, following the same path as the woman.

After Mass, I folded my garments neatly and hung them in the closet of the vestibule. The old priest, now dressed in a starched white T-shirt and dark slacks, came up behind me.

"What was going on back there?" he asked me.

"Nothing, Father," I said.

"Wasn't that man in the back of the church your father?" he asked. "Thought I recognized him."

I turned my face away from the priest and bowed my head.

"No," I said. "You're wrong. That wasn't my father."

"You sure?"

"Yeah," I said. "Very sure."

I quickly pulled my sweater over my head and rushed out the door.

"You're scheduled to serve a memorial Mass after school tomorrow," the old priest called out after me. "Please, try not to forget."

The next morning, I walked into Monsignor Burke's office and resigned from the altar boys.

My mother's son Anthony lived with us on and off during our years in Hell's Kitchen. He had first come to stay three days after my fourth birthday. He was sixteen then, thin, pale, painfully shy and unsure of both himself and his surroundings. His English was poor, a fault immediately seized upon by my father and his family.

As they so often did to my mother, they would speak about Anthony, many times in his presence, using words they knew he did not understand.

"They didn't want me there," Anthony remembered. "Any more than I wanted to be there. I came over because of my mother, no other reason. In some ways, I still find it hard to forgive her for putting us both in a situation that was unlivable."

My father, especially, had a difficult time with Anthony. Long gone were the words spoken to the members of my mother's family, promising the best for a young boy growing up fatherless. My father viewed Anthony in the same manner he viewed all men who came through our door, as a threat and a challenge to my mother's affections.

"I don't like him," my father said to me, talking about Anthony. "I think he's a Communist. Why the hell should I work to support him? Fuck him. I'm throwing the bum out."

Less than six months after his arrival in the United States, Anthony found himself alone, living in a basement apartment, working in an A&P supermarket after school to earn his rent money.

"It broke my heart," my mother said. "That, more than anything your father ever did to me. Knowing that I had a son out there, scared, alone and for no reason. No reason at all. What harm would it have done to let him live with us? Who would it have hurt? No one. But his family didn't want it and your father always did what his family told him to do."

My mother washed and ironed my half-brother's clothes every Thursday afternoon, using our landlady's apartment so as not to arouse my father's suspicions. Anthony would come by on those days, in the free time he had after school and before his supermarket shift began, and spend time with his mother.

"It was hard on both of us," Anthony said. "It would have been easier had we not seen each other at all, if maybe I had moved to another city, or even gone back to Italy. The way it stood, it honestly felt as if we had both done something terribly wrong, sneaking around, meeting the way we did, afraid to be seen by him or by someone else in his family. We were living like escaped prisoners. It's a time I'll never likely forget."

On occasion, my father's stance against my half-brother would soften and he would consent to have him return to our apartment, always with the stipulation that Anthony pay table money for his share of the food and rent.

"He can come back," my father would say, often after another one of my mother's tearful tirades. "But if you think for one minute that I'm gonna get up every morning and go work just to feed his fuckin' face, you got another think comin', baby. I make myself clear?"

"He works," my mother would always say. "And he's quiet and he doesn't eat much, you see how skinny he is. Between school and work, he won't even be here most of the time. He won't be any trouble at all. I promise you."

"All right then," my father would say. "Call him up. Tell him to come get his ass back here. Not too late, though. I gotta get some sleep."

One stay lasted just under two years. Another totaled less than a week. Regardless of the length of time, each visit was always tension-filled, the atmosphere primed for physical and verbal confrontations.

"He was always testing me," Anthony said. "Waiting for me to say or do what he felt was the wrong thing. The worst moments for me were when he fought with Mom. The fights always happened at night. I would lay in bed and pretend not to hear him hit her, not hear the punches or the slaps thrown at her. Not hear him cursing at her. Mom never cried or screamed or said a word. The next morning, when I would say something about it to her, she would deny that anything had happened. Believe me, living like that takes something out of you. Takes a lot out of you."

Anthony and I were never close. My father had convinced me that Anthony was a threat to my mother's affections, that she cared for him in a much deeper, broader way than she cared for me. I would then look at the two of them together, see how she seemed to dote on him, and see every word my father told me come to life.

"She don't give a fuck about us, One-punch," my father would often say, holding me on his knee after dinner, staring out an open window, looking down on Tenth Avenue. "Always remember that. That prick is all she cares about. You can tell just by the way she looks at him. You can't trust him. You can't trust her. There's one person you can trust and you know who that is, don't you?"

I nodded.

"You bet your ass," my father said. "I'm the one. I'm the only one and don't ever fuckin' forget that. No matter what anybody says, I'm the one."

Anthony and I were direct opposites. He was moody and temperamental, his personality closed and quiet. I loved to talk and, despite the constant problems at home, usually kept an upbeat mood.

"He's like his father," my mother said. "And, I'm afraid to say, you're like yours. The apple falls only so far from the tree. I don't worry about him, he doesn't go looking for trouble. Anthony's quiet, minds his own business. But I do worry about you. You're never quiet and you never mind your own business. You always got something to say. That habit could get you in a lot of trouble. Especially around here."

My half-brother and I spent very little time together and, to this day, don't really know each other as well as two brothers should. I suppose the twelve-year age difference that exists between us contributes to our overall lack of communication, as did my father's determination to do all he could to keep us apart.

These two problems, however, were ones he and I could have easily overcome had we both wanted to do so. But it's clear we didn't. It was much easier to allow those reasons to keep us apart than it was to search out the real motives behind our behavior. In truth, neither he nor I have ever felt comfortable in one another's company.

These days, we seldom see each other, except for a rare family dinner at either his home or mine. He does not remember his own father and despises the memory of mine. He is still quiet and reserved, content to let the bitter past fade from his memory. Anthony has always found it amusing that my father, for all his years of abuse and torment, would brag about him openly, talking with apparent pride about the banking executive he had helped raise as his own son.

My half-brother and I hardly ever seek each other's counsel or advice. There has never been a reason for us to do so. He is not someone I would call if in trouble, nor am I first on his list. Undeniably, though, a bond between us does exist. Each of us, by employing very different means, has survived.

That fact, as much as blood, welds us together.

In the spring of 1968, when I was thirteen years old, my parents decided it was time to move out of Hell's Kitchen. There were a number of factors that led to their decision. Prime among them was what my father saw as a one-shot opportunity for me to go to a first-rate Catholic high school, Mount St. Michael Academy, in the northeast Bronx.

"The neighborhood was starting to change," my father said. "And

I didn't care for the changes. All that sixties horseshit that was on TV almost every fuckin' night was startin' to show up on our streets. I could live with the long hair and all that other shit. But I wasn't gonna live with drugs. Not me. And not you. So I told your mother to find us a fresh place to live."

Within a month, my mother had found an apartment that fit my father's limited specifications—small and cheap. It was a three-room basement apartment at 4327 Boyd Avenue, well within walking distance of the school. The rooms were tiny and cramped, the floors cement hard, with the only heat coming from two large ceiling pipes located off the kitchen entrance.

"From the first he saw it, your father loved it," my mother said. "He saw it as a perfect place to keep his family. It was so small, we could never have anyone over for coffee, let alone dinner. There was no room to have guests, which kept your brother from ever visiting. The more crammed in we were, the more comfortable your father felt."

We were scheduled to move out of Hell's Kitchen in late April. My father had decided that the best way to let everyone know we were leaving was to throw a neighborhood block party, the biggest one the Kitchen had ever seen.

It was planned for the Sunday after Easter.

"I borrowed from everybody," my father said. "Hit on everybody I knew. I figure, what the fuck, when am I gonna see these humps again. I ordered steaks from Murray Baker and fish from a guy down on Fulton Street. Fruit, ice cream, games, rides, you name it. Even got some fuckin' guy to come in with a pony, sellin' rides a dime a pop. Your mother was really pissed. No surprise. She didn't know shit about style."

The party began at eight A.M. on a sky-clear Sunday morning. Small booths and makeshift stands had been set up along Tenth Avenue, a handful of them filtering down into 50th and 51st streets. Half-bed trucks loaded down with Ferris wheels and merry-go-rounds were parked up against the curb on the corner of 52nd and Tenth, right next to a van packed with cut-up chunks of watermelon resting on top of large, dripping blocks of ice.

Different musical sounds intermingled up and down the streets, from Frankie Valli and the 4 Seasons on 50th to Dion on 51st to

Domenico Modugno on 52nd, each new track blasting from the back of a stolen stereo system. Vitalis-pomped and permed street-corner soloists competed with the recordings, mixing in with their own versions of Frank Sinatra, Tony Bennett, Vic Damone and Motown.

Open-air barbecues, hamburgers, hot dogs and London broils simmering on top, were scattered, one every fifty feet, right alongside coolers filled with cans and bottles of cold beer, Pepsi, 7UP and crushed ice. Large half-gallon jugs of homemade wine, red and white, sold for two dollars apiece, three plastic cups included.

My father was dressed for a football wedding: sharply tailored blue slacks, starched and ironed red polo shirt, brand-new gray fedora tilted down to freeze out the sun. He had a big smile and a warm hug for anyone who crossed his path, happy to be, at least for this one short day, the center of everyone's attention. The undeclared King of Hell's Kitchen.

I stood by his side, dressed in a short-sleeve white-on-white button-down Arrow shirt, gray shorts cut just above the knee, thick white socks and spit-shined, laced-up Buster Browns. I also wore a fedora, similar to the one my father had on, and was biting down on a large, red-coated candy apple.

The cool morning breezes soon gave way to a hot springtime sun and warm dry air. The rising temperatures, combined with the smoke from the grills and the large number of people crowded onto the streets, began to make walking around uncomfortable.

"It's hot, Dad," I said to my father. "I mean, it's really hot."

My father looked down at me and smiled.

"You think so, One-punch?" he said.

"I know so," I said.

"All right, then," he said, laughing. "Turn 'em on."

"How many?"

My father looked up and down the avenue and shrugged his shoulders.

"What the hell," he said. "Turn 'em all on."

Within an hour, the fire hydrants lining Tenth Avenue had all been opened, ice-cold water streaming down the streets, cooling off everyone in sight. Children threw themselves headfirst into the water flow, while women took off their shoes and lifted up their skirts as they walked past.

I stood with my back to an open hydrant, drenched, water dripping down my head, into my eyes and mouth. I had stripped down to just the shorts, the rest of my clothes tossed into the hallway of an apartment building. I saw my father, standing across the way in front of Dick's Deli, one hand wrapped around my mother's waist, the other holding a snow cone as he winked at me, a huge smile spread across his face.

I walked over toward my parents, shaking off the water running down my forehead. When I was close enough, my father bent over and hugged me, kissing me several times on both cheeks and the top of my head.

"I love you, One-punch," he said. "I love you very much."

"I love you too, Daddy," I said. "I love you very much, too."

My father stood back up, still holding me to his side.

"Look at this, One-punch," he said, his arm running up and down the crowded avenue, taking it all in. "I don't want you to ever forget this place. Never forget how beautiful it all is. How special."

I looked out at the people of Hell's Kitchen, smoking, drinking, laughing, enjoying a rare day in the sun. I saw my friends from school jumping into the spray of the hydrants, tossing fire crackers at stray cats, playing Johnny-on-the-Pony against a tenement wall. I knew I would miss them, and I did. I missed them even more when, years later, I learned that many of them had died, tragic victims of drug overdoses, stick-up shootouts, suicides and the Vietnam War.

I looked at their parents, dressed in the best clothes swag money could buy, hard people with hard faces holding hands, freed for a few moments from the drudgery of the fights and struggles of their lives. They were faces I had grown to trust, and they, too, would be missed.

I spotted the Sacred Heart clergy, brothers and nuns loosely huddled in a corner in front of Mimi's Pizzeria, sipping drinks from plastic cups. They had taught me English when no one else would bother and had put up with my rampant truancy and lies, never losing their focus, always quick to forgive, regardless of the crime.

"Isn't this great?" my father said. "Isn't this fuckin' great? Who has this? Tell me that, One-punch. Who the hell has what we have?"

"Don't know, Dad," I answered.

"Nobody, that's who," my father said. "Look how fuckin' beautiful it is. Listen to it. This is what it's about. This is what makes us better 'n anybody. This. You understand?"

"I think so."

"Well, you better, because you ain't never gonna find a better place than this Kitchen," my father said. "I don't give a fuck where you end up. This is as good as it gets for people like us. This is your home. No matter where you wind up livin', this will always be your home. Remember that, One-punch. Promise me, you'll remember."

"I promise, Dad," I said. "I'll remember."

"Good boy,"my father said. "That's just what I like to hear."

In the distance, above the din of the crowd, Frankie Valli and the 4 Seasons could be heard singing "Walk Like a Man," the sound of his clear falsetto voice floating up and over the Hell's Kitchen tenements, helped by a trio of hi-fi speakers.

"Listen to that," one of the neighborhood old-timers said, a smile crossing his lips. "Will ya' listen to that little fuck. Christ, what a voice. He sings like a fuckin' angel."

VIII

I stood by my mother's side, in front of a jet plane, helping her hold on to a large white banner. We were both nervous, anxious to board the plane and begin our first trip to Italy together.

It was late June, 1969, New York hot and sticky, my chest and back wet with sweat, caused, in part, by the shirt, tie and wool jacket my mother insisted I wear.

We had bought our discount tickets from a travel agent in the Bronx who hooked us up with a religious charter group that flew Alitalia regularly and charged less than $150 for a round-trip fare.

We posed for a few group photographs, each member of the charter standing behind the difficult-to-hold white banner, the name of some Italian saint stenciled in blue script across the front. Between shots, the photographer screamed out a long series of Italian obscenities aimed in the direction of the passing jets.

I helped my mother buckle her seatbelt and watched as she made the sign of the cross, then opened her purse and took out a set of black rosary beads and a battered prayer book. She looked over at me and patted my hand.

"You should say a short prayer before we take off," she said. "Maybe one to St. Joseph."

"Why?"

"In case we die," she said.

It was cloudy and overcast as we pulled into the port of Ischia, both of us standing on the top deck of a lemon boat piloted by an old sea hand named Rumore. I stared at the oddly shaped houses dotting the port area, as the boat slowly inched its way backward into its designated berth.

A full eighteen hours had passed since we first left New York City, and all of it had been spent in travel.

It had taken nine hours by plane, three by train, nearly two on a boat and two long cab rides in between to get to this point in our voyage.

We had been met in Rome by my aunt Anna, my mother's youngest sister, a tall, bubbly woman filled with an overabundance of energy and good humor. She had prepared a veal cutlet lunch, complete with tossed green salad and red roasted peppers, all packed neatly inside several clear plastic canisters. She had even brought along plates, glasses and silverware, and carried everything in a large straw bag she kept flung over her shoulder.

We ate our lunch on the train, the simple green farmlands of the Roman countryside passing in a blur by our half-open windows. My aunt told me about the members of the family waiting to meet me in Ischia, cousins, uncles and other aunts I barely knew existed.

She told me about the tour buses, cabs and motor-taxis my mother's two brothers owned and operated, and how crowded with

German tourists the island had become, in part, because of their success.

Throughout the trip, my mother, always a reluctant traveler, slept.

I stood in front of my aunt, waiting to walk off the boat, holding a red and blue Mount St. Michael gym bag in one hand and my sweat-stained wool jacket folded around my other arm. My aunt had a hand on each of my shoulders.

"This is the place where your family comes from," she said, leaning over, edging closer to my ear. "Your mother, your aunts, uncles, grandmother, grandfather, everyone."

"My father, too," I said, not bothering to turn my head.

"Yes," Aunt Anna said. "Your father, too."

Those first weeks in Ischia were an awakening for me. I was surrounded, for the first time in my life, by people who didn't begin each day with a scam, who seemed to thrive on the very simplicity of their ordinary lives. The men I met were all awake before sunup and were at work before the morning dew had lifted. By the same hour, the women had hung their wash out to dry, had fed their families and had begun preparation for the afternoon meal.

Everywhere, there was singing.

Old women, stretching clean white sheets across a thin rope hanging from vine and post, sang Neapolitan love songs at full volume, often joined by their middle-aged daughters. Around crowded piazzas, teenagers sang the songs of their idol Johnny Murandi, heartfelt ballads played out to a soft rock 'n' roll beat. In front of the open doors of their homes, children skipped rope in time to the beat of Italian nursery rhymes.

My mornings were spent at the beach, six blocks from my mother's apartment building, swimming in the clear Mediterranean water. Afternoons, after lunch and while most of the island inhabitants napped, I would spend a few hours visiting my maternal grandmother, Maria Mattera.

She was a short woman, with thick white hair and a crooked smile.

There were a handful of teeth left in her mouth, and she walked with a slight limp, favoring her right side. She always dressed in widow's black, regardless of weather or temperature. Her hands were rough, hard, accustomed to work and adversity. She was quiet, with little time or patience for gossip or innuendo.

Grandma Maria owned a two-story stone house, walking distance from a beach she had never been to. She had given the first floor of the house over to my great-aunt Nanella, her husband's very ill sister and the woman who had originally introduced my parents to each other. Nanella had been living there since 1957, and in all that time the two women, enemies since their youth, had never exchanged a word.

"She had nowhere to go and no money," my grandmother said, when I asked about the situation. "No one wanted her. She had been trouble to a lot of people. The rooms downstairs weren't being used, so I had her stay here."

"But you don't talk to each other," I said.

"There's nothing to say," Grandma Maria said. "If there was, we'd say it."

I sat in a straight-back wooden chair next to a table in the middle of a high-ceilinged living room, the walls decorated on all sides with large framed pictures of my grandfather Gabriel and my late uncle John. The house was quiet, my two young cousins asleep somewhere in one of the back rooms. Grandma Maria was in the kitchen, preparing coffee, strong, bitter espresso, which she served with two drops of Stock 84 liquor and a small chunk of Italian chocolate.

"It's good for your heart," she said. "Wakes it up."

My grandmother placed the cup of coffee in front of me, dug a hand into her long white apron and pulled out three almond cookies wrapped in a table napkin.

"Eat these," she said. "They're good for you."

She sat down next to me and watched as I sipped the coffee and bit into a cookie. I looked over her shoulder and up toward my grandfather's picture. Gabriel Carcaterra was a tall, handsome man with a thin moustache and thinning hair. I never met him, his death coming three months prior to my birth, and knew him only through the stories my mother had told me.

"Do you miss him?" I asked my grandmother, nodding my head toward the picture.

"Of course," she said. "He was my husband."

Gabriel Carcaterra and Maria Mattera first met on a chilly spring afternoon next to a church in Ischia Ponte. She was sixteen, with long brown hair tied in the back with a ribbon. She was wearing a blue housedress and dark sandals, and carried a large wicker basket filled with fresh figs. She wore no makeup and had a small scratch just above her right eye.

Gabriel was dressed in work pants topped by a white wool sweater and a dark brown peak cap. He was eighteen, a hard-working young shepherd trying to make a go of the family business. He held his lunch under his right arm, a thick slice of bread and a fresh slab of provolone cheese wrapped with white linen. He had a red handkerchief tied in a knot around his neck.

"They fell in love at first sight," another of my mother's sisters, Nancy, said. "They never lost that feeling over the course of their lives. They were crazy about each other. Lovers till they died."

Gabriel and Maria were married in June of 1914, and two weeks later moved into the stone house where they both would eventually die. Their first child, a girl, was stillborn, and their second died a month after birth. Their third child, my aunt Francis, was born in 1917, and was a month old when Gabriel was drafted by the Italian Army and sent off to fight at the tail end of World War I.

"He came back with a bad ear," Grandma Maria said. "It got worse as he got older. He was entitled to government money, but never bothered with it. He was embarrassed. He felt there were people with more serious wounds than the one he had, so let them have the money. Can't do anything about that. That's just the way he was cut."

In the decade following the end of the war, Gabriel and Maria would have six more children, five of their own and one, my uncle John, whom they adopted at birth. My grandfather continued to work as a shepherd, tending to both his flock and his lands, and then, in the summer of 1930, he and Maria opened a large salumeria, an

Italian deli, in the middle of La Via Nuova, the port area's main thoroughfare.

"Like many people in Ischia, we didn't have much money and had to work hard for what little we had," Aunt Anna said. "But we did laugh a lot. Every day, no matter what, Poppa would always make sure of that."

The laughter had its base in simplicity.

"He would have the children take turns shaving his beard or trimming his moustache," Grandma Maria said. "He always kept change in his shirt pocket, knowing the children would somehow get soap in his eyes and reach for the money. When they did, he'd jump from his chair, wipe the soap from his eyes and chase them around the house. They loved it and he loved it."

The only enemies Gabriel Carcaterra had were certain members of his own family. He neither trusted nor liked two of his sisters—Nanella and Raffaela, my father's mother—and regarded them as gossips intent on causing trouble. While he remained civil and respectful to both, he did his best to avoid any involvement with either one.

"They were always a problem," my mother said. "From the start, they had it in for my mother and did all they could to aggravate her. They talked behind her back, spread lies, started rumors. But it got them nowhere. Mamma never said a word, about them or against them. She was as silent as stone."

My mother scratched at the back of her hand and chased a fly from her face before she continued.

"It's amazing how, through the years, those two women remained so much a part of Mamma's life," she said. "One living in her house and the other across the hall from me. Both still causing trouble."

Grandma Maria poured me another cup of coffee. She looked at me and smiled as she added the chocolate and whiskey.

"Aren't you having any?" I asked her.

"No," she said. "Doctor told me I had to choose between coffee and wine. Can't have both. I like wine better."

I drank the coffee and watched as she spread a pound of lentils on top of the table and began sorting them, weeding out the green and black ones.

"Have you ever thought about visiting us?" I asked. "Stay in America for a while."

"No," she said.

"Why?"

"It's not my country," she said. "My home is here."

Grandma Maria worked in the black market during the darkness of World War II. It was the only way she knew to keep her family alive and fed.

"Every morning she would take the boat to Naples," Anna said. "Leave in the dark and come back the same way. There, she'd deal in bread, oil, butter, milk, whatever there was that was available. She never came back empty-handed. It was dangerous work, with German soldiers everywhere, but she never came home without food."

My grandmother sometimes traded milk, taken fresh from the few remaining goats my grandfather had, for meat. Other times, she would barter the sheets and linens her daughters had sewn for candles or flour. Every transaction was handled in secrecy, since few people were known well enough to be trusted.

"Mamma got off the boat one night and walked right into a waiting truckload of German troops," Aunt Nancy told me. "She walked on the dock, ten pounds of cheese hanging in a pack over her shoulder, and stared at a young German soldier with a cocked machine gun in his hand.

" 'May I see the bag, Signora?' he asked her. He was a boy, no older than my brother Johnny.

" 'Will you kill me if I don't?' Mamma asked him.

"The soldier looked at Mamma, looked right into her eyes, uncocked the machine gun and lowered it.

" 'No, Signora,' he said to her. 'No. I won't kill you. You may go.'

"Mamma smiled at him and went on her way. She wasn't a woman that scared easy, that's for sure."

Grandma Maria never liked to ask questions, nor did she feel compelled to tell people what to do with their lives. She cared for her children, doted on her grandchildren when allowed and kept a respectful distance from all but a handful of lifetime friends.

I was fascinated by my grandmother and found her to be unlike anyone I had ever met either on the streets or in the apartments of Hell's Kitchen. She had a knack for practical jokes, hated telephones and had never in her life been inside a movie theater. She also had little time or patience for church, despite being surrounded by women whose lives were dominated by religion.

She never spoke to anyone about family matters, maintaining a grip on her privacy that was rare on an island that thrived on talk and idle chatter. She was incredibly stubborn, insisting on doing things her own way, which always meant alone and without outside interference. She never lied, but would evade the truth when the issue was one she did not care to discuss. She was the most independent member of the family and, though living in a world where women took a second seat to the men around them, was headstrong enough to run both a family and a business well into her middle sixties.

We finished our coffee and walked out into the fading sunlight of a warm afternoon. She had on an old straw hat and carried an even older straw handbag, the wood handles looped around her right shoulder, two white handkerchiefs, a Hershey bar with almonds and a pack of gum tossed inside.

Grandma Maria never carried any money and always walked at a brisk pace.

"Where would you like to go?" I asked her.

"The cemetery," she said. "You should see where your grandfather is buried."

"Can you walk that far?" I said.

"If I can't, it would be the first time," she said.

The cemetery of Porto D'Ischia was situated high on a grassy hill, overlooking both the small town and the quarter-moon harbor that encircled it. A heavy black fence, spiked at the top and surrounded by thick growths of pine trees and fresh flowers, lined the cobblestone entrance.

The headstones were small and lined up evenly in four rows of six, anchored on both sides by a series of white-columned family mausoleums, the dates on most of them going back to the eighteenth century.

An old gardener in a wool work shirt stood off to the side, a few feet past the entrance, raking dirt in even strands. He waved as my grandmother and I walked past.

My grandfather was buried on a low ridge overlooking the sea, in a sliding drawer next to his adopted son. He had been moved there in August of 1956, two years to the day after his death.

"His body was dug up and the coffin opened for the last look," Aunt Anna said. "The remains were then placed inside an air-tight steel box and placed in one of the family drawers. It's the way things are done here."

Grandma Maria ran her hand over her husband's name, which was hammered into the clear marble. She took a handkerchief from inside the front pocket of her black dress and wiped at first the marble and then her eyes.

"Fourteen years," she said. "Fourteen years next month."

"I'm sorry, Grandma," I said.

"So am I," she said.

Grandma Maria walked to a stone bench, spread her handkerchief out and sat down, facing her husband, her back to the port below. I walked behind her and leaned against a thin pine tree, its shade helping to cool what had been a hot afternoon.

"My mom told me lots of stories about him," I said to her. "That one time he gave away all your clothes."

Grandma Maria looked up at me and smiled.

"Our winter clothes," she said. "It was the summer after the war. He heard about some families in the mountains who were short on food and clothing, pretty much starving to death. He came home, found out where I kept all the winter clothes, took them and packed them all on the back of an old mule. He handed them out, came back home and never said a word about what he'd done to anyone."

"Didn't he think you'd find out?" I asked.

"I don't know," she said. "Knowing him, he probably just forgot all about it. Anyway, October comes and I can't find the winter clothes anywhere. I tore the house apart, convinced I had misplaced them. Then, your mother comes in and tells me she saw a young mountain girl in the store wearing a dress just like the one she owned. We both turned and looked over at your grandfather. He was sitting by the wood stove, drinking coffee. He put the cup down, walked over to where I was standing and kissed me on the cheek.

" 'We can buy more clothes,' he said. 'They can't.'

"What can you say after that? We went out and bought more clothes."

We sat quietly for a while, my grandmother lost in thought, remembering other times, happier ones. Her eyes never once moved from my grandfather's resting place, the straw fan in her hand held on her lap, an old woman mourning a man she loved.

I watched her, my back resting against the tree, one leg folded over the other. I saw my grandmother get up, walk over to the grave, bend to her knees and kiss the marble, mumbling a series of words as she did. I got up, walked over and stood behind her, crying over the body of a man I had never met.

She stood up slowly, turned to me and put one arm under mine.

"Let's go home," she said. "It's getting late."

"Thanks for bringing me here," I said.

"It's good for you to know where it is," she said. "It's where I'll be soon. You can visit us both."

We walked out past the gate together, waving our goodbyes to the old gardener we had seen on our way in.

"I'll do that," I said. "I promise."

"You don't have to promise," she said. "Just come. And remember, no flowers. I hate flowers."

"Okay," I said. "It's a deal."

Grandma Maria stopped and smiled, looking once more over her shoulder at the cemetery.

"I never understood flowers," she said.

Aunt Anna lowered a plate of pasta onto my place mat while my mother hovered behind her, spooning out Romano cheese and fresh pepper.

"There's plenty more," my mother said, running a hand through my hair. "Eat as much as you want."

I had never seen my mother as happy as she was during those first few weeks in Ischia. She was relaxed and free, so much so that she seemed to be another woman, no longer resembling the frail and frightened person who was unwilling to leave her Hell's Kitchen apartment.

She didn't scream at the slightest provocation, nor did she shake visibly whenever she heard a phone ring. I had grown up with an image of her trembling on a chair in our apartment, rosary beads wrapped around her hands, a crumpled tissue on her lap, tears running down her face. To see her now, planning family picnics, talking with friends, telling them jokes, laughing at their stories, was a special surprise.

She looked younger, her walk brisker, filled with a newfound energy. She ate better, no longer complained about her health and could be found most mornings at the beach, lying under the sun, a towel across her back, talking to one of her sisters.

"This is the Raffaela we know," my aunt Francis said. She sat across from me, twirling a forkful of thick pasta onto a tablespoon.

"We don't know the person you described to us," she said, chewing the pasta. "That woman is a stranger. But if she is the way you say she is back in America, then who do you think can be blamed for that? What he's done to her, what he's turned her into, isn't that a crime?"

"He doesn't mean it," I said.

"Maybe," my aunt said. "But whatever his reasons, he's nearly destroyed her. It's unforgivable."

"Things will get better," I said. "He needs time."

"Time for what?" she said. "It's been almost fifteen years and the situation has only grown worse. Your father will never change. Never. Not until he dies."

"I don't need to hear this," I said, trying to hide my anger. "You're not there, you don't know what goes on. There's no way for you to know."

Aunt Francis leaned across the table, reached for my two hands and held them in hers.

"No," she said. "But *you* do know what goes on. You know and can do what is necessary to change it."

"I can't change anything," I said.

My aunt released my hands, leaned back in her chair and poured us both a glass of red wine.

"Then there's nothing to be done," she said. "Except wait."

"Wait for what?"

"Until one of them dies," she said.

I made three very close friends in that first summer on Ischia, all of them boys my own age or close to it. My cousin Paolo from Pisa was the youngest, while Pepe from Rome was the oldest, and Gasperino from the island had the same birthday as I did.

The four of us all shared similar interests, except when it came to sports. In that respect, they lived for soccer, while I cared only about baseball.

"How can you watch that annoying game without falling asleep?" Pepe asked, walking by my side on the Via Nuova, as he licked the drippings off a chocolate ice-cream cone.

"It's not boring," I said. "You just don't understand it."

"What's to understand?" Paolo asked, handing Pepe a napkin. "You throw. You hit. You catch. Sounds simple."

"And boring," Pepe said. "I'd rather go to funerals than watch baseball."

"Have you guys ever seen a game?" I asked. "I mean a real game with real ballplayers."

"You mean Americans?" Gasperino said with a laugh, shoving three pieces of bubble gum into his mouth. "No, never with Americans, only Italians."

"I saw a team from Bari play one from Pisa last summer," Paolo said. "The game seemed as long as surgery."

"And half the fun," Pepe said.

"Well, look, make fun if you want," I said. "But there's a big difference between watching Bob Gibson pitch and watching some overweight bartender from Bari pitch."

"Who's Bob Gibson?" Gasperino asked.

"Don't you ever listen?" Pepe said. "Bob Gibson is an overweight bartender from Bari."

For most of that summer, the four of us were inseparable.

We swam at the beach together every morning, played soccer or shot pool every afternoon and went to outdoor movies followed by long walks in the evenings. We grew close to each other and I learned just from being in their company.

If we ever did argue, it was usually over which movie to see or which girl we should go out of our way to impress. We exchanged novels and magazines, discussed over iced coffees what for us were the new and serious issues of politics and sex and talked about our futures, about what we each wanted from life. The conversations were always long, involved and animated, and I could never imagine having them with any of my Hell's Kitchen friends.

"You have your eye on Franca, don't you?" Paolo asked me one morning as we walked past the Riva Mare Hotel, its top decks crowded with German tourists sunning themselves, heading for the beach.

"How do you know that?" I asked.

"What do you mean how do I know?" he said with a loud laugh. "I'm Italian."

"So?"

"Italians know everything about women."

"Cut the shit."

"No, I'm telling the truth," he said. "And besides, I overheard our mothers talking about it last night."

"What did they say?"

"Oh, the usual," he said. "You know, how happy everyone would be if you two ended up married. Franca's family and ours being as close to each other as they are. That sort of talk."

I reached over and grabbed Paolo's arm, stopping both of us near the beach entrance, next to a crowded snack bar.

"Were they kidding?" I asked.

"You'll learn, cousin, that in Italy no one kids about marriage," Paolo said. "Especially our mothers."

"I asked her to a movie," I said.

"Uncle Mario offered his wife a cup of coffee," Paolo said. "Barely knew her. Three months later they were in Florence on their honeymoon. Think he wasn't surprised?"

"I'm fourteen years old," I said.

"Relax," Paolo said. "They're only talking about it. It won't be a problem until next summer. If you're still with her."

"Jesus," I said.

"Stop worrying," Paolo said. "Let them talk all they want, what difference does it make?"

"It's annoying," I said. "To me, anyway."

"Don't let it bother you," Paolo said, staring at a German woman lying in the sand, her back to the sun, the thin straps of the top half of her two-piece bathing suit hanging loose off her shoulders. "Her father won't let you marry her anyway."

"Why not?"

"He doesn't want his daughter living in America," Paolo said. "Thinks it's a terrible place."

"How do you know that?"

Paolo pulled a thousand-lira bill from his shirt pocket and checked his watch.

"I asked him," he said. "Now, how about a pastry before we swim? I just saw Guiliano bring in a fresh batch."

In the three weeks I'd been in Ischia, I had written my father a letter a day, and wondered why I hadn't heard from him. In the letters, I had talked about my new friends and the different places and cities I had seen in Italy. I wrote about the tours I'd taken and the new foods I had tried and liked. I asked him how the Yankees were doing and how he was holding up in the New York heat.

In each letter I always told him that I missed him and loved him and wished he were with us.

"Do you think he gets the letters?" I asked my mother one day, watching as she fried eggplant in my aunt's kitchen.

"The mail here is slow," my mother said. "It isn't like in America. He'll get your letters. It will just take time."

"Can we call him?"

"If you want," she said. "Trouble is, we never know when he's home."

My mother sat down, letting the eggplants simmer on the stove, crossed her legs and looked out the double doors of the kitchen, past the terrace and the pine groves and out beyond, toward the sea.

She was tanned and looked younger than I had ever imagined she could. She sat erect in the chair, not stoop-shouldered as was her custom back home. Her face was clear and her eyes no longer carried a sad look.

"Do you miss him?" I asked her.

"Who?"

"Dad," I said.

My mother looked at me and shrugged.

"There really isn't all that much to miss, is there?" she said.

"What about home?" I said. "The apartment."

"That's not home," she said. "This, this island, this building is my home. This is where I belong. That other place is just somewhere to sleep."

"Do you want to stay here?"

"Why ask that question?" she said. "Of course I want to stay here, but I can't. Someday, maybe. But not now."

"Why not now?" I said. "I can go to school here and Dad could come over, find a job."

"Doing what?" she said.

"I don't know," I said. "Be a butcher. Or work with Uncle Mario on the buses. Anything he wants."

"And how long do you think that will last?" she said. "How long before your father does here what he does back there?"

She stood up, walked back over to the stove and turned the heat up on the eggplants. She looked over at me and smiled.

"It's nice to dream, especially at your age," she said to me. "As long as you remember that your dreams never come true. Not for us."

IX

The island of Ischia is a forty-eight-mile-wide province of Naples, with a general population hovering around fifty thousand. In the high tourist season of July, August and September, more than two million people cram its beaches, restaurants and hotels. More than 80 percent of the tourists are German, a holdover from World War II, when the island, for the better part of two years, was under Nazi occupation.

By and large, the citizens of Ischia languished in poverty during the postwar years, their livelihood determined either by the sea or, in the upper regions, by the farmlands. A scattering of hotels existed, catering to a small but loyal tourist clientele.

A dozen taxicabs were all that was needed to service the entire island. Horse-drawn carriages rumbled down the empty cobblestone streets. Restaurants were never crowded and evenings, regardless of the time of year, were always silent.

The attractions that now draw millions to the island each summer, including the mineral baths, the white sand beaches, the architecture and the food, were largely ignored during those lean times.

Then, in the summer of 1962, Elizabeth Taylor brought the poverty to an end.

"They made *Cleopatra* here," my aunt Anna said. "Everything was quiet during the first month, the movie people keeping to themselves, handing out a lot of work. Then, Taylor left her husband for that English actor and everything got crazy. The island turned insane, people rushing about everywhere. Boats filled with tourists arrived every hour, day and night. Forget about getting a cab or finding an empty hotel room. It was so crowded that it could take me as long as a half hour to walk the six blocks from the port to the house. It was unlike anything I've ever seen."

The island grew and prospered from that moment on. When I arrived in that summer of 1969, there was plenty of work to go around, with everyone, from merchants to plumbers, lining their pockets with tourist dollars.

Dozens of newly built, large-scale hotels crowded the horizon, restaurants were numerous and filled with customers, while the entire port area had been taken over by double lines of Mercedes-Benz taxis, all waiting to drive arriving tourists to their expensive suites.

My mother's brothers, Mario and Giovann Guisseppe, had, in a short five-year period, gone from struggling cab drivers to owners of the largest and most successful tourist transportation business on the island.

"I used to sleep in my cab," Uncle Mario told me. "Ate there, too. It was more than a business, it was my apartment. Now, thank God, we're doing well. I move my buses and cabs all over Europe. I guess, in a way, I owe it all to Elizabeth Taylor. You know with all that she did, I've never even seen one of her movies. Not even *Cleopatra*. I don't think it played here."

Aunt Anna held her two children by the hand as she bartered with a toothless and overweight livery driver. Four other children hovered around her, while two more stood next to me.

"I'm afraid it will take two carriages, Signora," the driver said. "Two. To take everyone safely."

"I know it will take two," Aunt Anna said. "What I don't know is how much two will cost me."

"I'm sure an honest person such as yourself will come up with a fair price, Signora," he said. "You were born in these parts, you know how difficult a working man's life can be."

"Please, do yourself a favor and save the working-man speech for the tourists," Aunt Anna said. "The ones who don't know about the three apartment buildings that you own."

"The bank owns them, Signora," he said. "I run them."

"My error," she said.

One of the children, my eight-year-old cousin Anna Maria, grew tired of the wait and walked over to the driver's carriage. She climbed its two iron steps and sat down on one of the thick cushions propped against the brim, her feet resting on the saddle step.

"Wouldn't it be easier if he just gave her a set price," I said to Paolo.

"He can't," Paolo said.

"Why not?"

"Because there is no set price," he said. "Never has been. Each driver gets whatever he can get. And besides, set prices take away from the fun. Stand back and watch. This is better than a Bud Spencer movie."

"You're being unreasonable," my aunt said. "I can't discuss anything, much less money, with an unreasonable man."

"Signora, if you want the ride for free you should just ask," the driver said.

"And if you wanted to rob me I would have handed you a gun," my aunt said.

She turned away from the driver and gathered the children around her.

"Let's go home," she said to them. "This was a bad idea. We'll come back some other time. Maybe after I've robbed a bank."

"Oh, no, please, Zia," one of the children said. "Please, take us for a ride. You promised."

The driver stepped forward and tapped my aunt on the shoulder.

"Signora," he said. "One moment, please. For the children."

"I cannot pay seven thousand lira per carriage," she said.

"And I cannot take two thousand," he said. "But, I will take five thousand lira each. For the children."

"I will give you four thousand lira each," my aunt said. "For the children, of course."

"Always," the driver said. "Four thousand it is, providing you also agree to buy four bags of carrots for my horses."

"Agreed," she said. "So long as the children can help feed them."

"I would have it no other way, Signora."

My aunt piled into the lead carriage, taking the youngest children along with her. Paolo and I boarded the second carriage, handled by a younger and thinner version of the main driver, three children snuggled by our side.

"Forward, Italia," Aunt Anna yelled from the front.

"Viva Mussolini," the driver said, as he clicked the horse into motion.

"Mussolini?" Paolo said.

Our driver turned sideways to look at us, an unfiltered cigarette hanging from his lower lip.

"Don't worry," he said. "My uncle's not a fascist. Mussolini's the name of his horse."

The two old tour-weary horses began the steep climb into the hills of Ischia, the first leg of our two-hour journey across the five main boroughs of the island. The port on my right quickly disappeared, replaced by a bold view of the sea below and the mountains above.

A half-dozen islands, from Capri to Sorrento, dotted the light blue horizon, while an array of wild flowers surrounded us on all sides. Birds whooped and chirped, the people we passed on the way smiled and waved, and the children in both carriages giggled and laughed aloud.

"It's beautiful," I said to Paolo. "I've never seen anything this beautiful."

"Heaven can't look this good," he said.

"I don't know much about heaven," I said, holding my cousin GianCarlo closer to my side. "I only know about hell."

"What do you mean?" Paolo asked.

"Nothing," I said. "That's just what they call the New York neighborhood where I grew up. Hell's Kitchen."

"That's in another part of the world," Paolo said. "As far away from here as you can get."

The drivers stopped their carriages next to a large, overripe fig tree. They leaped down from their seats, each holding a long, thin horsehair brush, and wiped away the thick white foam that had formed on the sides of their horses.

My aunt moved between the two carriages, handing out club rolls filled with marinated eggplant, smoked beef and sun-dried tomatoes. After the sandwiches, she handed out the drinks—sodas for Paolo and myself, wine for the drivers and Orangina for the children.

The older driver, standing by the side of his carriage, took a large bite from his sandwich and threw his hands to the sky.

"I can die now," he said. "I have tasted the greatest sandwich in the world. Magnificent, Signora, magnificent. There's no other word for it."

"Grazie," my aunt said.

We ate our food quietly, the sea to our back, the mountains leading up to Mount Epomeo facing us, warding off the slanting rays of
the sun. Occasionally, a Fiat sped past, the driver honking his horn,
waving a hand outside his window. It was as peaceful a place as I'd
ever seen.

Aunt Anna came up beside me, holding a small basket filled with
fruit.

"How about a peach?" she said.

I shook my head.

"Maybe later," I said. "I'm full."

I watched as she handed one to GianCarlo, smiling at him as he
took it. Nothing seemed to please Aunt Anna more than watching
people eat.

"Thanks for this," I said to her.

"It's a simple lunch," she said. "Nothing special."

"Not just the food," I said. "Everything. I'll remember it for a long
time."

She patted my leg and nodded her head.

"So will I," she said. "It's a nice memory to have of each other."

Paolo leaned past my shoulder, took Aunt Anna's hand and kissed
it.

"I don't mean to put a cloud over everyone's memory," he said.
"But, there's a slight problem."

My aunt looked at him and shrugged.

"What is it?" she said.

Paolo pointed a finger past the carriages and toward the fig tree.

"Our drivers are fast asleep," he said.

We looked over and saw the two of them sitting in the shade, their
legs spread apart, their mouths opened, their heads tilted to one side,
eyes closed shut.

My aunt lit a cigarette and laughed.

"It must have been the eggplant," she said.

"The bottle of wine didn't help them much either," Paolo said.

Aunt Anna picked up her youngest child and rested his head
against her shoulder.

"You know, maybe our two escorts have the right idea," she said.
"A short nap might do us all a world of good."

"Here?" Paolo said.

"What better place," she said. "There's plenty of shade, a beautiful view and hardly any traffic. It's perfect."

"Where will we all sleep?" Paolo asked.

"The children next to each other in the carriages," Aunt Anna said. "You boys can find yourselves a nice spot under one of those trees."

"That sounds good," Paolo said. "So long as it's nowhere near any of the horses."

Aunt Anna laughed.

"I'm sure they feel the same way about you," she said.

We slept there, thick Italian pines blocking out the strength of the sun, for a little more than an hour. Paolo and I shared the base of a tree, our shoulders touching, a dark red horse blanket spread across our legs. The children were evenly divided among the two carriages, a small mangle of arms, legs and faces brushing against each other. The two drivers were still in their place, snoring into their second hour.

Aunt Anna was the only one who didn't sleep.

She sat in the front seat of the lead carriage, the horse's reins held loosely in one hand, a lit cigarette in her other. She had a letter from my father on her lap, still folded inside the envelope my mother had torn it from earlier that day.

Anna let the cigarette smoke filter through her nose and mouth as she gazed over at the sleeping children. She moved her head farther to the right, until her eyes settled on me. She looked at me for quite some time, her face sad and weary, still undecided over whether to tell me about the letter and its contents.

Aunt Anna took a deep breath, jumped down from her seat and tossed her cigarette to the ground. She walked over to where Paolo and I were sleeping, bent down and gently nudged us awake.

"Let's go, boys," she said. "Time to go home."

I was an hour late for a wedding reception, celebrating the marriage between two family friends. On my way there, I was supposed to pick up a large fruit basket my mother had ordered from Minicucci's Café and to place the card she had written on top of it.

"Remember to get there before one," my mother said. "That's when he closes for lunch."

"I won't forget," I said.

I was dressed for the reception in my Ischia best: black slacks, blue button-down short-sleeve shirt, black loafers, no socks and a light gray jacket borrowed from my cousin Paolo. I was wearing cologne given me by Uncle Mario and had a pocket full of candies and mints, supplied by Grandma Maria.

"I'm never going to eat this much candy," I said to her, watching as she stuffed my pocket until it looked swollen.

"Maybe you'll meet someone who can," she said.

I left Grandma Maria's house shortly after noon, ran past the church, quiet on this early Sunday afternoon, made my way through a pair of narrow side streets and stood in front of Minicucci's. Rafel, the owner, spotted me from behind the bar and waved me over to him.

"Will you look at the American?" he said with a smile. "Are you sure you're not the one getting married?"

"Not yet," I said.

"Good," Rafel said. "There's still hope for my daughter."

"Your daughter is too beautiful for me," I said. "And I'm too poor for you."

"You learned a lot from your grandma in a short time," he said with a laugh.

Rafel moved out from behind the counter and stood next to me, one arm draped over my shoulders.

"I have made a wonderful fruit basket, just like your mother asked," he said. "Come, let me show you."

We walked together toward the back of the café, the air inside cool and sweet, heavy with the smell of fresh baked pastry. The dark marble floors were polished to a shine, as was the giant silver espresso machine in the corner, resting on a half-moon table, surrounded by cups, spoons and saucers.

A dozen circular tables, three chairs to each of them, were scattered throughout the café, one line of them next to the large front window that covered the run of the bar. Six more tables were outside, Cinzano umbrellas opened above them, hooked at an angle.

"How long have you had the café?" I asked.

"Six years," Rafel said. "Opened it the year before my wife died."

"Sorry," I said. "I didn't know about that."

"No way for you to know," he said, shrugging. "Just as there was no reason to know before this summer that the two of us would end up as friends."

"How did she die, Rafel?"

"Drunk driver," he said. "Crashed into her right out on the street there. She was dead as soon as she fell."

"I'm really sorry," I said.

"She was such a beautiful woman," he said. "Tall and thin, with a wonderful smile. My daughter looks just like her."

Rafel turned away from me and yelled out to a young boy in the back.

"Franco," he said. "Bring me out that fruit basket. The one for Signora Carcaterra. It's over in the corner, by the brown table."

"It's ready, Zio," Franco said. "I'll bring it right out."

Rafel stopped by the espresso machine and poured out two cups of coffee, one for each of us. He stood by the window, looking out at the slow-moving street traffic outside.

"I had a difficult few years," he said. "After my wife died, I lost interest in the business, in my family, in myself."

"What changed?"

"Time helped," he said, stirring two splashes of Sambuca Romano into his coffee. "Your grandma helped more."

"How?"

"She came to talk to me one morning," Rafel said. "She sat down, said what was on her mind and left."

"What'd she say?"

"Nothing that a lot of other people hadn't come by to tell me," Rafel said. "With your grandma, though, it just seemed to make more sense. She's a hard woman to ignore."

"I know," I said. "She's seen so much, been through so much. Half the time, I can't believe she's still alive."

"She has a survivor's understanding of life and death," Rafel said. "Maybe that's it. I don't know. Whatever it is, it worked. At least for me."

Franco came out from the back room, the largest fruit basket I'd ever seen cradled in both his arms.

"Here we are," Rafel said. "I hope your mother will be pleased."

"I'm sure she will," I said, reaching a hand into my wallet, pulling

117

out a fifty-thousand-lira bill my mother had given me. "Take what we owe out of this."

"No need," Rafel said. "Already taken care of."

"What do you mean, someone already paid?" I said. "Who?"

"Italians never discuss money with Americans," Rafel said, laughing, patting me on the back. "Now go, you don't want to be late for the reception."

"Thanks, Rafel," I said, taking the basket from Franco's arms.

"For nothing, my friend," Rafel said. "For nothing."

The reception was held in a restaurant in Ischia Ponte, a fifteen-minute walk from the café. I was running late and decided to take side streets to cut down on time. The basket was heavy and the day hot, but I knew my mother would be upset if I showed up after the bride and groom had arrived.

I passed by a ten-foot-high gate, its wrought iron freshly painted a dark shade of green. I could see the restaurant on the other side of the gate; a six-piece band led by a short man in an evening jacket was busy performing a soft rendition of "Parla Mi D'Amore, Mariu."

The nearest opening to the gate was four blocks away and walking to it would delay me even further. The only sensible thing to do, it seemed, was to climb up and over the gate.

I hooked the basket over my right shoulder, tearing a hole in the tin foil which covered the top. I moved slowly up the gate, my hands reaching for the top spikes, my legs loosely wrapped around the thin bars. Across the way, facing me and watching the climb, was a squat old woman, who was tossing out a half-empty pail of dishwater into dense green shrubbery.

"Be careful," she said to me. "You're going to get hurt. Be careful. Please."

"Don't worry," I said. "I'll be all right."

I got my left leg over the top, slipping it between two sharp, thick spikes. I moved across slowly, carefully switching the fruit basket from my right arm to my left hand and then dropping it down the few feet to the ground. It landed, top up, in a clump of high grass, the fruit intact.

I tried to move my left leg over, looking to hang-drop from the top of the gate. One of my pants legs scraped against two of the iron curls that jutted out just below the spikes. I could feel the pants starting to tear and reached down to help move the leg along.

Then I lost all balance.

I toppled over the gate, my body half-hanging from the top. One of the green spikes had pierced through my shirt, jacket and the fleshy part of my right arm.

The pain I felt was sharp and intense, the lower part of my arm suddenly chilled with sweat and warmed from the rush of blood. I looked up, the sun partially blocking my vision, and saw the blood flowing past my arm and running onto my shoulder and neck.

My feet hung inches from the ground.

The old woman, now standing by her open kitchen window, saw me and screamed.

I grabbed at the gate with my left hand, hoping to climb back up and pull my arm off the spike. I turned my neck toward the old woman, saw her still standing there, both her hands held against her mouth, squashing back another scream.

"Jesus, my Jesus," she mumbled. "Jesus, Jesus."

"Get help," I said to her. "Please, get someone to help me."

The old woman disappeared from the window and was soon by my side.

"What should I do?" she said, looking up at me. "Oh, my God. There's so much blood. So much blood."

"Help push me higher," I said, trying not to think of the blood, trying to ignore the pain. "I got to get my arm off the damn spike."

The old woman put all her strength and weight against my legs, shoving them both up. While she did that, I reached for the top of the bars with my free hand.

"*Forza*, young man," she said. "Don't stop. You can make it. Just don't stop."

I grabbed onto one of the spikes and pulled myself up to where I was level with my bleeding arm. Slowly and painfully, I lifted the arm off the spike. I didn't look at the swelling, fought through the burning sensation it was causing and let it drop to my side.

"Come to me," the old woman said. "Drop down to me."

I let go of the gate and fell to the ground, on my side, inches from the old woman's feet.

"Don't move," she said, leaning over me, caressing my face with her hands. "I'll get a doctor."

"I don't need a doctor," I said. "Get my mother. She's in that restaurant on the corner."

"Emilio's?"

"Yes," I said. "Go and get her. Please."

I felt the old woman leave my side, heard her footsteps crunching down on the dirt around me and stared up at the cloudless sky. I touched the wound with the palm of my free hand, numb and raw from the blow, the blood still flowing from the quarter-size tear in the jacket.

I closed my eyes and rested my head against the base of the fruit basket, convinced that my wounded right arm would never again be what it was before the attempted climb.

"What a jerk," I said to myself. "What a fuckin' jerk."

I woke up in a bed on the second floor of the Porto D'Ischia clinic, dressed in a short hospital gown, my right arm heavily bandaged from the shoulder down to the elbow. My mother sat in a small wicker chair to my right, rosary beads in her hands, a concerned look on her face.

"How long have I been here?" I asked her.

"A few hours," she said.

She stood up and walked over to the light brown two-drawer bureau next to my bed. She took a white washcloth from a bedpan filled with ice and water, squeezed the cloth dry and rested it on my forehead.

"Your arm will be okay," she said. "The doctor said the tear looks worse than it is. There was no nerve damage. It should heal up fine. He said you were very lucky."

"How long do I have to stay here?"

"Overnight," she said. "They want to make sure it doesn't get infected. God willing, you should be home by late tomorrow afternoon."

"Good," I said. "I hate hospitals."

"So do I," my mother said.

She walked over to the open window, a warm evening breeze

parting the thin white curtains. She looked out at the line of people passing below, well-to-do tourists dressed in long gowns, short skirts and tailored slacks, out for a night of dinner and discos.

"You okay, Mom?" I asked.

She turned to face me, her right shoulder resting against a corner of the white wall closest to the window.

"There's trouble at home," she said. "Your father wants us back there as soon as possible."

"What kind of trouble?"

"What kind of trouble do we always have?" she asked me. "Money. Isn't it always money? Your father borrowed from some people who want it back. If they don't get it back they are going to kill him."

"How do you know this?" I asked. "Did Dad call you?"

My mother reached into the front pocket of the light blue house-dress she was wearing. She moved away from the window and came closer to me, to the side of my bed, a folded letter and a torn envelope in her right hand.

"No, he didn't call me." She handed over the letter. "This came for you three days ago. It's from your father. I wasn't going to show it to you."

"Why are you showing it to me now?" I said.

"I wanted to wait," my mother said. "See if the things he wrote you were true."

"Are they?"

"I don't know," she said, walking away from me and back toward the window. "Your father knows how to cover his lies. You should know that by now. If you know anything at all, you should know that."

I pulled the letter from the envelope, unfolded it and began to read what my father had written. I quickly recognized his half-scrawl, half-print writing style inked across three sheets of yellow legal paper. The incomplete sentences coupled with the poor spelling and weak grammar made the letter difficult to follow, but it was clear enough for me to tell that my father was in serious trouble.

"Please come home," the letter concluded. "I need you and I need my baby. I love you both very much. Very much. I want to see you both again before I die."

I read the letter twice before refolding it and placing it back in the envelope. I put the envelope on the bureau to my right and looked at my mother.

"Were you gonna wait until they killed him?" I said.

"Nobody's going to kill him," my mother sighed. "Don't believe everything you read."

"How do you know that?" I said, raising my voice. "Tell me, Mom, how the hell do you know that?"

"If your father was going to be killed by *anyone*, it would have happened a long time ago. Over something more serious than anything he's talking about in that letter."

"That's what you want, isn't it?" I asked my mother. "That's really what you want. That's what you pray for every day, every night. That they find him dead. Am I right? Tell me the truth, Mom, am I right?"

My mother stared at me a long time before she answered.

"Yes," she said finally, putting on her white sweater and picking up her black handbag. "It's not only what I want, it's what I need. For me, your father's death is my chance."

"Chance for what?"

"To escape," she said. "With my own life."

Paolo broke off a large piece of Italian bread, cracked it open and dunked it into his glass of wine.

"Don't spoil your appetite," his mother, my aunt Nancy, said. "Wait for everyone to get here."

"I'll be an old man by the time everyone gets here," Paolo said. "Old and hungry."

Grandma Maria came out of the kitchen, carrying a large bowl of spaghetti blanketed in a red meat sauce. She placed the bowl directly to my right.

"Get some food into him," Grandma Maria said to my mother. "He just got out of the hospital."

My mother held my plate in her hand and silently scooped out a large helping of meatballs and pasta. She placed it back in front of me and returned to the kitchen to help her sisters prepare the fruit and the salad. We had not said a word to each other since the previous evening in the hospital.

Paolo nudged me with his elbow, watching my mother walk past him.

"What's going on?" he asked me.

"Nothing," I said. "It's nothing."

"You want to go out after dinner?" he said.

"Sure," I said. "Where do you want to go?"

"Oh, you know, the usual," he said, looking over at his mother and smiling. "Any place that can give us an abundance of sex, drugs and rock 'n' roll."

Aunt Nancy picked up a hand towel and threw it at him.

"Delinquent," she said, trying to hide her smile. "I'm raising a delinquent."

"I'm sorry, Mom," Paolo said. "What was I thinking? Forget the music. No loud music. I swear to you."

Aunt Francis brought out a platter filled with roasted chicken parts, covered with oven-baked skinless potatoes, hot peppers, stuffed mushrooms and assorted spices.

She laid the platter in the center of the table, leaned back and slapped Paolo on the arm.

"Stay away from women," she said to him. "They'll melt your hammer."

"Melt my what?" Paolo said.

"You know what I'm talking about," Aunt Francis said. "Don't play dumb with me."

"You don't mean *all* women, do you?" Paolo asked, now playing to the room.

"All women," Aunt Francis said. "Especially the German ones. God only knows about them."

"What about the French?" Paolo said, egging Aunt Francis on. "The French are nice."

"Try to find a clean one," she said, sitting down and pouring herself a cold glass of white wine.

"The kind of girl I like . . ." Paolo said.

"The kind of girl you like you can usually find in jail," Aunt Francis said, as the laughter around the table grew louder.

"No, Zia, no that's not true," Paolo said. "I only go out with girls I meet at the beach."

"Oh, those angels," Aunt Francis said. "Sitting there all day, their breasts in the sand, their ass in the air."

"That's them," Paolo said.

"Tell me, who in the name of God would want to be seen with women like that?" Aunt Francis said.

"I wouldn't mind," her husband, Uncle Ciccio, chipped in.

Aunt Francis playfully slapped her husband on the head and shoulders. Paolo clapped his hands, applauding his uncle.

"Bravo, Zio," Paolo said. "Bravo."

"I did nothing," Uncle Ciccio said. "I simply answered a question."

I looked over at my mother, sitting in a corner seat to my left, her pasta untouched and growing cold. She stared at me, her eyes still angry, her manner subdued, ignoring the laughter growing around her.

My mother sipped some water, pulled her chair back, stood up and walked away from the table, heading for the terrace outside. I finished my wine, wiped my mouth with a napkin and followed her out into the warm air.

"I'm going back," I said to my mother, as I stood by her side, both of us looking down at four boys in shorts and T-shirts playing a loose game of soccer. "I'm leaving day after tomorrow."

"That's up to you," my mother said. "I'm not going to stop you, if that's your concern."

"You want to come with me?"

"No," my mother said. "Your father asked for you, not me."

I turned away from the boys and faced my mother.

"Maybe you should never come back," I said to her. "Stay here. With your family."

"My return ticket is dated September sixth," my mother said. "I have until then to decide."

"He needs us now," I said. "He needs *you* now."

"He doesn't need me *or* you," my mother said. "He needs money and he'll take it from anyone who'll give it to him."

"God, I can't believe how much you hate him," I said.

"I don't hate him," my mother said. "Believe me, I don't hate him."

"What is it then?"

"I'm just tired," she said. "I can't do it anymore. Can't live like we've been living anymore."

"Does he know that?"

"I tried telling him," she said. "I called the other night and tried to tell him how I felt."

"What'd he say?"

"He never heard me," she said. "He started yelling, accused me of having boyfriends, of living off his money, of ignoring him. The usual. It's nothing we all haven't heard a thousand times before. And there will never be an end to it."

"I still think you should come back," I said.

"Why?" my mother said. "What's there for me?"

"I'm there for you," I said.

"You?" my mother said with a half laugh. "You've never been there for me. Never. Not once."

"What?" I said, surprised at the level of her anger.

"All you know, all you see, all you care about is your father," my mother said. "Nothing else is as important to you as that man."

"That's not true," I said.

"I'm afraid that it's all very true," my mother said. "He's turned you into a smaller version of him. He's got you so wound that you never see his weakness, only his strength."

"He's my father," I said. "Do you want me not to love my father?"

"Of course you should love him," my mother said, reaching over to cup my face in her two hands. "But don't *be* like him. Please, God, be anything in this world, but don't ever be like that man."

My mother bent over and kissed me on both cheeks.

"His family hated to see me doing that," my mother said.

"Doing what?" I asked. "Kissing me?"

"I could never do it when they were around," she said. "Try to imagine that. Try to imagine what that feels like, what that does to a person."

"I can't," I said.

"Few can," my mother said, looking away, silent for a moment. "Anyway, we've talked enough for one night. Go, now. Young Paolo's waiting for you."

"Don't wait up for me," I said.

She ran a hand through my hair and smiled.

"I'm your mother," she said. "I'm supposed to wait up. So, do us both a favor and try not to be too late."

"I'll try," I said, turning away and going back inside Grandma Maria's house.

My mother lingered on the terrace, her fists braced around the black hand railings, her head down, her eyes filled with tears.

Her sister Anna walked up behind her, a cup of coffee in her hand. She tapped my mother on the shoulder and handed her the coffee.

"Sugar's in already," she said.

"It's not the sugar that worries me," my mother said. "It's the chocolate Mamma puts in every cup."

"Keeps your heart pumping," Aunt Anna said with a smile.

My mother laughed and drank her coffee, staring past her sister toward the full table of relatives halfway through their dessert, the men arguing over soccer, the women gossiping about their friends.

"You know you have to tell him, Raffaela," Aunt Anna said. "The time has come for him to know."

"The time has come," my mother said. "How can I be sure of that? How can I know I won't be making a big mistake by telling him?"

"He's old enough," Aunt Anna said. "And he asks questions. It's only been luck that he hasn't found out yet. But he will. And soon."

"He adores his father," my mother said. "In his eyes, he can do no wrong."

"That's all the more reason to tell him," Aunt Anna said.

"You know what you're asking me to do?" my mother said. "To pit a son against his own father."

"No, sister, that's not what I'm asking," Aunt Anna said. "Not at all."

"What then?" my mother asked, choking back a fresh onslaught of tears.

Aunt Anna reached over and embraced my mother, both women crying openly, leaning against the terrace rail.

Aunt Anna whispered into my mother's ear. "I'm asking you to tell the boy the truth, Raffaela. Tell him the truth now."

*   *   *

I didn't want to leave Ischia without my mother, believing that my father needed her as much as he needed me. If my father was indeed in trouble, I could only comfort him. My mother could, as always, somehow bail him out.

I let another week pass before calling him. I went to Grandma Maria's house to use her phone, staring out at the summer rain falling outside her living-room window, waiting until the fourth ring, when my father picked up.

"Dad?" I said. "Hey, Dad. It's me."

"Hey, One-punch," he said in a tired voice. "Long time."

"How are you, Dad?" I asked. "How are you feeling?"

"When you guys coming home?" my father said, ignoring my questions.

"September, Dad," I said. "Mom wants to stay until September."

"That's her," he said. "What about you?"

"I want to stay, too," I said. "Unless you need me to be home."

"Need you?" my father said, his voice distant and cold. "Why the fuck would I need you? I don't need you. I don't need anybody. Never did."

"Are you still in trouble, like you wrote in your letter?" I asked.

"Forget all that," my father said. "I took care of it on my own. Just more bullshit."

"You sure?"

"Very sure," my father said. "No, you go ahead. You and your mother have yourselves a good time. On me."

"Dad?" I said.

"So long, One-punch," my father said. "And don't bother calling here anymore. I'll see you when you get back. *If* you get back."

"I love you, Dad," I said, as my father slammed the phone back into its cradle.

I would never say those words to him again.

It was noon on July 15, 1969, when my mother told me about my father and his first wife. In less than a week's time, Neil Armstrong would walk on the moon and the New York Mets would begin their unbelievable quest for a baseball championship. None of that would matter much to me, none of it would register with the impact such events would normally have had on a fourteen-year-old boy enjoying his first summer away from home.

My mother and I stood by the shoreline of the white sand beach behind the Church of San Pietro, both of us shivering despite the hot summer sun glaring down. The words she had spoken seconds earlier still echoed in my ears, the truth behind each one etched both on my mother's face and in her eyes.

"How did he kill her?" I asked, watching as the tears welled and then eased their way down my mother's cheeks.

"Please," she said, her voice choked. "Leave it at that. For now."

"How did he kill her?" I said. "Tell me."

"With a pillow," my mother said. "He put a pillow over her face. In a hotel room."

"When?"

"A long time ago," my mother said. "Such a very long time ago."

I spent the rest of the day in a quiet rage. Angry at my father for hiding his crime from me so well and for so many years. Angry at my mother for waiting until now to tell me. Angry at myself for being so stupid, so gullible, never once questioning my father about his own life, his own past.

Many different feelings and emotions ran through my mind that day, all of them colored by an overwhelming feeling of being betrayed. The relationship my father and I had enjoyed would never again be what it was now that his crime was known to me. Yes, he would still always be my father. Nothing could change that. But he could never again be my friend. The murder of his first wife had changed that.

Most of all, however, I could not lose this new image of my father that had been freshly imbedded in my mind—a fierce, vicious thug suffocating the life out of a half-naked woman. A woman who happened to be his wife.

*   *   *

Grandma Maria put the pot of coffee on the table as soon as she heard me walking up the stairs to her house. I walked past her, pulled a chair out and sat by the table.

"You hungry?" she said.

"No, not really," I said. "Coffee's fine."

Grandma Maria made her way to the kitchen. She moved slowly against the late afternoon heat, holding a balled-up white handkerchief in one hand and a Chinese embroidered paper fan in the other.

She came back out carrying a tray that held an espresso cup and a plate full of miniature Italian pastries. She poured out some coffee and moved the pastry plate closer to me.

"They're fresh," she said. "Got them early this morning."

"Thanks, Grandma," I said. "I'm just not hungry."

"You shouldn't have coffee on an empty stomach," she said. "Especially my coffee."

We sat in silence. I drank my coffee, ignoring the hot slanting rays of the sun coming through each of the front three windows and the open door. We were both sweating, the heat in the room thick and oppressive. Neither one of us seemed to mind.

"Did you know?" I asked her, placing my empty cup back in the tray. "About my father?"

"Yes," she said without any hesitation. "I've known since you were born."

"Why didn't you tell me?" I said. "Why didn't anyone tell me?"

"Your mother asked me not to. She asked us all not to tell."

"Why?" I wanted to know. "What was she so afraid of?"

"She didn't want you to end up hating him."

"I don't hate my father," I said, defensively. "I don't hate him, so she was afraid for nothing."

"Not now," Grandma Maria said. "Not yet. The wound is still fresh. It takes time to hate."

"Do you hate him?" I asked. "For what he did?"

Grandma Maria stood up, wiped her upper lip with her handkerchief, walked over to one of the windows and lowered the blue Levolor blind, partially blocking out the sun.

"Do you, Grandma?" I said to her back. "Do you hate my father?"

Grandma Maria turned and looked right at me, standing parallel to the framed photo of Grandpa Gabriel.

"Your mother was carrying you when my husband was in Naples, dying," she began. "My daughters would take turns spending the night with him, helping him sleep through the pain. Each night, before they left, I would hand over a five-thousand-lira bill. That was to buy morphine for my husband, for his pain."

Grandma Maria moved to the table, pulled out her chair and sat down.

"One night, your father asked if he could spend the night with my husband," Grandma Maria went on. "Give everyone a break. I thanked him for his concern and handed him a five-thousand-lira bill, telling him what it was for. Your father kissed me and left. That night, my husband never got his morphine."

"What happened?"

"Your father met a nurse he liked," Grandma Maria said. "Bought pizzas for her and her friends, with the money I gave him. Left my husband in his bed, alone with his pain. All night. After that, my husband never wanted to see your father again. And he never did."

Grandma Maria poured me another cup of coffee, strong, old hands holding firm and steady.

"Now," she said looking directly at me. "Do you still want me to answer your question?"

The Feast of San Gennaro, the largest held on Ischia, began during the second week of August. Aunt Anna and Grandma Maria decided to have a full family dinner at a local restaurant on the first night of the feast, calling in relatives from as far away as Pisa, Florence and Udine in Northern Italy. In all, close to 250 people were expected.

"This is going to be bigger than last year's party," Paolo said, sitting at a small table in an outdoor café, facing the Mediterranean, drinking from a glass of Coke filled with two large lemon slices. "And last year's was huge."

"What's the big deal?" I said, still brooding over what had been told me about my father almost a month earlier. "It's about a saint, right?"

"It's about a lot of things," Paolo said. "Besides, it's a party and it'll be fun. Anything wrong with that?"

"Not from where you're sitting," I said.

Paolo finished drinking his soda and put his glass down on the wooden table, pushing it closer to the center.

"You don't have to go," he said. "No one is forcing you to go. At least no one I know." He leaned across the table, facing me, his face flushed and angry.

"Look, someone should say this and I guess I'm the one," he said.

"Then say it," I said. "Don't wait."

"You're acting like an asshole," Paolo said. "Since you got the news about your father."

"Got the news?" I said. "Is that what you call it? News?"

"I don't know what to call it," Paolo said. "And if it happened to me, I don't know how I would react. Maybe the same."

"So, what's your point?"

"That you're taking it out on us, the ones who love you. And that's a wrong thing to do."

I looked over at my cousin who had, in such a short span of time, grown to be a most trusted friend. His honest eyes and open face were lined with concern, his soft hands held together, his youthful body tense with emotion.

"I'm angry," I said. "I'm so angry I can't figure out what to do."

"There isn't much you *can* do," Paolo said.

"You don't understand," I almost shouted. "I should be doing something about this. I should be finding out more about it. As much as I can."

"Why?"

I put down my glass of Coke hard against the wood surface.

"How the hell can you ask me such a stupid question?" I said. "What do you mean why?"

"It's not a stupid question," Paolo said, pushing his chair back and standing up to leave. "You know everything you need to know right now. Anything else is just trouble. For you and for everybody else."

He put his chair in its place, picked up his half-empty glass of soda and finished his drink.

"You and I should not talk about this anymore," he said, resting his glass next to a crumpled napkin. "Not if we are to stay as friends."

He left the café, easily melding into the slow-moving tourist traffic. I sat there alone, suddenly unsure of myself and of my surroundings.

I looked around, saw couples at the other tables laughing, holding hands, telling stories, at ease and happy with one another. Living their lives openly, as if they had nothing at all to hide.

There now was only one vision in my head that mattered to me, and only one thought running steadily through my mind. The two were united together as one and were as painful as any headache, following me every step of my day. Over and over in my mind's eye, regardless of time or place, I would see a picture of my father, a pillow held in both hands, a woman squirming under the bulk of his weight.

Nothing I did could make that vision and that thought go away. On those few nights when I could sleep, I dreamt about my father and his first wife. When I went swimming at the beach, looking away from sand to shore, it would appear, as clear as ever.

It was now nearly a month since my mother had told me about the murder. I couldn't read a story in the paper or go to a movie or read a book without somehow linking my father's face to what I was doing. I couldn't bring myself to either call or write my father, unsure of the words I would use, afraid of the visions that such attempts would conjure up.

There seemed no way for me to escape from it.

I closed my eyes, my hands tightly held over them, anxious to clear my head, eager to move away from my seat. I felt closed in, short of breath and frightened, the vision of my father's crime pounding at me, beating at my head and eyes.

I stood up, my shirt wet with cold sweat, briefly looked to my left and right, trying to focus my gaze and silence the noise. I held the base of the wooden table with both hands and glanced at a woman walking past me, barefoot in a short green beach dress, a lit cigarette hanging from one hand.

I lifted the table from its umbrella stand and flipped it over, sending it to the ground in a loud explosion of chairs, glass and splintered wood.

I put my hands in my pockets and slowly walked away, leaving the angry shouts and startled murmurs behind me.

*　　*　　*

Multicolored fireworks lit up the night sky, exploding in timed bursts throughout Ischia. It was the first day of the feast; relatives and friends were crowded more than three hundred strong inside Gennaro's restaurant, the hugs and kisses flowing as freely as the local wine.

I stood next to an open window, looking out at the fireworks above and the still waters below, holding a plate filled with warm food. Aunt Anna stood to my left, one hand cupped under a bowl of pasta in tuna sauce, the other twirling a fork filled with linguini.

"What do you think so far?" she said, putting the fork to her mouth.

"It's pretty," I said.

"It gets prettier," Aunt Anna said. "At midnight, they'll be shooting fireworks from the mouth of Mount Epemeo. Then the boats will come into the harbor, all of them lit up, and form a circle around the one that's carrying the statue of San Gennaro."

"Why is he so special?"

"He's the patron saint of the island," Aunt Anna said. "Of Naples, really. But we adopted him some time ago. In troubled times, he's the one who we can always turn to for help."

"Does it work?" I asked her, picking at a thin slice of fried eggplant.

"Sometimes," she said. "If it's meant to help."

The fireworks outside grew in intensity and volume, each burst spraying out an array of vibrant colors. The narrow streets around the restaurant were packed with tourists browsing past expensive shops or buying delicacies from booths that had been set up near the hill by the church. The locals were dressed in their Sunday outfits, the mothers trying to corral their children, the men walking behind them, smoking constantly, talking in low voices to friends at their side. Everyone heading for the water to stand or sit as they waited for the statue of a saint to be hoisted above an explosive sea.

"Is it always this crowded?" I asked Aunt Anna, handing my now empty plate to a passing waiter.

"Gets worse every year," she said, finishing off the last of her pasta. "Do you want to go out, get a closer look?"

"Maybe later," I said.

Aunt Anna lit a cigarette, took a deep drag and blew the smoke toward the open window we were both facing.

"I heard about your little escapade in the piazza," she said. "Was the drink not to your liking?"

"Who told you?" I said.

"This island's a hard place to keep a secret. Especially if it's done in broad daylight."

"I guess it was pretty stupid," I admitted.

"Doesn't matter much now," she said. "It's done."

She bent over and reached for a glass ashtray from one of the tables, took a last pull from the cigarette and snubbed it out. She looked back at me and smiled.

"It's a bad habit," she said, brushing traces of ash from her fingertips. "I don't know why I do it. I don't even like to smoke."

"I'm sorry," I said to her.

"Forget it," she shrugged. "Grandma Maria took care of everything. She and the owner of the café have been friends for years."

"Not just about the table," I said. "About everything else. I've been acting a little crazy, I guess, since I found out about my father."

"To be expected," Aunt Anna said. "Your mother gave you a tough pill to swallow."

"I just don't know what to do or how I'm supposed to act," I said. "And I can't even think about what I'm gonna do when I see him again."

"You don't have to act different," Aunt Anna said. "That's silly. No one is going to think any less or any more of you because of this. You forget, *we've* all known about it for years. *You* just found out."

"What did you do when you found out?"

"I screamed," Aunt Anna said. "I felt like I was in the middle of a horror movie. It was frightening. What your father did may be a common thing back in America, but it's unheard of around here."

"You get over it?"

"Never," she said. "I worry about your mother. Worry about her safety. About her life. And why shouldn't I worry? You kill one wife, why couldn't you kill two?"

"I can't get it out of my head," I said. "You know, I don't even know what my father's wife looked like, never saw a picture of her, never asked him about her, nothing like that. But boy do I see her now. Clearly. In my head. Every damn day."

Aunt Anna reached over and surrounded me with her arms, the top of my head resting against the base of her chin. Waiters rushed by on both sides, setting trays filled with food down onto a large buffet table. Others, in sauce-soiled white jackets, jumped from group to group picking up empty plates and dirty forks.

"Forget it for one night," Aunt Anna whispered in my ear. "Just this one night. Find Paolo and the other boys and go out and have a good time."

I lifted my head and moved away from her arms.

"Paolo said they were thinking of going out on one of the boats," I said.

"Good," Aunt Anna said. "You should join them. It sounds like fun. Your father can wait."

"What do I say to him?" I wanted to know. "When I see him again."

"About the murder?"

"Yes."

Aunt Anna flipped open the handbag hanging from a strap on her shoulder. She reached in with one hand and pulled out a cigarette and a small box of kitchen matches.

"You may not say anything," she said. "It might not be the right time."

"The right time," I said, shaking my head. "The right time to ask my father about killing his wife. I can't think of a right time for that."

Aunt Anna stroked the left side of my face, the cigarette hanging from inside two of her fingers.

"You'll know when," Aunt Anna said. "Believe me, little one, you will know. The moment finds you. It always does."

* * *

I zippered the last of my suitcases shut and placed them on the top of the outside steps. I checked to see that my passport and tickets were all in order and then sat in a corner chair, waiting for Grandma Maria to come up from the basement.

She walked slowly, taking each step two feet at a time, a small cardboard box held under her right arm. She nodded her head in my direction when she saw me.

"Waiting long?" she asked, making her way past me and into the cool shade of the apartment, tossing the box on top of an empty side table.

"Long enough to pack," I said. "Wanted to get it out of the way."

"I've never packed," she said. "In my life. Never went anywhere that I needed more clothes than I had on."

I walked toward her, handing her a white cloth napkin from the table. She took it, folded it and wiped droplets of sweat from the center of her forehead and above her upper lip.

"You've never been on a vacation?" I said with a smile, knowing what the answer would be.

"The next one I take will be my first," Grandma Maria said, smiling back.

I poured us both large glasses of cold water and pulled two chairs away from the center of the table. I sat down next to her and handed her one of the glasses. She drank in large gulps, finishing the water in four quick swallows. She placed the glass next to her feet, sat back and slapped open the paper fan she kept hidden up her sleeve.

"I'm gonna miss you," I said, watching as she fanned herself. "More than anybody else here."

"You'll be back," she said. "And I'll be here. With a little luck."

"I wish I didn't have to go," I said. "Wish I could stay here. With you."

"Not possible," Grandma Maria said. "You have a life in America. A place. It is your country."

"It's not going to be the same," I said. "Not after what happened this summer."

"Nothing happened," Grandma Maria said. "You grew up, that's all."

"I've only been here three months," I said. "Seems more like three years."

"That's Ischia," she said. "The clocks here tick slower than other places."

She stood up and headed for the kitchen.

"It's time for coffee," she said as she walked.

"It's gotta be over a hundred degrees outside," I said.

"Then coffee's just what you need," she said, disappearing behind the kitchen door.

I stirred my coffee and watched as Grandma Maria poured in the two shots of Stock 84.

"No chocolate?" I said.

"It's already in there," she said. "Drink it fast, before it cools."

"I promise you one thing," I said.

"What?"

"I'll never drink coffee like this with anyone else but you," I said. "Especially in the summer."

Grandma Maria laughed, exposing a massive shortage of teeth. She dabbed at her forehead with the folded napkin held in the palm of her hand.

"Promise me something else," she said.

"Name it," I said.

"Face up to your father," she said.

"That's not an easy one, Grandma," I said. "Don't know if I can do that."

"You can," she said. "And you will."

"What makes you so sure?"

"I've watched you," she said. "Since you found out about the murder."

"It made my summer ugly," I said.

"You have to learn to carry it around with you," Grandma Maria said. "Your father's crime is a part of your life. And it will be from now on."

137

I stood up and walked over to the window, hands inside my pants pockets, tears running down my face.

"What do I do, Grandma?" I said, looking at the stone house across the way, trying hard to smell the sea less than a quarter mile away.

"Whatever needs to be done," she said. "You'll have the answers, don't worry. When the time comes."

Grandma Maria walked over to the old brown bureau in the corner of the dining room, opened the top drawer and pulled out a large yellow envelope.

"Take this," she said.

"What is it?"

"A start," she said.

"Can I open it?" I asked.

"Yes," she said. "But not now. Wait until you're back in America."

I slid the envelope into the back pocket of my slacks and looked at my watch.

"It's time to go," I said. "You have no idea how nervous Mom gets when we have to travel."

"Knowing her," she said, "I can imagine."

I looked around the room, trying to record everything, my eyes stopping momentarily at the picture of Grandpa Gabriel.

"I'll never forget you, Grandma," I said, not wanting to leave.

"You never have to," she said.

We hugged and kissed in the summer heat, Grandma Maria caressing my face, wiping away my tears.

"Remember this place, this island," she said. "It's as important to you as any one person. Your history is here. Your blood."

"I won't forget it," I said.

"Good," Grandma Maria said. "Now go. Don't miss your plane. I don't need to hear your mother yell at me. Not at my age."

I picked up my suitcases and made my way down the curving stone steps, putting them down again when I reached the base. I turned and waved a final goodbye to Grandma Maria.

"Remember," I yelled up to her. "You promised to save that coffee for me."

"I have to," she said with a laugh. "Can't get anybody else to drink it. Especially in this heat. They're afraid they'll die from it."

"Gotta die of something," I said.

"Gotta die of something," Grandma Maria agreed, turning away from me and walking back, head down, into the only home she had ever lived in.

Book Two

I'VE LEARNED, MR. GITTES, THAT AT ANY
GIVEN MOMENT IN HIS LIFE, A MAN IS
CAPABLE OF ANYTHING.

—John Huston to Jack Nicholson
in *Chinatown*

I

My father, breathing heavily, tasted the blood flowing down from his mouth. An elderly white-haired man in a torn shirt hovered over him, rubbing Vaseline over my father's face, staring into his eyes.

"This is your round, Mario," the old man said. "He's yours. He's all yours. Take the cocksucker out."

"He hits hard," my father said. "Takes what I give him."

"Fuck all that," the old man said. "Hook to his heart and then come across with that right of yours. That'll send him down. Fuck yeah, that'll send him down for damn sure."

The bell for the third and final round was about to ring. My father, still sitting on a short three-legged stool in his corner, briefly scanned the stuffy, smoky Connecticut auditorium, amazed at how many people could fit inside such a small place.

"There would be at least six, seven hundred in a hall that shouldn't have held more than two hundred," my father told me. "Everybody screamin' and smokin', tossin' money back and forth, betting not only on the fight but on the round and even the number of punches we were gonna throw."

My father called them "whiskey bouts," held up and down the East Coast in places where a young man with a hard punch could fight as often as three times in one night using three different names.

"I would be introduced as Mario Jones in the first fight," my father recalled. "Mario Smith in the second and Mario whatever in the third. By that time, it was so late and they were so drunk that nobody gave a shit about your name, so long as you had on gloves and were ready to kick the shit outta somebody. If you won, you got fifty bucks a bout, plus a cut of the action my old man was taking in from his seat. If you lost you got shit. Some nights, you could take home as much as four hundred dollars for just a few hours' work."

My father and his opponent, a thick-muscled, heavyset Irishman from Jamaica, Queens, circled around each other near the center of the ring. They each flicked a few soft jabs in the air, both looking to move in closer, to land some solid blows. My father bit down harder on his mouthpiece, causing his split lip to open up even more, the blood now streaming past his chin and onto his chest.

"Move it," his corner man yelled. "Move it. Wrap it up. Stop fuckin' around. Wrap the bastard up."

My father was hit just above the right eye with a short, choppy right hand and then ducked under the follow-up left hook. Another right, this one landing flat against his face, forced my father to take a step back.

"C'mon, Mario," the corner man pleaded. "What are ya doin'? Fight this fuck, will ya please."

My father moved in closer, lowering his right shoulder into his opponent's side and shifting his feet to give his punches more leverage. He swung a sharp hook into the body, then another and then a third.

"I wanted to take the fuckin' air out of his lungs," my father said. "Bring the prick's arms to his sides. Get ready to drop him down. I knew I could take him. It was just a question of when and how."

The punch, a powerful overhand right, caught my father by surprise and landed flush against his mouthpiece, splitting his lower lip in half. Blood sprayed out from my father and onto his opponent's face and arms. The force of the blow and the loss of blood dazed my father and forced him to hold on, the two fighters clinched away in a corner right above the official timekeeper.

"Bleed to death, you prick," my father's opponent said to him. "Bleed to fuckin' death."

My father pushed away and spit out his mouthpiece. The lower half of his face and top half of his chest were blanketed with his blood. He squared off against his opponent and threw a right hand that just grazed the man's face. Then a body blow, a hard left directed right under the heart, found its mark.

"That was the one," my father said. "That punch took everything outta him, right then and there. The prick couldn't breathe and I went in to finish it. I knew there wasn't that much time left in the round."

My father landed a right cross to the jaw and another left hook to the body, then a vicious left-right combination that shattered his opponent's nose. A bruising series of raging punches sent the man staggering against the ropes, my father fast on him.

"Finish him off, Mario," the corner man said, his voice cracked from screaming. "Finish him off."

Six unanswered blows all found their mark, each causing welts to form. The final punch, a belt-high uppercut, sent my father's opponent flat down against the bottom two strands of the ring ropes, his eyes glazed and his head wobbly. My father brushed his right forearm past his lower lip, spit out a mouthful of blood and walked off toward his corner, his night's work completed.

A frail-looking ring physician, liver spots dotting both his hands and thick glasses resting on a chain around his neck, stitched my father's lip in the dressing room.

"How many you think he needs, doc?" the corner man asked.

"About a dozen," the doctor said. "Give or take. He's lost a lot of blood."

"No shit," my father said, trying to ignore the pain and looking at anything but the doctor's shaky hands.

"Can he fight next week?" the corner man asked. "We got a date in Bridgeport."

"No," the doctor said. "A month is what he needs. Then give it a shot."

"How about two weeks?" the corner man said.

"Forget it," the doctor said. "A month. Anything less, you're asking for trouble."

"We're gonna be in enough trouble, we don't show up in Bridgeport next week," the corner man said.

The doctor sewed in the last of the stitches.

"There you go," he said to my father. "It's not pretty, but it'll hold."

"Thanks, doc," my father said. "Okay if I shower, get dressed?"

"Yeah, no problem," the doctor said, reaching into the front pocket of his tattered brown jacket. "Here, take these. It'll help the pain."

The doctor handed my father four red capsules, placing them in the palm of his still-taped right hand.

"I'll pass, doc," my father said, moving off the bench and toward the shower. "Pills make me sleepy and I got plans for tonight. Big plans."

One hour later, my father stood under a dim streetlight, fully dressed, his hands at his side, occasionally checking his watch, waiting for a man walking in the shadows, slowly making his way up the street.

"Hello, prick," my father said when the man stood close enough to be seen.

"What the fuck do you want?" my father's ring opponent said, startled, a hint of surprise in his voice.

The man had thick strips of tape stretched across both his eyes, and his cheeks and lips were discolored and swollen.

"I owe you," my father said.

"Owe me for what?" the man said.

"For this," my father said, pointing to his stitched lip.

The man took a step back, holding his hands palms up.

"Hey, c'mon, will ya," he said. "Let's keep it to the ring, okay?"

My father moved closer to the man, away from the glare of the overhead streetlight.

"Listen, I was gonna go down to Duggan's," the man said. "Have a beer. Come along if you want. Otherwise, get outta my way."

The force of my father's right hand, closed into a fist, landed flush against the man's taped-over right eye. The left that immediately followed it forced blood to seep through the strands of white tape. Two quick and powerful shots to the body removed any chance the man had of defending himself.

"Nobody cuts me," my father said, kicking the man in the chest and back just as he was beginning to sway to the ground. "Nobody. I don't give a fuck who it is. *Nobody* cuts me."

My father then grabbed the man from behind and began to pound his head against the concrete sidewalk closest to the streetlight. He turned him over, blood now flowing from the back of the man's head, and began pounding at his face and neck with kicks.

"Nobody cuts me," my father kept repeating. "Nobody anywhere fuckin' cuts me."

My father stared down at the man, saw all the blood, heard the gurgling attempts to breathe and stopped kicking. He reached into his pants pocket and pulled out a small roll of bills, tens at the top, singles down the rest of the way. He peeled off a ten and two singles, bent over and stuffed them inside the front pocket of the man's blood-soaked shirt.

"You can go to Duggan's now," my father said to the man. "My treat."

In the spring of 1940, my father was twenty-three years old and living at home. He had no steady job, little in the way of money and gave no thought at all to what he might want to do for a living.

"I liked having a good time," he told me. "I went dancing every Friday and Saturday, shacking up for the night with whatever girl I got lucky with. I lived day-to-day. If I needed money I would pull in a couple of days' work down the docks, unloadin' produce. Otherwise, I'd just ask my mother for a few bucks. She was always good for it."

My father didn't drink or smoke, and exercised for a full hour every day. He weighed less than 160 pounds, all of them evenly spread out across a five-foot, seven-and-one-half-inch frame. He was

147

balding, with thin strands of brown hair resting across the top of an unlined scalp. He was quick to fight and was thought to be one of the best jitterbug and fox-trot dancers on the West Side.

"You never knew the man had no money," says Angela, a now seventy-year-old woman who dated my father for a two-month period in 1940. "When we went out we always went in style. He treated me good. Very good. Sure, he was always ready and willing to fight. Who the hell wasn't in that godawful neighborhood? Tell you the truth, though. I was as surprised as all get-out when I heard about the jam he got himself into. With the wife, I mean."

My father did not, by all appearances, seem the type of man eager to settle down. He had slept with his first woman when he was sixteen and since that awkward night had bedded more than he could count. If he couldn't convince a woman he met in a bar to spend the night, he would pay one for the pleasure. It didn't seem to matter much to him either way.

He had been fighting for money since he was fifteen, trained initially by the former flyweight champion of the world Fidel La Barba. Mastoid surgery was performed on my father's left ear when he was five years old. The botched result cost him 70 percent of his hearing and kept him out of both the army and the professional ring.

"Everybody thought I couldn't hear because of the punches I was takin'," my father said. "Had nothin' to do with that. Nothin' at all. But I could never convince any doctor of that. Couldn't get licensed, that's why I fought in the whiskey bouts. I tell you something. If I coulda turned pro, my life would have turned out to be totally different. You can bet your life on that."

My father was the second oldest in a family of three boys and two girls that was ruled by a mother quick to spoil and a father quicker to slap. My father tolerated his brothers and doted on his sisters, especially the youngest, Mary.

"My oldest brother, Danny, would always brush past me," Aunt Mary said. "Never say anything other than 'Go away. You bother me.' Mario was different. He would tell me stories, take me to movies, give me the loose change from his pockets. And because of his reputation on the street, no one ever bothered me. They knew if they did, he would go looking for them."

My paternal grandfather, Lorenzo, worked on the "pistol piers," 62 and 67, which were controlled by mobster Albert Anastasia's younger brother, Tony. There were no steady shifts, no posted hours, the hard manual work dictated only by the number of ships in port and the regularity of payoffs made to the various union officials on hand.

"The old man was almost never home," my father said. "He usually worked for four straight days without stopping, then came back to the apartment and slept for two or three days. That was his week. We didn't talk or see each other all that much. If my mother told him that any of us had done something wrong, he'd come look for us and beat us until he was tired. Other than that, he went about his business and we went about ours."

There was no time for laughter, and family gatherings were, more often than not, an excuse to do battle.

"That family was always fighting," said the super of the building where my grandparents lived. "Shouting and screaming, every damn day. Never a break. There was no peace coming out of that place. Holidays were the worst time. That's when they really went at it."

Dinner was just about over. My father's mother, Raffaela, and her oldest daughter, Anna, were in the small kitchen, washing dishes and putting water on for coffee. My grandmother sang a love song as she scrubbed the inside of a blackened old pot, happy that her sons were together at her table to share a holiday meal.

My father sat hunched forward on a shaky wooden chair at a large table in the middle of a crowded dining room. He was wiping at the corners of his plate with a thick slice of Italian bread. My father put the bread in his mouth, picked up a fork and speared a last piece of chicken off a platter in the center of the table.

"Hey, what's with you?" his brother Daniel said, reaching for my father's arm.

"What?" my father said. "What's your problem?"

"I was gonna have that piece," Daniel said.

"Well, now you ain't," my father said.

"Give me the chicken, prick," Daniel said. "You can't just take it from me."

"Fuck you," my father said. "Next time move faster. Now, I just as soon give it to a bum on the street as give it to you."

"Hey, why don't you two relax, okay?" my father's youngest brother, Albert, said. "It's only a fuckin' piece of chicken. God forbid you would split it."

"Split shit," my father said.

"The only thing I'm gonna split is his fuckin' face," Daniel said.

Daniel reached across and grabbed my father by the collar of his blue sport shirt, pulling him closer to his end of the table. Albert stood up and backed away, not eager to interfere. My grandfather sat at the head of the long table, not moving, sipping from a glass of red wine.

My father took a wild swing aimed at the top of Daniel's head, knocking over two empty glasses and a half-filled bottle of water. At the noise, Raffaela and Anna came into the living room, their hands dripping with soapy water.

"Stop them," Anna said. "Please, somebody. Stop them."

My father and his brother left the table and headed out the door.

"I'm gonna beat you up and down this fuckin' block," my father said.

"Say goodbye to this scumbag," Daniel said to his family. "It's the last time you're gonna see him alive."

"I'm makin' coffee," Anna said. "Sit down. Stay for coffee."

"*Dove vai?*" my grandmother screamed. "Stay here. No go out."

"I'll be back, Ma," my father said. "I gotta teach your son some fuckin' manners first."

"Let's go, prick," his brother said, standing outside the open apartment door. "I ain't got all fuckin' day."

"I'll make more chicken," Anna said. "There's plenty. Just sit down and relax."

"That's not a bad idea," my father said, putting on his hat and walking out of the apartment. "Go ahead and do that. I won't be long."

Albert walked to the open door and closed it, wiping off his shirt as he did, leaving my father outside. He picked up a chair and sat down next to my grandfather. He reached for a jug of red wine and poured out two glasses worth.

"*Salute*, Pop," he said. "Here's another fuckin' Thanksgiving that's come and gone."

My father was standing in the middle of a crowded CYO dance hall, chewing two pieces of Juicy Fruit gum and drinking from a short-neck bottle of Coke, when he first saw the woman he would marry and then murder. She was wearing a flowered dress, small white buttons down the front and a silk half-moon blue bow on the back. She was average height and ten pounds away from thin, with thick brown hair hanging just off her shoulders, her hazel eyes shiny and bright when matched against the revolving dance-hall lights.

Her name was Grace Monte.

"The minute I saw her I knew," my father said. "She was the prettiest girl in the world. There was none better."

My father dropped his gum inside the now empty Coke and laid the bottle cap up against a wall. He straightened his black shirt inside his khaki pants and checked the shine on his shoes. He walked across the hall, careful not to bump into any of the dancers swinging past to the beats of a Benny Goodman tune, and stood before Grace.

"Hows about a dance?" my father said.

"Sure," she agreed.

"This one too fast?" my father asked. "Wanta wait for the next?"

"This one's okay," she told him.

They twirled around the dance floor, easy and light. She was a good dancer, her shapely legs responding to the furious riffs of the swing band, her body comfortable with the movements, her dress wiggling itself around her thighs, my father's hands loosely held in hers.

"She could really move," my father said. "She was always the first one out on a dance floor. Music was like drugs for her. That first night, we didn't talk all that much. Danced mostly. To everything that was played, from Goodman to Chick Webb. The happiest times the two of us had, we had on a dance floor. It was that way from the beginning. Stayed that way right up to the end."

*　　*　　*

151

My father bought her a Coke and poured it into a plastic cup over-flowing with ice. They were both still breathing heavily from the dancing, sweat glistening on their faces and foreheads, the back of my father's shirt glued to his shoulders.

"It's an oven in here," my father said. "How about we take a walk outside. It'll cool us off."

"Okay," Grace said. "I have to go to the bathroom first. I'll be back in a minute."

"No problem," my father said. "I'll wait for you here."

They walked together, barely inches apart, on Tenth Avenue, heading away from the CYO hall and up toward 54th Street. There was a chill to the air, the hard breezes instantly cooling their bodies, forcing them to turn to their jackets for warmth.

"You okay?" my father asked.

"Yes," Grace said, looking at him and smiling. "I'm fine."

"Hungry?" my father said. "We could go grab a coupla burgers. Up the block. At the diner. They're not bad."

"I don't think I can," she said. "It's getting late."

"Then let me take you home," my father said.

She slipped an open hand into his and they both clutched on tight.

"Thanks," she said. "That would be nice."

By all accounts, Grace was the most sought-after girl in Hell's Kitchen. She was sixteen when my father first met her, her walk still girlish, her manner shy and uneasy, especially when surrounded by adults.

"She was quiet," my father said. "Until you said or did something she didn't like. Then, she wouldn't be quiet at all. She'd tell you exactly what was on her mind. She was what you'd call a ballsy broad. I liked that about her. Shit, I liked a lot of things about her."

One week after that first dance, Grace and my father began to keep regular company. They went to the movies together, ate late dinners in empty diners and danced whenever and wherever opportunity presented itself.

What little they knew about each other was all that seemed to matter. They both liked Cagney over Bogart, bebop over cool jazz,

Chick Webb over Gene Krupa and boxing over baseball. Neither one drank, and both would, on occasion, smoke a cigarette.

On their seventh date together, in a small Southern Italian restaurant on West 48th Street, after having paid to see a Ronald Coleman movie they both hated, my father and Grace first talked about marriage.

"She wore a blue dress that night," my father said. "Small pink dots running up and down the front and back. She looked as beautiful as a movie star, like a Grace Kelly or an Ann Sheridan. I couldn't imagine anyone having anything on her. I was hooked, as in love as any guy could be. I knew I had found the right woman for me. I was set. Fallin' in love with her seemed such an easy thing to do. Lookin' back on it, maybe it was too easy."

My father had no full-time job and no money saved and had yet to tell anyone in his family about his marriage plans. He had often talked about having children of his own and had always wanted to marry a neighborhood girl.

"That's the way things worked back then," he said. "You fucked around with as many broads as you could get your hands on and then, when the time was right, you settled down with a girl no one else had been with. You never married someone's reject, a hand-me-down woman. In my time, you grew your own. It was the right thing to do."

Grace felt secure around my father. In her youthful eyes, my father was a handsome and willing adventurer ready and eager to do or try anything. He was, if nothing else, confident, openly bragging about the millions he would one day make and the properties he would own, all of it to be handed over to her care.

"For you, Gracie," my father would say. "It would all be for you. Nothin' too big or too small."

Grace wanted out of Hell's Kitchen, had grown weary of living in a four-room cold-water apartment that overlooked the back end of a warehouse, and was old enough to know that having money was the best way to ensure that escape. So, she bought into my father's dreams.

She ignored the cold treatment she received from my father's family and the warnings that were issued by members of her own. She turned away from the steady whispers and rumors regarding both my father and his mother, the snide talk of lend-outs, of fast hands and slow minds. None of that mattered to her.

Grace was sixteen and in love.

Grace and my father were married on a rainy morning in a sedate City Hall civil ceremony, united in matrimony by a tall man with a slight stutter. They had ignored the angry requests from both sides of the family to wait, to delay the marriage until my father held a steady job, one that would enable him to support a wife and an eventual family.

"Everybody thought we were in a hurry to get married because Grace was pregnant," my father said. "That was bullshit talk, started by a prick with time on his hands. We just wanted to be together and didn't see why the hell we needed to wait. For anybody. No more fuckin' mystery to it than that."

My father wore black slacks on his first wedding day, topped by a black two-button jacket with thin lapels and a white-on-white shirt buttoned to the top. He wore no tie and combed back what was left of his hair with a brush drenched in warm water.

Grace wore an off-white dress, hand-knit, given to her by her favorite aunt. Her auburn hair was freshly cut and curled, and hung just above the rim of the neckline. She had on red nail polish, red lipstick, cream-colored pumps and her grandmother's white shawl, also hand-knit.

Her brown eyes were framed by mascara, her left hand gripped my father's arm and her wide, little girl smile helped to hide the nervous feeling in the center of her stomach.

"Her teeth were shakin'," my father said. "Mine too. I couldn't get over it. Guys like me don't end up with girls that look as good as her, let me tell you."

They giggled as they said their vows, Grace using a cough to disguise her laughter. My father kept the wedding band he had bought with borrowed money in the middle of a curled-up white handkerchief, which he would occasionally remove from a front pocket of his trousers to wipe his wet brow. He had two twenties, a ten and two singles folded inside his wallet, tucked next to three tightly wrapped packets of Trojans and a small crumbling picture of his mother.

The rain had stopped by the time Grace and my father walked back outside, reduced to a fine mist, the streets gleaming and wet. They walked slowly, stopping every few steps to kiss and hug, heading for a downtown diner and a cheeseburger, french fries and two Cokes lunch.

"The diner was an old one," my father said. "Dirty, the windows all kinda misty with grease. God knows what the fuck kind of meat they used to make the burgers. But it didn't matter. None of that shit matters when you first get married."

They walked uptown to the bus depot and the long ride to the Rustic Cabin, a motel on the far end of the New Jersey shore, for the start of a honeymoon weekend. My father paid cash for their round-trip tickets and sat with his wife in the last seat of a battered, rusty old bus, both of them kissing, hugging and giggling throughout the length of the trip.

The driver, a thin, middle-aged man with a four-inch scar across his forehead, sang an old Irish love ballad to the newlyweds on board, hitting full volume as the bus cleared its way past the Wee-hawken cliffs.

"You married, buddy?" my father shouted to the driver once the song was over.

"You bet," the driver said. "As married as any man."

"How long?" my father asked.

"First time or second?" the driver said, tilting his head to one side, keeping his eyes focused on the stretch of road ahead of him.

"Pick one," my father said.

"Twelve years," the driver said. "Second time was the better one."

"Why's that?"

"First one didn't like music or drinkin' or anything else that amounted to fun," the driver said.

"Why'd the hell you marry her?" my father said.

"Didn't know I'd meet the second one," the driver said, laughing and turning the big wiper blades on to brush aside the drops of fresh rain.

My father fell quiet for a few moments, holding Grace close to his side, watching as the bus made its way past a three-mile stretch of New Jersey factories.

"How long before we get to where we goin'?" my father said, turning away from the silent smokestacks.

"What's your rush?" the driver said. "You got the rest of your life."

"We're gonna go hear Sinatra sing, over down at the Rustic Cabin," my father said. "Don't wanna miss it."

"Don't worry," the driver said. "I been on this job eight years and ain't missed an arrival time yet. Don't plan on doing it tonight, either."

"What you think of him?" my father said.

"Who?" the driver said. "Sinatra?"

"Yeah."

"He's good," the driver said. "Now, mind you, he ain't no Crosby. But he's almost as good. The young kids seem to have taken a shine to him. Must be the way he holds on to that mike, hangin' over it like he's gonna fall. You ever see him do that?"

"Yeah, I have," my father said. "Coupla times. At the Paramount. In New York."

"Then you know what I'm talkin' about," the driver said. "It's a gimmick, I suppose. People are bound to get tired of it soon enough."

"That don't matter to me," my father said. "So long as it don't happen before tonight."

The thin curtain strands separated in the chilly breeze that came through the open window. My father reached over and pulled the top of the white comforter over his wife's bare shoulders.

"This'll keep you warm, baby," my father said.

Grace reached out her arms and held my father close to her.

"I don't need anything to keep me warm," she said, a bride now for just over six hours. "Just you."

"You know that's the truth," my father said. "That will always be the truth."

Grace fingered the wedding band on her left hand, still adjusting to the feel. She brushed loose a few locks of hair from her eyes and stared over at her husband.

"Are you sorry?" she asked.

"About what?" my father said. "Gettin' married?"

"Yeah."

"What, you kiddin' me," he said. "Smartest thing I ever did was hookin' up with you."

"I know, but . . ."

"But what, baby?" my father said. "What's wrong?"

"Your family," Grace said. "I'm just sorry they didn't come to see us get married."

"Hey, fuck 'em," my father said. "Fuck all of 'em. They don't mean shit to me. You're the only one, baby. The only one that counts. You understand, baby? Just you."

"It woulda been nice, though," she said. "To have them there."

"Like I said, fuck it," my father said. "Don't even think about it. Now, c'mon, get dressed. I got a surprise for you."

"What is it?"

"Just get dressed," my father said. "And leave the rest of the night to me."

The cabin lights dimmed, and the couples gathered at tables around the small stage put down their glasses and reached for hands to hold. The lit candles at each table gave a glow to the women's faces as the orchestra, awash in darkness, began playing the opening strings of a love ballad they all knew.

A rail-thin, curly haired young man in a dark tuxedo walked across the stage, heading for the lone mike placed in the center of the floor. He grabbed it and sang only three words before the screams from the women and the applause from the men drowned out his sound.

"He opened with a Hoagy Carmichael song," my father told me. "It was called 'I Get Along Without You Very Well.' I looked across at all the tables, watching people move closer together, the women wiping tears from their eyes. Never saw anything like it before. It was like being in a church."

Frank Sinatra held a glass in his hand and wiped his brow with a folded handkerchief. He had just finished singing his fourth number of the evening.

"I understand there are quite a few newlyweds among us tonight," he said, putting the handkerchief back in his jacket pocket. He smiled and bowed at the applause coming from the dozen freshly married couples in attendance, lifting his champagne glass to them.

"Would the newlyweds all rise, please," Sinatra said. "And would everyone else kindly join me in wishing them much happiness through all their years together. *Cent'anni di salute. Cent'anni a tutti.*"

"*Cent'anni*, baby," my father said, holding his arms around his wife and kissing her on the cheeks and lips. "I love you, Grace. I'll always love you."

"I love you too, honey," Grace said. "Always."

My father reached into his pocket and pulled out a long, flat black box and handed it to his wife.

"Here, Gracie," he said. "Here's the surprise I had for you. I hope you like it."

Grace took the box and opened it. Her eyes moistened when she saw the double-strand pearl necklace.

She put her arms around my father, kissed him twice and whispered in his ear.

"Dance with me, baby," she said. "Dance with me now."

Grace and my father stood next to their table, holding on to one another, dancing slowly, quietly, listening as Frank Sinatra sang them a song called "Street of Dreams."

II

Gabriel Carcaterra sat back in his chair, a cup of hot coffee to his left, looking at the hand he had just been dealt. He was one of six players around a wooden table inside a near empty café, playing cards at half a lira a deal by candlelight. A tall, somber young man, in a plaid hunting shirt and work pants, stood against the bar, sipping a Bacari bitter, trying to ignore the table.

Gabriel reached for his cup of coffee, blowing away some of the steam before he drank. The player to his left, a chunky old man with horn-rim glasses and a two-day stubble on his face, moved his chair closer to my grandfather.

"I hear there's a man in town with his eye on one of your daughters," the old man whispered.

"Which one?" Gabriel said, not looking away from either his coffee or his cards.

"The quiet one," the old man said. "Raffaela."

Gabriel put his cup down and turned to the old man.

"Who is this man?" he said. "Do you know him?"

"He's a new face on the island," the old man said. "Transferred over from the North."

"Transferred how?" Gabriel asked. "You mean a banker?"

"No," the old man said. "He's not a banker. He's a caribanieri. A policeman."

"Gabriel, my friend, we are here to play cards," the overweight man across from my grandfather said, an unlit cigar dangling from his mouth. "Let our wives plan the weddings. It is their job, their enjoyment."

"There is no wedding to plan," Gabriel said.

"Raffaela likes him," the old man said. "Very much. And he feels the same about her."

My grandfather tossed his cards onto the table and stood up from his chair.

"There is no wedding," he said. "Not between my daughter and any policeman from the North. Tell this caribanieri that when you see him."

"You can easily tell him yourself," the old man said. "He's standing behind you, that young man at the bar."

My grandfather turned away from the table and toward the bar, watching as the man walked over to him.

"Signor Carcaterra," the young man said, reaching for my grandfather's hand. "My name is Mario Scubla. I am the caribanieri your friend was attempting to tell you about."

"He wasn't doing that good a job," Gabriel said, looking over at his friend. "Perhaps you should take over for him."

"I would like that, sir," Mario said.

159

"How long have you been a police officer?" Gabriel asked.

"A little over a year," Mario said. "I was initially stationed in Salerno, and now here."

"How long have you been on Ischia?"

"Five months."

"And my daughter?" Gabriel said. "How long have you been seeing her?"

"Four months, sir," Mario said. "It will be four months tomorrow."

"Ah, an anniversary," Gabriel said. "You and I should talk. Away from here. Alone."

"I think so, too, sir," Mario said.

"You don't need to call me sir," Gabriel said. "I'm a shepherd. Gabriel suits me well."

My grandfather turned to his friends at the table, placing one hand across Mario's broad back.

"This young man is a caribanieri," Gabriel announced. "Stationed here. Name is Mario Scubla."

Mario and the men shook hands and nodded their hellos to each other.

"You've met the old ones," Gabriel said to him. "Now, let's go for a walk and talk about the young ones. My daughter Raffaela in particular."

My mother wore white on her first wedding day, a long veil covering a face that had no makeup. She was seventeen and nervous, not yet comfortable with the idea of living away from her friends and family.

"You are with him now," her mother had said to her at dinner. "Where he goes, where he lives, is where you go and where you live. That is what you have chosen. Good or bad, it is your life now."

My mother had wanted to wait to marry, at least until the war in Europe was at an end. It was the summer of 1940, and throughout Italy, young men, including her brother John, were leaving home to fight for reasons no one truly understood.

"I'm scared," she said to Mario, a week before her wedding day. "What if something happens?"

"Nothing will happen," Mario said, sipping a glass of wine. "I will take care of you. Don't worry."

"We don't know anything," my mother said. "We're just like the sheep my father takes care of. Someone tells us to fight and we go. No one even stops to ask why."

"It is Mussolini's war," Mario said. "Let him fight it."

"It is our war, too," my mother said. "And it's getting closer. My friend Maria told me that the English are going to attack us. Here, in the South."

"That's crazy talk," Mario said. "And it has nothing to do with us."

"I'm just scared," my mother said. "For both of us."

"All the more reason why we should be together," Mario said, his arm around my mother. "Then nothing can hurt us."

The church at San Pietro was crowded as my mother made her way down the center aisle, the organist keying the wedding march, her sisters crying, her father at her side. My mother looked away from her relatives and up to the main altar, at her soon-to-be husband. Their eyes held until she was by his side, sliding one arm carefully under his.

Mario Scubla was twenty years old on his wedding day and resembled royalty in his full dress uniform, topped by two sets of couplets on his shoulders and a battery of colorful ribbons across his chest. He stood tall and confident, his dark Northern Italian features easily highlighted in a church filled with the rays of the sun. He smiled over at his bride and winked at his uniformed friends lining the front pew.

"It was the kind of wedding every Italian girl dreams about," my mother said. "A handsome husband, a proud family, a beautiful church. Nothing else seemed to matter to me on that day. The war was miles away. So was everything else that was bad. But I was a kid, what could I have known? How could I have guessed what would happen? The happiness of that day would not last. Not for me or for my husband. Or for the children we would have. Or for anyone who was there. But, no one sensed it. No one felt it. Not on that day."

Six months into their marriage, my mother and her husband bought a house in Salerno, along Southern Italy's Amalfi Coast. Her husband had grown restless on Ischia, weary of the peaceful nature of the island and its inhabitants, and seemed eager to work actively as a police officer again.

"He was young and bored," my mother said. "In the time we lived in Ischia, he grew close to my father and a few of his friends. But they were all so much older. He also felt as if he wasn't doing the job he was paid to do. There's never been any kind of crime on Ischia. Especially back then. It's difficult to be a police officer in a situation like that."

They had saved enough money to buy a two-bedroom stone house five miles to the north of Salerno's center. The large kitchen had a bay window that overlooked two acres of pine groves and the small barn that housed two milk cows and a chicken coop. The rear bedrooms had ten-foot ceilings and a winter view of the sea. A black iron wood-burning stove ate up a corner of the large dining room and helped heat the entire house.

"It needed work," my mother said. "The ceilings were chipped and cracking. The marble floors were split and the doors to all the rooms needed to be replaced. We had no furniture, and all our money had gone toward buying the house. Despite that, my first weeks in that house were the happiest ones I've known."

Anna came up from Ischia to help my mother with the work that needed to be done. My mother also hired two local handymen to fix up the barn and paint the outside of the house. She set aside three months to complete her dream project, hoping to have everything in place by Easter Sunday, 1942.

"She was a real taskmaster," Aunt Anna said. "We were both up before the sun. We washed in cold water and dressed by candlelight and drank our coffee huddled around the wood stove. By six, she had breakfast waiting for her husband and a list of things for us to do. She didn't even allow time to have a morning cigarette."

My mother bought two used bicycles for herself and her sister, and each morning they rode into town together, gathering all the supplies needed to complete the day's work. My mother scrubbed down the walls and floors, while Anna handled the chipped ceilings and all the broken fixtures. They also bartered for as many pieces of inexpensive furniture as could be found.

They all sang as they worked, a large pot of thick red sauce boiling away atop the stove, a waiting reward for a fair morning's labor.

*   *   *

My mother stepped down from a ladder spread open between the dining room and kitchen. She removed a thick pair of workman's gloves and walked toward her sister.

"The cows need to be milked," my mother said.

Anna was on the top step of a ladder in the middle of the dining room, paint chips spread about her like stars, her face dotted white.

"What?" she said, looking down at my mother.

"The cows haven't been milked," my mother said.

"That's too bad," Anna said.

"Why don't you take care of that," my mother said. "I'll finish with what you're doing."

Anna began her climb down from the ladder, stopping when her right foot rested on the last rung.

"Are you crazy?" she said. "You want me to milk your cows? I wouldn't know what to do. I'm not a farmer."

"You're not a painter either," my mother said. "But you seem to be doing fine with that."

"Raffaela, I came here to help you fix up your house," Anna said. "I did not come here to milk cows. So, please, let's go on to the next subject."

"Well, somebody's got to do it," my mother said.

"Fine. You do it."

"I can't," my mother said.

"Why not?"

"I don't know how," my mother said.

"What's there to know," Anna replied. "You grab a tit and pull. Stop when the bucket is full."

My mother suddenly threw a right hand over her mouth and rushed out of the room and into the kitchen, her head lowered over the top of the white enamel sink. Her sister came to her side and held the back of her head and neck, waiting as she vomited out her breakfast.

"All right, Raffaela, you made your point," Anna said when my mother had finished. "I'll milk the damn cows."

My mother lifted her head from the sink, her body leaning against the sharp base.

"It has nothing to do with the cows," she said, wiping her mouth with a damp cloth. "I'm pregnant."

"Are you sure?"

"I've been sick every morning for three weeks now. And I haven't had my period for two months."

"Sounds pregnant to me," Anna said. "But what do I know? I haven't even been kissed yet."

"Believe me, Anna," my mother said. "I'm going to have a baby."

"Oh, Raffaela, I'm so happy for you," Anna said, reaching out her arms to hug my mother, tears beginning to stream down her unlined face. "So happy."

"Thank you," my mother said. "I'm happy, too. And a little nervous. We barely have enough money to take care of this house. Now with a baby. I don't know how we're going to do it. It's going to be rough."

"Does Mario know?"

"Not yet," my mother said. "I wanted to have the house ready before I told him anything. It would make for such a nice surprise."

"He seems preoccupied lately," Anna said, pouring herself a cup of coffee. "Not himself."

"It's the war," my mother said. "There's a lot going on he doesn't tell me. But I know. I hear the talk in town. I know how frightened people are. In so many ways, this is the worst time for me to be having a baby."

"You can't think that way, Raffaela," Anna told her, placing her cup on top of the sink. "Things will work out, you'll see. This war is like all wars. It will come and it will go."

"I hope you're right," my mother said. "For everyone's sake, not just mine."

"Anyway, we don't have time for all that silly talk," Anna said. "We have something more important to decide."

"Like what?"

"Like what color do we paint the baby's room? Pink or blue?"

"White," my mother told her emphatically. "We paint the baby's room white."

"Why white?"

"It's the only color the painter sells," my mother said. "And it's the only color we can afford."

"Well, white it is," Anna said. "It'll match the other rooms."

III

Grace stood with her back to the open window, her two hands cupping the bottom of her stomach, eight months pregnant with her first and only child. My father sat on a cracked wooden chair, his legs spread out, one foot over the other. A small rotary fan whined atop the kitchen table to his left, spreading a warm breeze through the cramped and steamy apartment.

"What are we going to do?" Grace said.

"I'll take care of it," my father said. "Don't worry about it."

"How?"

"How? What do you give a fuck how?" my father said. "So long as it's all taken care of. That's all you should give a shit about. Nothin' else."

"Well, I'd still like to know how we're gonna pay the rent and take care of a baby with no money," Grace said. "I'm curious, that's all."

My father uncrossed his legs, stood up and moved quickly toward his wife, grabbing a handful of her hair.

"What do I have to do, bitch?" he said, twisting her face toward his. "What do I have to do to get through to you?"

"Honey, don't," Grace said. "Please. I'm sorry."

"Save that 'honey' shit for when it counts," my father said, loosening his grip. "For now, just shut the fuck up and let me do what I gotta do. Understand?"

"I'm worried," Grace said.

"Well, don't be," my father said. "'Cause there ain't nothin' to fuckin' worry about."

Grace moved away from the window and closer to the stove.

"You want a cup of coffee?" she asked my father. "I'll make a fresh pot."

"Forget the coffee," my father said. "How about something to eat?"

"It's not even four," Grace said, glancing at her watch.

"So what," my father said. "I'm hungry."

"You wanna go out and eat? Get the hell out of this oven?"

"You were just bitchin' about no money," my father said. "Now you wanna go out and eat. I can't figure you, Gracie. Sometimes, I think you say things just to break my balls."

"What do you want from me, Mario?" Grace said, anger in her voice, strands of hair shading one of her eyes. "I'm pregnant, in case you hadn't noticed. I'm hot and I'm broke and there's no food in the house, if you can call this shithole we live in a house. And I have no idea what's gonna happen next. But I don't think it's gonna be anything good."

My father moved three steps forward to his left and backhanded Grace across the face, his knuckles landing just below one of her eyes. He grabbed the back of her dress and pushed his wife up against the sink, her head down, shoving her under the rusty faucet.

"Shoulda told me you were hot," my father said, turning the cold water on, watching it pour over the back of Grace's head and dress.

"Let go!" Grace roared, her hands and arms swinging wildly above her. "You fuck! Let me go!"

"Soon as I cool you off," my father told her.

Grace's mouth, open and gasping for breath, caught the side of my father's right hand. She bit down onto the fat part of the skin and held it hard.

"Fuck," my father said, pulling his now bleeding hand away. "Fuck. That's it. You're finished now, you bitch."

My father began punching his wife on top of her head, the force of the left-handed blows slamming Grace against the wash-basin side of the sink. He then pulled her hair back and tossed his wife to the floor.

"Get up," he said, kicking Grace on the arms and rear. "Get the fuck up."

"Stop it," Grace said, screaming out the words through her tears, trying to deflect the kicks with her hands. "Please, stop it. The baby. You'll hurt the baby."

"Shut up." My father sucked hard on his bleeding hand. "Shut up before I fuckin' kill ya."

My father got down on his knees, turning his wife around to face him, her shoulders pinned down by the force of his weight.

"That's it," he said. "You understand, that's it. No more lip. Just shut the fuck up and do what you gotta do. Makin' myself clear?"

Grace nodded, shivering from the cold water and the tears.

"I don't hear you," my father said.

"Yes," Grace said.

"Yes what?"

"You make yourself clear," Grace said. "Now get the hell off me."

My father stood up, walked over to the kitchen table and pulled a white napkin off a plastic ring. He wrapped the napkin around his hand.

"You bit pretty deep," my father said. "I think I need stitches."

"Don't worry," Grace said. "I'm sure you'll live."

"Here," my father said, tossing Grace a hand towel from the sink. "Wipe yourself off. You look like you just got out of a shower."

"No thanks to you," Grace said.

My father watched as his wife dried off her face, hands and arms with the towel. He then walked over toward her and took the towel from her hands.

"Let me help you," my father said, wiping dry her forehead. "You better change outta these clothes. Before you get a cold."

"I know," Grace said. "I will."

"You still hungry?" my father said, holding the tip of Grace's face with one hand. "I mean, you still wanna go out?"

"Yeah," Grace said. "I'm hungry and I still wanna go out."

"Okay," my father said. "Go get dressed."

"Where we gonna go?" Grace said. "We still don't have any money."

"We'll eat down at John's," my father said. "I can owe him for the dinner."

"Why not?" Grace shrugged. "We owe everybody else in the neighborhood."

"Hey, you gonna start again?" my father said. "Let's just go out and have a good time."

"All right," Grace said, putting a hand on her husband's shoulder. "But we gotta do somethin' soon, Mario. We gotta get up from under all this shit."

"Tomorrow, baby," my father said. "I promise. Tomorrow we start takin' care of bills. Now, c'mon, go get dressed. It's early enough we can still catch a movie after the restaurant. Cagney's playin' over at the Beacon."

*   *   *

Well into the first year of his marriage my father had yet to secure a full-time job. When strapped for cash, he would turn in a Pier 62 all-nighter, emptying cement sacks from the bowels of a docked liner, working on his father's crew. He spent one, sometimes two weeks a month behind the grill of a West Side diner, cooking hamburgers and hash for the working poor of Hell's Kitchen who were too tired to cook for themselves.

"It all added up to shit money," my father said. "I mean, we're talkin' what, forty, maybe forty-five bucks a month. That's nothin'. Not for what we needed. Not for a wife and kid and a ton of fuckin' bills. Shit, I was payin' out more in vig, in interest payments to loan sharks, than I was bringing in in table money."

My father and Grace lived in a three-room furnished apartment on the third floor of a dark and decaying West Side tenement walk-up. There was no real kitchen, only a double sink and a hot plate with a wraparound bent rail. A torn green curtain on plastic hooks served to separate it from the combination living and dining room. A cracked wooden door, minus the inside knob, blocked off the cramped bedroom, whose only window looked down on a narrow alley lined with silver-lid garbage cans.

The bed was small, a thin mattress thrown across a creaky spring stand. An ashen Jesus on a cross hung above the dark brown headboard. Next to the bed, on a tiny end table backed up against a wall, my father kept his wallet, loose change and framed picture of his mother.

Grace's clothes covered a far wall, dresses and slacks draped over hangers on a makeshift rack, shoes lined up underneath. Her photo album was hidden behind a black wool winter coat.

There were few lights in the apartment, and no overheads. Each room was painted in an oil-based off-white, the edge of the walls covered with thin lines of dirt and dust. Black roaches nested in the cracks around the leaky radiators in two of the rooms.

"Let's face it," my father said. "The place was a shithole. But it was all we could afford. The rent was near to nothin' and we were still behind on it. I don't really know what happened. I just couldn't seem to get off the mark. Get anything going. We were young, but felt old, you know. It was as if our life was ending, not starting. I don't know what it was. I just know it wasn't good."

My father was irrationally jealous about Grace, convinced that a number of neighborhood men had cast their eyes on his beautiful wife. There was a lot of talk in Hell's Kitchen, and my father managed to hear most of it. None of it was ever to his liking.

"Usual shit," my father said. "Great lookin' broad stuck with a deadbeat husband. I used to be on the other end of that kind of talk myself for years. I was always cattin' around with some married lady sick of the guy she was livin' with. I never knew if there was any truth to the talk around my wife. True or not, I just didn't like to hear it, is all."

IV

Sweat poured off Raffaela's face and body, her skin glowing by the flickering lights of the half-dozen candles surrounding her bed. Her nightgown was lifted to her bare waist, her legs up and spread wide. Four women, all dressed in widow's black, hovered about her, two of them holding my mother's arms.

"Stop the pain," my mother said to the widow at her left. "Do something, please. Just stop the pain."

"With time, little one," the widow said in a voice barely audible. "With time."

In the corridor just beyond the closed bedroom door, my mother's husband tried hard to ignore his wife's screams and cries. He lit an unfiltered cigarette and nervously stamped out the match with the edge of a black boot.

One of the widows began to pour ice water from a porcelain jug onto the top of my mother's head, watching as it spread from her hair down to the sheets and pillows. Another widow, her white hair combed back tight into a bun, her black woolen dress spotted with

169

blood, knelt upon the bed, facing my mother, one hand on her stomach, the other probing deep inside her.

"Get the cloth," the one pouring the water said. "Spread it around her. Catch all the blood."

"I need more light," the widow with her hand inside my mother said. "Hold a few candles around me."

"There aren't any more," one of the widows said. "We lit all we could find."

"Matches then," the widow on the bed said. "Lighters. Wood. Anything you find. Just do it quickly."

The shrill blast of the air-raid siren drowned out the last of the woman's words. The four widows nervously exchanged glances, anticipating the enemy bombs that might land within moments around them.

"Get the husband in here and any other man you can find," the widow on the bed said, power now added to her voice. "We'll need all the help we can get."

"Should we move her to the shelter?" one of the widows said.

"There's no time," another said. "The baby will be born here. Or die here. Those are the only choices left us."

"Please, dear God," a third widow said. "This one night. Be with us this one night."

The first bombs landed a mile to the south, their explosive force powerful enough to knock out half a bay window. Particles of dust were shaken out of corner walls, and three cups and saucers fell from the edge of the living room table to the floor. The oldest widow dropped to her knees in fear, and another wrapped a set of black rosary beads around her right hand.

"Are we going to die?" my mother asked the woman gripping her right hand.

"Not tonight, angel," the woman said, managing a wide smile. "Tonight this room is for living, not for dying."

The next explosion rocked the house and sent an uprooted tree crashing against the side door, one of its long limbs breaking through a panel window.

"We have to blow out the candles," Mario, my mother's husband, said. "They can see the lights from above."

"Every room but this one," the widow on the bed said. "We can't do what we need to do in the dark."

"You used to say you could deliver a baby wearing a blindfold," Mario said, dousing the candle to his right with a thumb and forefinger. "Tonight, we'll see if that's true."

The woman leaned closer to my mother and stared at Mario, her body rigid, her eyes harsh.

"It is your child I attempt this magic act with," she said to him. "Are you prepared for what may happen?"

"My child's life was in your hands *before* the bombs," Mario said. "Nothing's changed."

The old woman nodded her head in agreement, then turned her attention to the others around her.

"All of you, stay close," she said to the frightened women. "Look around you. Try to remember where everything is. And everyone, please, remain calm. Ignore what goes on around you. Think only of the child."

The old woman then turned her attention back to Mario.

"Blow out the lights in the room," she said to him. "And pray to the God above."

My mother's screams failed to drown out the confusion she felt. Above her the plaster from the ceiling shook and fell away in chunks, thick pieces landing on the bed near her head. The entire house was filled with smoke from the burning farmlands outside. She felt hands touching her, warm clothes placed on her hips and thighs, cold towels atop her head and across her face. The insides of her ears buzzed from the sounds of the falling bombs.

"I have the head," the woman in the center of the bed said. "Down low. Just a few more inches. Graziella, lean over and lay a warm towel under my hands."

"I've got it," Graziella said. "It's the last clean one we have."

"Push, Raffaela," the woman in the bed said. "Push down. With all your strength."

My mother squeezed and pushed, as hard and as steady as she could.

"Don't stop," the woman said. "You're almost finished. Don't stop."

"Five minutes," the woman sponging my mother said. "Five minutes more, Raffaela. That's all we need."

The wall above the bed cracked open, dislodging the bed and knocking the woman kneeling in the center of it to the floor.

"Don't panic," the woman yelled, crawling off the floor and back to her feet. "Don't panic. Help me back to the bed. We haven't much time."

The thick smoke made breathing difficult. Outside, fire engine and police car sirens rang out in all directions, sounds of church bells clashed with car horns, and everywhere screams and cries could be heard.

"I have it," the woman, once again on the bed, said. "I have the baby. Now, Raffaela, let's finish it. Let's finish it now, child."

My mother gathered her strength for two more surges downward, taking deep, smoke-filled breaths each time. Drops of blood began to stain the sheets and towels, both already soaked with water and sweat.

"Graziella, a towel, quickly," the woman in the bed yelled. "Clean or dirty. I don't care."

Graziella pulled a white cotton towel from the back of her wrap-around house apron.

"I was saving this one," she said. "For when the baby was born."

"That's now," the woman in the bed said. "Give it here."

The woman held the baby by the ankles, his cord still attached, blood and foam showering down on both her and my mother. She shoved three fingers in the baby's mouth, twirled them around and took them out, wiping them on the back of her dress. She then lifted her free hand and came down hard with a slap on the baby's rear.

For a long second there was silence in the room, and then a sound every woman there recognized as the healthy cry of a newborn.

"What is it?" my mother managed to gasp. "Boy or girl?"

"I don't need a light to tell you that," the woman in the bed said with a laugh. "It's a boy. A happy little boy."

"Mario," one of the women called out to my mother's husband. "Come closer. Come touch your son."

Mario walked slowly across the room, stepping on rubble and stone, felt for the bed and then touched the warmth of his son's head.

"Figlolo," he said in a near whisper. "My boy. You finally made it."

Graziella and the woman in the bed finished wrapping the baby, cooing quietly through the whole process. They undid pins in their hair and used them to clip the towel in place. The woman bent over and kissed the center of the baby's forehead.

"Bello, giovanni," she said to him. "Welcome to the world."

"What's left of it anyway," Graziella said.

The air-raid alarm blew four times, signaling an all-clear, the bombing for this night at an end. An old woman with a shaky hand ran a match along the floor and looked for a candle to light. Mario and another widow did the same.

"The baby," Graziella said. "Put a candle near the baby. So we can see him."

Four lit candles soon surrounded both mother and child. The women all moaned their approval while Mario stood off to the side and smiled, wells of tears forming in his eyes. Everyone moved closer to both sides of the headboard, watching as my mother leaned the baby's mouth to her exposed breast, feeding him his first taste of natural milk.

Mario kicked away some of the fallen furniture and opened all the windows, letting the early fall air take some of the smoke from the room.

"He's beautiful, Raffaela," Graziella said to my mother. "Such serious eyes."

"He's smart, too," one of the widows said. "Took to the breast right away. Some babies need time to figure out what to do."

"He had a rough ride," the woman on the bed said. "He worked up an appetite."

My mother looked up at the women around her and smiled.

"How do I thank you?" she asked. "For what you did. All of you."

"We simply did what we came to do," Graziella answered. "Nothing more."

"I can't believe it's over," my mother said, staring down at her son as he sucked on her breast. "It's a miracle."

"All births are miracles," the widow on the bed said. "This one a little bit more so."

One of the widows handed my mother a picture of St. Giovann Guisseppe and a small Bible, its binding torn and shabby.

"We had help in our work, Signora," she said. "We always have help."

The women gathered closer around the edges of the bed, reaching for the baby and bowing their heads in prayer.

"Will you lead the rosary?" the woman on the bed said to Graziella. "Pray for the child and for our families."

"Willingly," Graziella said.

My mother cried softly, clutching her son tightly about her, as the women mumbled the beginnings of the stations of the rosary, their faces lit by a small circle of candles at their sides, feeding off the warmth of the dust-filled room.

While the women prayed, my mother's husband, Mario, silently smoked and stared out through two panels of a cracked window at the ruin left by the bombs.

"It's going to take more than prayer to survive this," he said to himself. "A lot more."

V

The woman leaned across the bed and tried to shake my father awake.

"C'mon," she said. "Wake up. There's a call for you."

"Who is it?" my father said, his eyes still closed, both arms wrapped around a cotton pillow.

"I didn't ask," the woman said. "And they didn't say."

My father lifted an arm over his head and took the receiver from the woman.

"Yeah?" he said, one eye squinting at an alarm clock on the bureau next to him.

"Get down here, you piece of shit," a male voice said. "Get down here right now."

"Get down where?" my father said.

"The hospital, hump," the voice said. "Your wife just had a baby."

"You kiddin' me or what?" my father said.

"What, it's a fuckin' surprise to you?" the voice said. "She was pregnant, right? So what you think happens after that?"

"She all right?" my father wanted to know.

"The wife's good," the voice said. "So's the kid."

"What is it?" my father said.

"What am I, a fuckin' newspaper?" the voice said. "Get your fat ass out of that whore's bed and come find out for yourself."

My father cried the first time he saw his daughter, her face as round and as open as his. He stared in awe as she crinkled her hands and wiggled her feet and opened her mouth and cried, her fresh lungs filled with hospital air.

"What a doll she was," my father said. "What a fuckin' doll. Looked just like me. She was a heavy kid, you know, her mouth always going, cryin' over somethin' or other. It was great to see her, I'll tell you that. I never been as happy to see someone in my life."

Grace was in bed, a white sheet folded at her waist, still groggy from the delivery. Her head was resting against two plumped-up pillows, her eyes looking at a sugar-loaded IV dripping slowly into her left arm. She didn't hear my father walk into the room.

"Hey, baby," he said, holding his gray fedora with both hands. "How you doin'?"

"A little late, Mario," she said, her eyes not moving from the IV bag. "You shoulda been here yesterday."

"I was busy, baby," my father said, moving three steps closer to the bed. "Lining up a job."

"What was her name?" Grace said, turning to face my father. "And how much did it cost you?"

"I'm tellin' you the truth, baby," my father said. "I wasn't with no broad. I was gettin' a job. A good job."

"Yeah, right, Mario," Grace said. "That's you. Always looking for work."

"You bet your ass, baby," my father said. "I need work now. Got a kid to feed."

"That's right, Mario," Grace said. "You're a big boy now. With a wife and kid. You can't fool around anymore."

"I'm not foolin' with you, baby," my father said. "I'm serious. Steady table money from now on. You'll see. No more bullshit."

"I hope so," Grace said weakly, closing her eyes, giving in to the postbirth medication. "You better go now. I'm gonna take a nap."

"Sure, baby," my father said. "Whatever you want. I'll come back in an hour or so. That sound good to you?"

Grace didn't answer. She was sound asleep, her head turned away from her husband and toward the window, the traffic three floors below at a standstill.

My father walked toward his wife, reaching out for her when he stood by her side. He lifted her hand with his and kissed it softly.

"I love you, baby," he said to her turned-away face. "I love you so much."

He put her hand to his eyes, tears dripping onto her fingers.

"Everything's gonna be okay," he said. "You'll see, baby. Everything's gonna be just perfect."

My father flipped over a hamburger and dropped two slices of rye bread into a toaster. His paper-thin white T-shirt was soaked through with sweat, his forehead glistened under the bare bulb lighting of the diner's kitchen and his feet hurt from the heat and the tight shoes he wore.

"Hurry up with that burger, would ya," a brown-haired waiter said to my father. "The guy's asked me three times for the fuckin' thing."

"It's comin'," my father said. "Tell him to have another cup of coffee."

"Just get the burger," the waiter said, swinging the kitchen door closed behind him. "Let me worry about what he's gonna be drinkin'."

My father lifted the burger onto a bun, shoved it onto an empty plate, and rang a tin bell to his right. He popped the toaster up, buttered the two slices of rye, cut them in half and laid them next to a scrambled-egg-and-ham platter.

The waiter came back into the kitchen and grabbed the burger platter from the cook counter.

"God, what a prick," the waiter said to my father. "Out there, cursin' and yellin' at everybody. Tough guy. I'd like to shove this burger right up his ass."

"This place is always filled with scumbags like that," my father said. "I don't know what it is."

"Maybe it's the way you cook," the waiter said, smiling.

"I think it's the way you serve," my father said with a quick wink of an eye. "Kills their appetite."

"Wish me luck," the waiter said, kicking the kitchen door behind him.

My father checked the order slips hanging above his head. He pulled one down and reached for a bowl of eggs, cracking two open over the grill. He pulled three strips of precooked bacon out of a pot, their fat ends curled up at the corners, and laid them next to the eggs, staring down at them as they cooked. He turned his head away when he heard the waiter coming up behind him.

"Put another burger on, Mario," the waiter said, tossing the platter with the first burger on it into the crowded sink.

"What happened?" my father said.

"Overcooked," the waiter said. "The guy wants it medium rare, not overcooked. Said for you to clean the shit outta your ears so you can get the orders straight."

My father wiped his hands on the short apron around his waist and handed a skillet to the waiter.

"Keep an eye on the eggs," my father said. "Over easy, bacon and white toast. Got it?"

"Got it," the waiter said, taking hold of the skillet. "What are you gonna do?"

"I'm gonna go see this guy," my father said. "See if there's anything else he needs."

"Easy, Mario," the waiter said. "Don't fuck around. You'll lose your job."

"Yeah," my father said. "What a fuckin' crime that would be."

"I shoulda kept my mouth shut," the waiter said.

"Too late," my father said, walking out of the kitchen.

"You got a problem with me?" my father said to a man sitting in a booth pouring three scoops of sugar into a cup of coffee.

"I might," the man said. "Depends on who the fuck you are."

"I'm the cook," my father said, watching as the man stirred his coffee with the flip side of his fork.

"You mean the asshole who burned my burger," the man said, smiling at his friend across the booth.

"That's me," my father said.

"The last cook this place had was half a retard," the man said, looking at his friend, ignoring my father. "That wasn't bad enough. They get rid of him and bring in this fuckin' shithead. Makes me wonder why the fuck I come in here at all."

"I know why you come in here," my father said, taking his apron off and tossing it behind him, over the counter.

"Yeah, fucko?" the man said. "Tell me, why's that?"

"They're afraid of you," my father said. "Everybody here is. You know it and they know it. So, you can come in here, run your mouth all fuckin' night and nobody says shit."

"And what?" the man said, his voice rising, loud enough for the half-dozen other customers to notice. "You got a bug up your ass about that? Don't want me in here no more?"

"You won't be able to come in here anymore," my father said. "Not after tonight."

"Hey, I've taken all the shit from you I'm gonna take," the man said, beginning his slide out of the booth. "Not only can't I get a good meal in this hole, but I gotta get lip from the jerk-off help."

My father reached over and grabbed a handful of the man's thick brown hair, pulled it back and then slammed his face against the top of the Formica table. My father's eyes never lost sight of the man's friend, who sat with his fists curled, not moving.

"Keep talkin', prick," my father said to the man. "While you still got teeth."

While he held the man's face down on the Formica, my father landed two hard rights hands against the back of his neck and then dragged him out of the booth, shoving him to the ground.

"You get in the middle of this and I'll leave you for dead," my father said, pointing his finger at the man's friend. "Hear me, prick?"

The friend nodded his head and uncurled his hands.

The man on the ground grabbed the aluminum legs of a stool near the counter, lifting himself halfway off the floor.

"C'mere, tough guy," my father said, bending down and squeezing one hand around the man's throat. "It's time for you and me to dance."

My father lifted him to his feet, his hand still wrapped around his throat, and swung three short, powerful left hooks under the man's heart, the air, like from a loose valve, quickly leaving him. My father took his hand away from the man's throat, grabbed him by the shoulders and began pounding his head against the countertop, knocking over ketchup bottles, sugar canisters and stainless-steel cream dispensers.

An older woman, eating a bowl of split pea with bacon soup, held a hand across her mouth and shuddered as she watched the fight develop before her.

"You'll kill him," she said, mumbling the words over her hands. "Sainted Jesus, stop it, you'll kill him!"

"Don't quit eatin' on account of me, Mamma," my father said to her. "Your soup's gonna get cold."

My father continued kicking and punching the man, whose face was now a mask shrouded with blood. The man's shirt was torn, his pants wet and one shoe, a black loafer, had come off and now rested against the back end of a booth. Three of the man's front teeth had been knocked loose and were sprinkled on the counter, resting next to a broken bottle of ketchup and a small pool of blood.

"Hey, Jimmy," my father said, calling for the waiter, who stood by the kitchen entrance, watching the fight. "Do me a favor, okay?"

"Sure, Mario," the waiter said. "Anything you want."

"Bring me that hamburger this prick said he didn't wanna eat," my father said.

"It's in the sink, Mario," the waiter said. "Got soap all over it."

"Even better," my father said. "Bring it on out here."

The waiter disappeared into the kitchen and came back out seconds later holding a platter with a soggy hamburger on top of it.

"Here you go, Mario," the waiter said with a smile. "Just like you ordered it."

My father took the platter from the waiter and placed it on top of the counter to his left. He then bent over and lifted the bleeding man to his feet, pushing him down onto a stool, the burger placed before him.

"Okay, tough guy," my father said. "Start eatin'. And don't move from that fuckin' stool till you're done."

The man's right hand was lined with blood and shaking, his entire body trembling from the beating he had just received. He held the hamburger, lowering his head in order to bring it to his lips.

"Take big bites," my father said to him. "I ain't got all fuckin' night."

My father walked away from the man, wiping blood-spattered hands across the front of his T-shirt and grease-speckled white pants. He went toward the back of the diner, heading for the coat rack, where he had left his fedora hanging at an angle.

"Take care of yourself, Jimmy," my father said, putting on his hat and reaching out a hand for the exit door, the top half of its glass window broken and taped over.

"You too, Mario," the waiter said. "And good luck."

"Thanks," my father said. "I'm probably gonna need it."

"What you want me to tell Bobby Mac when I see him?" the waiter asked.

"Tell him to shove this fuckin' place up his ass," my father said.

"And what about the guy out front?" the waiter said, nodding his head toward the bleeding man at the counter, still eating the soap burger.

"Tell you what, Jimmy," my father said. "Give him a break. If he can't eat it all, put it in a take-out bag. Let him finish the fuckin' thing at home."

VI

World War II had turned Italy into a country in ruin. Entire cities lay wasted, fresh food was in scarce supply, medical goods at a premium. In many of the southern cities, towns and islands, including Ischia and Salerno, a year-round blackout and an eleven P.M. curfew were in effect.

"The simplest things were the hardest to find," my mother said. "Flour for bread and pasta, cheese of any kind, fresh vegetables were all out of the question. And since we didn't have enough to feed ourselves, we couldn't feed the farm animals we counted on for milk and eggs. People all around us were starving, walking around with sunken and scared looks. It was horrible. Horrible."

For the people of Italy, the fall of 1943 was the worst time of all. Mussolini and the fascists were on the run, and the remnants of the Italian government had switched their allegiance away from the Axis powers, working now instead for the Allied cause. The Nazi high command, in retaliation for this perceived betrayal, ordered full-scale and continuous bombings and attacks throughout the whole of Southern Italy.

The thick smoke from those bombs blocked out the sun for most of the day, while the fires they set off helped light the dark nights. The cries of frightened and hungry children echoed through empty streets, many of them still in diapers, quite a few shedding tears over the body of a dead parent.

"Everyone was touched by that war," Grandma Maria said. "Not one person was spared. Widowed women and orphans were the only thing Italy mass-produced during the war. We made them by the thousands. Every day, in every part of the country. It was an ugly time for us. You cannot live through a time like that without a scar."

The soldier, young and in battle fatigues, leaned against my mother's front door, his chest and right arm covered with the blood pouring from an open wound just below his neckline. He had trouble breath-

181

ing, his body shaking and shivering from the cold. In his good hand, the left one, he held a gun, his fingers wrapped tightly around the butt.

My mother finished breast-feeding her one-week-old baby, Gabriel, and placed him face down, asleep, in his wooden rocker. Her other son, fifteen-month-old Anthony, played on the floor with a set of wooden soldiers given him by his father. The house was cold, the two small pieces of wood burning in the stove not enough to heat the rooms.

"Antonio, stay here and don't touch anything," she said to the boy. "Mamma's going outside to get more wood for the fire. I'll be right back."

My mother tossed a red and white shawl over her shoulders, covering the housedress from neck to waist, patted her son gently on the head and opened the front door.

She muffled a scream as the young soldier nearly fell on top of her.

"Help me," he whispered. "Help me, please."

My mother watched as the soldier dropped to his knees, face forward, heading for the cold comfort of the hard floor. His head came to rest inches from where Anthony was playing, a wooden soldier in his hand, another on his leg.

"Jesus," my mother said, bending to ease Anthony into her arms, then carrying him over to his playpen in the corner of the room, near the oak dining table. "Sweet God, what do I do?"

She knew from the cut of the man's uniform he was a German soldier, the high black boots and army grays a too-familiar sight in Salerno. She saw the gun, which had dropped from his hand when he hit the ground, resting under the crib and went over to pick it up. Her hands trembled as she touched it. She carried it over to a high shelf, laying it behind a half-empty bottle of Fernet Branca and a silver-framed photo of her husband.

She walked back over to the soldier, bent down and shook him by the tops of his shoulders without receiving any firm response. She felt the cold wetness on his neck, just above the uniform collar, and saw the blood staining through his shirt and jacket, torn at the back. She caught a sidelong view of his face and knew he was no older than twenty and probably much younger.

"Giovanni," my mother said. "Young man. Can you hear me? Can you hear what I'm saying to you?"

The soldier only mumbled, blood and spit bubbles forming at his lips, a glazed look to his half-open eyes. My mother tried lifting him and couldn't, concerned about getting him face up and on the bed in order to tend to his wound. She looked over at the playpen where Anthony, like his younger brother, had curled up in a far corner and fallen fast asleep.

There was no one around to call for help, and her husband wouldn't be home until well after dark. My mother paced nervously around the fallen soldier, trying to decide what to do next. She ran across the room, pulled open the bottom drawer of an old wooden hutch and took out all that she owned in the way of medicine and bandages.

She placed the two gauze pads, three small towels and bottle of rubbing alcohol on top of the table and then went back over to the soldier.

"Young man," she said, making one final attempt to shake the soldier awake. "Young man, please, get up. Please."

My mother again looked around the house, and saw both her children still sound asleep. She stayed crouched on her knees and made the sign of the cross, mumbling a short prayer to St. Jude, the patron of lost causes.

My mother then rubbed both her hands against the front of her housedress and placed them under the young soldier's arms. She began to drag the soldier slowly across the floor, heading for the couch in the center of the room. The soldier moaned and grimaced, the front of his body and my mother's hands both wet with blood.

She got his head and one arm on top of the couch, the soldier's bleeding body immediately darkening the light gray cushions. The baby began to cry just as my mother got one of the soldier's legs onto the far end of the couch.

"Dear God, give me strength," my mother said, looking over her shoulder at her baby. "Let us all make it through this day."

The soldier opened his eyes, wary of his surroundings, conscious of his wounds. His shirt was off, crumpled on the floor by his side, his chest covered with alcohol-soaked white gauze and towels. He looked to his left and saw my mother sitting on a straight-back wooden chair, breast-feeding a baby.

"Who are you?" he asked her in German.

The words startled my mother who stood up, turned her back, pulled the baby from her breast and buttoned her dress. She turned again to the soldier and pointed to his chest.

"You are hurt," she said, hoping he understood Italian. "You need a doctor."

The soldier looked at his wound and nodded.

"How far am I from Salerno?" the soldier asked.

"Five kilometers," my mother said, guessing at what he had asked, holding up all the fingers of her right hand. "Straight down the main road."

"I can't go that far," the soldier said, shaking his head, his voice breaking, his legs numb from the loss of blood.

"I know," my mother said, walking over toward the soldier, lifting the cold towels from his wound. "You will die before you get to town."

The opening around the soldier's wound had hardened, the bleeding slowed to a trickle, pink flesh visible beneath the shattered skin. The color from the soldier's face was fading, an off-white pallor setting in around his eyes and cheekbones. His lips were dry and turning purple, and the veins at his neck twitched whenever he swallowed.

"He was dying," my mother told me later. "And there was nothing more I could do for him. He was so young. So very young. I put my baby back in his crib and checked on my other son. Then I walked back over to the soldier, sat next to him on the couch, and held his hand. It was all that was left for me to do."

The hand felt cold. The soldier's body shuddered whenever he took a breath, the blankets my mother had wrapped around his legs and chest proving of little use. The soldier stared up at my mother, his hazel eyes beginning their slow drift away from life. He gradually lifted his right hand from under the red and black patterned blanket, reached up and touched my mother's face.

"Your name," he said to her. "What's your name?"

"Raffaela," my mother said, pointing to herself. "And you? What are you called?"

The soldier did not answer. His eyes were half-opened, the lids not moving. My mother looked at his chest and saw that his breathing had stopped, his body no longer trembling.

My mother bent down and rested her head against the soldier's chest, which was still caked with blood, her cheeks laced with tears over the death of a young stranger. She held his body to hers, resting quietly with him into the late afternoon, as both her children slept.

VII

The apartment was without heat, semicircles of ice forming on the locked windowpanes, rolled-up white towels shoved around their cracks. The walls were cold to the touch, an icy breeze easing itself up from the cracked floor boards. The only warmth in the apartment came from the bare forty-watt bulb in the bedroom.

My father sat on a slant-board wooden chair, his six-month-old baby daughter wrapped tightly in his arms. He was wearing a blue pullover sweater and a gray hat, lid up. The baby was in Dr. Denton's, asleep against my father's chest, her body hot and her face flushed from a high fever.

Grace was asleep in the bed next to where my father sat, trying to stay warm under two thin blankets and a wool coat. She was shivering, her lips shaking, her 101-degree temperature only three degrees less than what her daughter was suffering with.

"Grace, you up?" my father said, staring down at his daughter's face.

"I'm trying hard not to be," Grace said, from under the blankets.

"The aspirin we gave her is not doin' a fuckin' thing," my father said. "She's boiling hot."

"Give it time, Mario," Grace said. "It takes time for aspirin to work."

"We ain't got time," my father said.

"That's all we got," Grace said. "Now leave her alone and let her sleep. She needs her rest."

"Maybe I should call the doctor again," my father said. "Maybe there's something else he could give her."

"For Christ's sake, Mario, it's three in the morning," Grace said. "Bring the baby into bed and let's all get some sleep. There's nothin' else we can do until the morning."

"No, it's okay," my father said. "You sleep. I'm not tired. I'll stay up. Keep an eye on her. In case."

The baby's fever did not go down, topping out at 104.8 on the early side of dawn. My father laid his daughter on the bed, her head resting near her mother's curled-up feet, and changed her diaper, tossing the soiled one in a lined canister near the door.

"Enough of this shit," he said to his daughter. "We're goin'."

Grace turned over on her side and looked at her husband.

"Where you goin', Mario?" she said. "It's still dark out."

"I'm takin' her to the hospital," my father said. "Get dressed and meet us there. We'll be in the emergency room."

"Can't you just wait a few more hours?" Grace asked, sitting up in the bed. "Then we can all go back to the doctor."

"Fuck him," my father said. "I'm not waitin' for him, you or anybody else. We're out the door."

"You're crazy," Grace said.

"Remember," my father said. "The emergency room at Polyclinic. See you there."

"How long has she had a fever?" the nurse asked my father.

"Too long," my father said.

"That's not the answer I'm looking for," the nurse said.

"I don't give a fuck about any answer you're lookin' for, sister," my father said. "I'm lookin' for a doctor for my kid and I better see one quick before I turn this whole fuckin' place upside down."

"Calm down," the nurse said. "I want to help you."

"Good," my father said. "Then get my kid a doctor."

The nurse, a tall, slender woman with thick black hair, leaned across my father and felt the baby's forehead.

"She's very hot," the nurse said.

"That's exactly right, sweetheart," my father said. "She's hot and only gettin' hotter. Now, let's stop wastin' time and get a fuckin' doctor over here."

"Wait right here," the nurse said, pushing her chair back and shoving the plastic curtain behind her aside. "I'll see if I can find him."

"We ain't goin' anywhere, sister," my father said. "Believe you me."

The doctor, a young intern with a bad cold, carefully examined my father's daughter.

"She's a cutie," he said, his voice clogged and hoarse. "Beautiful eyes."

"Thanks," my father said. "How bad is she?"

"Well, her lungs are congested and her fever's high," the doctor said. "And her throat is red as licorice. Has she had trouble sleeping?"

"No, not really," my father said. "She shakes and shivers but sleeps pretty well."

"That's all part of it," the doctor said. "Real bad cold, that's all it is."

"What about the fever?" my father said.

"We'll give her something to help bring it down," the doctor said. "And we'll give you some to take home to give her. One dose every four hours, if she needs it. Other than that there isn't much more to do except wait it out."

"How long you figure?" my father said.

"Three to five days," the doctor said. "She should be good as new by the end of the week."

"Thanks for everything, doc," my father said, shaking the intern's hand. "I appreciate it."

"No problem," the doctor said. "Bring her home and put her to bed. She needs to rest. You may as well join her. Looks like you could use some sleep yourself. Have your wife baby the both of you."

"Yeah, nice idea, doc," my father said with a smile. "Now, all I gotta do is get my wife outta fuckin' bed."

"She sick, too?" the doctor said.

"Says she is," my father said. "Who the fuck knows."

Grace was waiting for them outside the emergency room entrance, shivering under her thin brown wool coat. Her eyes were tearing and her hair was combed straight back, held there by a trio of black bobby pins.

"So, what'd they say?" she asked my father when he came out of the hospital.

"Where the fuck have you been?" my father said, walking past his wife, heading toward the corner. "You shoulda been here, Gracie. We needed you."

"Cut the drama, Mario," Grace said. "Just tell me what the doctors said."

"I don't have to tell you shit. Not a fuckin' thing. Hear me, baby? Nothin'."

"What did they say, Mario?" Her voice high, angry, brittle from her cold.

"Don't raise your voice to me, you fuckin' cunt," my father said. "I'll put this kid down and beat you all over this fuckin' avenue."

"You're crazy, Mario." Grace, stopped in the middle of 52nd Street and Tenth Avenue, began yelling at the back of my father's head. "You're crazy. Just crazy."

"Don't come home, bitch," my father muttered over his shoulder, not bothering to look back at his wife. "Don't come home. 'Cause I'll kill you if you do."

My father wrapped the white blanket tighter around his daughter and crossed the street, holding the baby's face closer to his.

"I'm gonna kill that bitch," he said in a low voice. "I swear to God, one day I'm gonna kill that bitch."

VIII

My mother gripped the rosary beads with her right hand and squeezed them as tight as she could, holding back tears with a great deal of difficulty.

"I'm very sorry," the doctor said. "We'll do what little we can."

"Is there any medicine he could take?" she asked. "Any pills? Anything?"

"Raffaela, please," my mother's husband said. "Calm yourself."

The doctor stood up from behind his desk, a large yellow folder under his arm. He lit a cigarette and walked over to my mother and her husband, who were sitting on two rickety wooden chairs in his cramped and foul-smelling office.

"It's a disease we know very little about," the doctor said, his voice low, smoke filtering through both nose and mouth. "Can't find either the cause or the cure. We do know it spreads quickly. Especially the kind we think you have."

My mother reached over and held her husband's hand.

"How quickly?" he asked.

The doctor took a deep breath and raised his shoulders up and down.

"Three months," he said, staring at my mother's husband. "Six months at the very latest. You wouldn't want it to go beyond that."

"Will there be pain?" my mother's husband asked.

"Not at first," the doctor said, leaning across his desk to crush out his cigarette.

"When then?"

"You'll begin to lose weight," the doctor said.

"I already have," her husband said. "Don't seem to have much of an appetite."

"That will come and go," the doctor said. "But the weight will stay off. You'll begin to feel weak, tired. The pain will then begin to increase."

"Can you give me anything?"

"Yes, of course," the doctor said. "Painkillers. Morphine. You can start on them now if you wish."

"There's no need," her husband said.

"Call me if there's anything you want," the doctor said. "I'll try to get to you as soon as I can. This war has left us with an overabundance of bodies and a shortage of doctors."

My mother's husband stood up and reached his hand out to the doctor.

"You've done all you can," he said as they shook. "I thank you for that."

"I've done nothing," the doctor said. "I'm supposed to save lives. It's my job. Yet, I could not save yours."

"From what you told me, no one could," her husband said.

"It's this war," my mother said, her voice choked. "All these bombs. They've poisoned the air."

"Will you be staying here, in Salerno?" the doctor asked, trying to ignore her.

"I haven't decided," her husband said. "It's all happened so suddenly. I have family up North, in Udine. I may go there."

"Let me know what you decide," the doctor said. "I'll refer you to a physician in the area."

"Can I still go to work?" the husband asked.

"If you feel up to it, why not?" the doctor said. "Just try not to do too much. You'll need all your strength."

"For what?" my mother's husband asked, walking out of the doctor's office and back out onto the streets of Salerno.

The stomach pains had begun six months earlier, usually hitting him after each meal. Initially he dismissed them, writing them off as the price to be paid for his wife's spicy cooking. When the pain intensified and occurred more frequently, he turned to home remedies for a cure. When she could find them, my mother would boil up a mixture of lemons and oranges and force her husband to drink down the hot results.

"It will disinfect your system," she would say. "Cleans out all the germs. Drink it down, hot and fast."

"It tastes terrible," he would say.

"It's good for you," she would say. "It's supposed to taste terrible."

The recurring pains he initially felt were soon followed by severe muscle cramps, strong enough to double him over. More often than not, they would strike without warning, and were always followed by long bouts of nausea and vomiting.

"He usually ate one big meal a day," my mother said. "Pasta, if we had any, or thick soups in the winter, and fresh salads in the summer. He liked his wine, too. Always cleaned his plate and emptied his glass. But he could never finish a meal or a drink after he got sick. He became even quieter than he was normally, seldom spoke a word. He was twenty-six and dying. In front of me. In front of his children."

Two months after the doctor's visit and the confirmation of stomach cancer, my mother's husband, *carabinieri di prima grado* Mario Scubla, decided to go home to the hills of Udine in Northern Italy to die under the warm blankets of the bed he was born in.

"His face had lost all signs of life," my mother told me. "His skin was gray, the space around his eyes hollow. He was walking and working, but he was already dead. He didn't want anyone to see him. He wanted to be left alone and be allowed to die alone. He asked me to pack a few of his clothes. Said he was going up North to visit with his family for a few weeks. He sat in a chair by the bed, watching me pack his valise. That moment, on that day, I knew I would never see him come back again."

The train had just pulled into the Salerno station, heavy charcoal smoke rising from its front stack. My mother stood in front of the fourth car, the sliding door open, staring at an old woman gingerly making her way up the three black iron steps.

My mother held her baby son in the crook of her right elbow and kept her left hand under her husband's arm. Anthony was to her right, holding on to the pocket flap of her housedress.

My mother looked at her husband, feeling the weakness of his legs and body. His thick hair was beginning to recede, and his lower lip shook visibly. He was dressed in full uniform, determined to keep his appearance proper till the very end.

"Are you sure you don't want us to come with you?" my mother said.

191

"Don't be silly," he said. "We could both use the time away from each other. A break for both. I'll be back in time for the holiday."

"I'll try to find fresh rabbit," my mother said, unable to hold back her tears. "We haven't had it for some time."

"It would be a miracle if you could find a rabbit these days," he said with a smile, caressing his wife's face. "The slow ones are dead and the smart ones are underground. Waiting for the war to end."

"Mario," my mother said.

"Yes, *bella*," he said, still smiling.

"Please don't leave," my mother whispered. "Stay here, with us."

"I must leave," he told her. "I cannot stay. Not like this. Not anymore."

My mother leaned her head against her husband's shoulder, crying over what she was about to lose.

"I'll miss you," she said. "So much. The children, too."

"I'll miss you too, Raffaela," he said, kissing my mother on the lips and then bending down and carefully lifting his son into his arms. "But I leave you in good hands with this young man. And someday soon, they'll be strong hands."

Shrill whistles blew behind them as the conductors shouted for all passengers to board the train.

My mother and her husband stared at one another for a long moment, and then hugged for one final time.

"Take care of yourself, little one," her husband said. "Stay safe."

"Write me," my mother said, her hands trembling, her eyes swollen and red, watching her husband step onto the train. "As soon as you can."

My mother's husband waved at her and the children as he slowly made his way to the middle of the car, to an open seat by the window. As the train pulled away, he put a hand to his lips and blew his family one final kiss goodbye.

Three weeks later to the day, my mother received two pieces of mail. One was a long letter her husband had written her while on the train trip north. Over four thin sheets of paper, scrawled with a nervous hand and a near-empty ink pen, he told of his love for my mother and how lucky he was to have a wife who cared for him as much as she did. His only written regret was that their time spent together was so brief.

The second piece of mail was a telegram that had been delayed in getting to my mother. The short two-sentence statement told her that her husband, Mario Scubla, twenty-six years old, had died in his sleep, peacefully and without pain.

Burial had already been carried out.

IX

My father handed his wife an ice-filled glass of rum and Coke and sat back down to listen to the jazz band playing on the stage to his left. His hands casually played with a half-empty bowl of peanuts in front of him.

"These guys ain't bad," he said. "Next number, let's dance."

"Sure," Grace said. "I just need to use the bathroom first. You wouldn't know where it is?"

"In the back somewhere," my father said. "Off the side of the stairs."

My father watched as his wife walked past him, making her way toward the rear stairwell. She winked at him as she walked by.

"Hurry back, baby," my father said. "Don't wanna be without you too long."

"Two minutes," she said. "Be back before the song's finished."

Her high heels felt tight, the trim black dress snug around her waist and hips. Her hair was cut short, hanging just off her shoulder tops, swinging gently as she moved between the round tables. My father stared at her every move, smiling, munching on a handful of peanuts, relaxed and ready to enjoy a rare night out with his wife.

The Legion hall was filled with soldiers home on leave from their battles in Europe and across the Pacific. Even though the jazz band had been playing for less than an hour, most of the enlisted men were fast on their way to drunk, thanks in great part to the free beer given anyone in uniform.

"I didn't like being around soldiers," my father remembered later. "They were always blowin' smoke, pushin' their way around the women, braggin' about how many German or Japanese soldiers they killed. Tell you the truth, I never really gave a shit. Don't know why. Maybe because the army wouldn't take me, on account of my ear. Or maybe I just thought they were assholes. Either way, they didn't like me and I didn't like them."

Grace closed the door to the ladies' room behind her and started the crammed walk back to her table. As she made her way around a crowded section of the bar, she bumped into an army sergeant, a tall, thin young man with curly brown hair and a cast on his right arm, up to the elbow.

"Excuse me," she said. "Sorry."

"Not your fault, honey," the sergeant said, turning to face her. "This place's so damned crowded. Guess they're tryin' to take in as much money as they can."

"Guess so," Grace said. "Anyway, I'm sorry I bumped you. Hope I didn't get any beer on you."

"You did, a bit," the sergeant said. "But you can make it up to me in a real hurry."

"What do you mean?" Grace said.

"Dance with me," the sergeant said. "Just one dance. This next one."

"I can't," Grace said. "I'm with someone."

"He won't mind," the sergeant said. "Hell, it's only one dance."

"Oh, he'll mind," Grace said. "Believe me."

My father walked up behind the sergeant, standing there, hands on hips, facing his wife.

"You got a problem, mac?" my father said.

The sergeant turned to look at my father.

"None that I can see," the sergeant said.

"Good," my father said. "Then maybe you let the lady go where she's goin'."

"Fine with me," the sergeant said. "Just as soon as I get my dance."

"You don't understand," my father said. "She ain't dancin' with you. Not now. Not ever."

"What are you?" the sergeant said. "Her father?"

"Better than that, fuckface," my father said. "I'm her husband."

The sergeant grabbed a glass from the bar and swallowed down its contents. He wiped his mouth with the palm of his hand and turned his attention back to my father. Behind him, Grace lit a cigarette.

"Why aren't you in uniform?" the sergeant asked my father. "Everyone here is supposed to be in uniform."

"Maybe I lost mine," my father said. "Or maybe I ain't in the fuckin' army. Reason enough for you?"

"Why's that?" the sergeant asked. "Big, strong fuckin' guy like you. Why ain't you in the army?"

"I wanted to go," my father said. "But they wouldn't take me."

"Why not?"

"Said they were takin' all the assholes first. You know, guys like you."

"You want to go outside with this?" the sergeant said, placing his empty glass back on the bar.

"No," my father said. "I don't."

"Then we'll take care of it right here and now," the sergeant said.

"It's over," my father said. "Forget about it. But when your arm heals and you're still itchin', come look for me."

"I don't need two arms to beat a scumbag like you," the sergeant said. "Don't need an arm. Don't need anything."

"Look, chief," my father said. "It's over, okay? I'm not gonna fight you and you ain't gonna fight me. Not tonight anyways."

My father leaned over behind the sergeant and reached for Grace's hand, winking at his wife as he held her by the fingers.

"C'mon, baby," my father said. "I owe you a dance."

"Yes you do," Grace said, smiling as she walked past the sergeant, on her way to the dance floor.

"You led me on, bitch," the sergeant said to Grace. "Teased me up."

He grabbed the back of Grace's dress with his good hand, pulling her toward him and away from my father.

"Stay here," the sergeant said. "With me. Fuck him. Fuck that coward."

Grace swung a free hand and slapped the sergeant hard across the face.

"Take your hand off me," she said. "And keep it off."

My father turned his head in time to see Grace slap the sergeant. "What's goin' on?" he asked his wife. "What'd you hit him for?"

"I felt like it." Grace turned back toward the dance floor.

"I don't know," my father said, putting his arms around his wife's hips, still eyeing the sergeant at the bar.

"Don't know what?" Grace said.

"How the fuck we ever gonna beat the Germans," my father said, "if the soldiers we send over the side can't even take on a broad."

"I'm not a broad," Grace said with a smile.

"Yeah you are," my father said. "You're a broad. You're a great fuckin' broad."

My father and his wife danced close to one another until the band broke for the night.

X

The first bomb landed and exploded by the side of the train tunnel, sending rocks, dirt and debris skyward in three different directions. The second bomb splintered and uprooted a tree, sending branches bouncing toward the main road to town.

"Stay down," an old man said, pointing a thin finger at the overhead clouds. "They're still coming. Just stay down."

"We'll be killed," an old woman said, blood dripping down the right side of her face. "We'll all be killed."

My mother held her six-month-old baby in her arms, cradled close to her chest, her heart pounding, her hands and face cold and damp with sweat. She was six miles outside Salerno and three hundred yards from the inside of the train tunnel, the only place she knew would be safe from German bombs.

"It was such a beautiful day," my mother would later remember. "I was walking with a group of eight, mostly old people, heading to town to see if there was any food to be bought. We had heard that the

Germans had moved further up, to the north, and that the Americans were on their way in. And there hadn't been any bombing for several days. We all thought it was safe to go. We had no choice, really. We needed the food."

The German Spitfire, zeroing down on the scattered Italians, pelted the ground and the top wall of the train tunnel with machine-gun fire. Two people were left sprawled dead in its wake as the plane swooped back toward the skies. Another plane soon followed it, dropping down four bombs in rapid succession. The blast from one of the bombs sent a dislodged rock slicing against the side of my mother's leg, leaving her with a long gash and a heavy loss of blood.

"Raffaela," one of the old women shouted to my mother. "Hide the baby by the trees. He'll be safe there."

"No," my mother said, smoke from the bombs searing her eyes. "I won't leave him. He stays with me. We'll all be safe once we get to the tunnel."

"I won't make the tunnel," the old woman shouted. "I can't run. My legs."

"Grab hold of my arm," my mother said. "Run with me. It's not that far."

"Go without me, little one," the old woman said. "Save yourself. Save the baby."

"We'll all be saved," my mother said. "Don't stop. Close your eyes, keep your head down and run."

The bullet hit the old woman inches above her right temple. She fell to her left, against my mother's side, moaning as her legs crumpled beneath her.

"Angelina," my mother said, startled. "Angelina, what happened? Angelina, please? What's wrong?"

The old woman dropped to the ground, as three more German planes circled overhead. Less than fifty feet separated my mother and her baby from the tunnel entrance. My mother's upper body shook and her legs were weak. Her eyeglasses had been lost amid the turmoil, clouding her vision and confusing her sense of direction.

"It would have been so easy," my mother said. "Just to run to that tunnel. But I couldn't. I froze. A woman I had barely known was dead at my feet. There was smoke and fire everywhere. Women were screaming and men were crying. I held my baby in my arms, his eyes open, quiet, ignorant of his surroundings. I just stood there and prayed it would all pass me by."

The bomb landed to my mother's left, in the brush, up against the side of a hill lined with fig trees and pine cones. The explosion sent her and the baby sprawling to the ground, rocks and sand falling all about them. My mother landed face down, her cheek and forehead cut and bleeding, her right elbow twisted out of its socket, broken.

The baby lay silent, ten feet to her right.

My mother looked up, wiping the blood from her face, ignoring the pain in her arm and at her side, where a rib had cracked. She dug her hands into the soft ground and dragged her way to where the infant lay, his right leg twitching slightly. She touched his arm and rolled him gently onto his back. His white cotton pajamas were stained with dirt and blood. His face was smudged, his eyes closed, his lower lip cut.

"He looked like he was asleep," my mother said. "Like he was in a crib, in the middle of a dream. He was breathing and, except for a few bruises, looked okay. He stayed still and I moved closer to him, hugging him with my good arm. Then I saw the cut on his head."

The gash ran along six inches of soft skin and bled heavily, the flow moving down the back of the baby's head, past his ear and onto the ground to his left. The blow, caused by a fall against the sharp edges of a rock, was deep and already beginning to swell at the sides. My mother ran her hand along the cut, her fingers wiping away as much dirt as she could find.

My mother got to her knees, one arm held at her side, the other reaching down for her baby. She scooped him up into her arms and stood up, her legs wobbly, her vision fuzzy, her head aching and hurt. She heard the baby moan as she lifted his head onto her shoulder, bloody side up to the air.

"The planes had gone," my mother said, "their damage done. All around me, people lay on the ground, some injured, some dead. I had to find a doctor. My baby needed a doctor. I knew I didn't have much time."

My mother walked past a woman who was bleeding from a cut on her neck and crying over her husband's stilled body. She looked up at my mother as she passed.

"Do you see, Raffaela?" she said, her face wrinkled and washed with tears. "Do you see what those bastards did to my Arturo? Look. Look at him."

"Come to town with me," my mother said to her. "Tend to your wounds."

"I'm staying here," the woman said. "Where I belong. With my husband."

"We'll come back," my mother said. "We'll care for our dead later."

"You go," the grieving woman said. "I want to be with Arturo. Keep him safe."

"I'll send help," my mother said. "They may not be here till nightfall."

"I'll be here, little one," the old lady said. "You take care of your child. He should be your only worry."

The doctor tightened the bandage around the baby's head, securing it with a last piece of adhesive tape. Two nuns, both nurses on the clinic's staff, cared for the baby's other, more minor wounds, soaking them down with cotton swabs wet through with peroxide. The baby, crying and agitated, suffered loudly through the entire ordeal.

"Will he be all right?" my mother asked the doctor. "My baby, will he be all right?"

She was sitting on a wooden bench, the doctor working with his back to her, a short nurse dressed in blue attending to my mother's broken elbow.

"It's not too serious, is it?" she asked. "It didn't look too deep. There was all that blood and dirt, but it didn't look too deep."

The doctor turned away from the baby, looking across the room at my mother.

"Calm yourself, Signora," the doctor, a young intern with thick brown hair and a pencil-thin moustache, said. "The baby needs rest and attention. As do you."

"Can I take him home?" my mother said.

"Yes, of course," the doctor said. "Just as soon as your own wounds are tended. One of the nurses here will give you some medication, something to quell his pain."

"Does he have stitches?" my mother said.

"Fifteen of them," the doctor said. "Bring him back here in a week and I'll take them out. In the meantime, go home and get rest. Both of you. Doctor's orders."

"If the war allows it," my mother said.

XI

My father stood up from the chair, a glass of soda in his right hand, staring down at his wife sitting across from him.

"When the fuck are you gonna stop?" he said, his voice angry and low.

"Stop what, Mario?" Grace said. "I'm not doing anything. Not that I can see."

"Don't play dumb with me," my father yelled. "You know what I'm talkin' about."

"No, I don't," Grace said. "I have no idea what you're talkin' about, Mario. As usual."

My father reared back and threw the glass of soda against a far wall, to the right of an open window. It shattered on impact, streams of Coke flowing down the side of the wall, its cream-colored surface chipped and peeling.

Grace cringed at the violent toss, one hand instinctively held up to her face, her feet and legs bracing themselves against the base of her chair. She pulled herself back when my father leaned over the table, pointing a finger at her.

"This guy you been talkin' to," my father said, sneering. "Your boyfriend. That's what the fuck I'm talkin' about."

"My boyfriend?" Grace said. "I don't have *any* boyfriend. Why would you even think that?"

"I hear different," my father said. "I hear plenty different."

"Who do you hear it from?" Grace demanded. "Your mother?"

"Leave my mother outta this," my father roared. "This one's between you and me."

"That's right," Grace said. "I forgot. Can't talk about your mother. She's a saint."

My father lifted his right hand up above his head and came down with it hard against the side of Grace's face. He kicked the chair behind him farther away and grabbed his wife by the front of her dress, pulling her up close to his eyes.

"Who you layin' down for?" my father said. "Tell me, bitch. Before I leave you for dead."

"Nobody, Mario," Grace said. "I swear it."

My father slapped his wife again and then tossed her against the edge of the table. He picked up a chair from the floor and began slamming it on the ground, not stopping until all the legs and the back had shattered. He flung what was left aside and bent down, picking up a sheared-off chair leg.

"You gonna tell me or not?" my father said. "I'm through fuckin' around with you."

Their daughter, now four, asleep in the back room on her parents' bed, began to cry.

"Let me get Phyllis," Grace said. "I don't want her walkin' in here to see this."

"Don't worry about her," my father said. "She'll be fine. Now, answer me. Who is it? Who you been with?"

"Nobody!" Grace screamed. "Nobody, goddamn it. Nobody. Even if I wanted to be with somebody who would risk it? Everybody knows I'm married to a crazy man. Can't have any friends. Can't do anything. Can't go anywhere. Can't talk to nobody. The answer's no. I don't have a boyfriend. I only wish to God I did."

"You fuckin' cunt," my father said, swinging the chair leg high in the air and bringing it down against his wife's back. "I'll kill ya. I'll fuckin' kill ya today."

The second blow brought Grace to her knees. The third one sent her sprawling to the floor. My father held the chair leg so tight in his hand that his palm bled. He hit his wife three more times, on her legs and thighs, before flinging the chair leg over his shoulder.

He had bent down and lifted the back of Grace's head, holding her by her hair, ready to punch her across the face, when he heard his daughter's voice.

"Mommy," his daughter said. "Mommy, come here."

My father let go of his wife's hair, stood up and wiped the sweat off his face with the back of his arm. Grace got up to her knees, one hand reaching the table on her right side, looking for balance.

"Wait there, sweetie," she said in a low voice. "Mommy's comin'."

Grace stood up, her legs wobbly, her eyes red, her face flushed.

"We're outta here, Mario," she said to my father. "Both of us. For good. We've had enough from you. Do what you want. I don't care anymore. Just stay the hell away from us."

My father stood there, both hands, knuckles in, resting on his hips, his head down, eyes to the floor.

Grace walked across the room and carefully lifted her daughter into her arms.

"C'mon, honey," she said to her. "Let's go."

Grace picked up her black purse from the table and slung it over her right shoulder. She straightened out the back of her dress and opened the door leading out of the apartment.

"Goodbye, Daddy," Phyllis said as the door closed softly behind them.

My father was left there, one fist punching down steadily against his right knee. His breathing was heavy, his pulse racing, his eyes hard and angry.

"Bitch," he said. "Fuckin' no-good bitch. No good. That's all. No fuckin' good."

He punched at his leg harder, both his hands balled into tight fists. His ears were red, his upper body showered in sweat. He walked to the window, looking out, the slight breeze that came in feeling good against his chest.

He turned away from the window, reached down and picked up the discarded chair leg. He held it in his hand, looked at it, turned it over a few times and tossed it out the window. Then he walked toward a kitchen chair that was half-broken and laying on its side, picked it up and threw it out the window as well.

He pulled out bureau drawers crammed with clothing, walked them over to the window and dropped them down. Pillows, dishes, towels, more chair parts, hats, jackets and any piece of furniture he could push through were all fed out the window.

"Nobody leaves me," my father said to himself, throwing out two pairs of his wife's shoes. "*Nobody* leaves *me.*"

He walked into the rear room, pulled the white cotton blanket off the bed, rolled it into a ball and stuffed it under his arm. With a free hand he grabbed as many framed pictures as he could, headed back to the open window and threw everything he held out.

"Fuckin' bitch," my father said. "I hate her."

Neighbors from the other apartments banged on my father's door, pleading with him to stop what he was doing. An elderly woman on the second floor, frightened by all the noise, phoned the police. A man living in the apartment below my father yelled at him, his bald head twisted up and out from his open window.

"What the fuck's got into you, you crazy bastard," the man shouted. "You're gonna kill somebody, you don't stop."

"Here," my father said, dropping a piece of a chair in his direction. "A present for you. Shove it up your wife's ass."

"You're crazy," the man screamed. "Hear me? Crazy. You belong in the fuckin' bin."

"What's your problem?" my father said, looking down at the man. "I'm just cleanin' the place up a bit. It was gettin' too crowded in here."

"Go get a job, you lazy bum," the man said, ducking his head back inside the apartment, slamming down his window.

The apartment door was slowly opened, the landlord and two uniformed police officers standing in the doorway.

"I'm sorry, Mario," said the landlord, a square-shouldered man with the pinky finger missing from his left hand. "Somebody called them. I hadda let them in."

The older police officer, his hat slightly tilted back, one hand resting on his gun belt, stepped into the doorway, surveying the damaged apartment.

"Who you think you are?" he said to my father. "Lon Chaney?"

"I ordered new furniture," my father said. "They can't deliver it until I get rid of the old stuff."

"Fuckin' comedian," the cop said. "This neighborhood's full of comedians. The jails are, too."

"Why you here?" my father said, leaning against a far wall. "I break the law? Something like that?"

"Maybe," the cop said. "If you call hittin' an old lady over the head with a chair from a coupla flights up breakin' the law."

"I didn't hit anybody with a chair," my father said. "Especially no old lady."

"No, you didn't," the cop said. "But you could have."

"Could have ain't a crime," my father said. "Last time I looked."

"You through?" the cop said, kicking aside one of my father's shirts lying sprawled, collar up, on the floor. "Get it all outta your system?"

"Maybe," my father said.

"Yes or no, wise guy? I'm not here to play any fuckin' games with you. People in this building are scared shitless. You're a fuckin' menace. I could bring you in just on that alone. Now, answer my fuckin' question. You through here or not?"

"Yeah," my father said slowly. "I'm through."

"Good," the cop said, his voice softening. "Why don't you get outta here then. Take a walk. Cool down. Whatever it is, it'll blow over."

"It's my wife," my father said. "Took my kid and left me."

"This the first time?" the cop said.

"What, that she left me?" my father said. "Yeah. It is."

"She'll be back, then," the cop said. "Give her some time. She needs to blow off some steam, same as you."

"You married?" my father asked the cop.

"Know anybody my age who ain't?" the cop said, a smile across his face. "Now, c'mon, let's both get outta here."

"I got nowhere to go," my father said.

"You'll think of someplace," the cop said. "Maybe take in a movie. You like movies, don't you?"

My father nodded. "Gangster movies. You know, stuff with action in it."

"Not today," the cop said.

"What you mean?" my father asked.

"Find a comedy," the cop said. "Somethin' to make you laugh. That'd be a better bet. For you. For all of us."

XII

Raffaela's baby did not respond to any of the medication he was given. He lost weight in the weeks following the bombing attack, indifferent to both food and drink. My mother, due to the seriousness of her own injuries, was unable to breast-feed her son, her milk not forming as well as it normally would.

"We only believed in breast-feeding in those days," my mother said. "You couldn't trust the quality of the formula, especially during the war. Since I couldn't breast-feed him for awhile, three women from around the area were called, women who had just had babies of their own. And they fed him. Within a few days, he got an infection from one of them. It didn't help that he was already weak. His wounds were slow to heal. Soon he had a high fever and became very sick. I was so ignorant. We all were. And he was so innocent. We really never gave him much of a chance."

One month after the bombing outside the train tunnel, Gabriel Scubla died, five days past six months of age. On the last day she held her baby in her arms, my mother dressed him in a neck-to-toe all-white cotton gown. She combed down his few strands of dark brown hair with a blue comb soaked in warm water and soap. She put soft white socks on both his feet, and a silver bracelet around his right wrist. A creased picture of St. Giovann Guisseppe was spread across his chest, his hands folded above it.

My mother kissed his hands, feet, cheeks and lips before handing him to a funeral director with a thin frame and sagging shoulders.

"They laid him down in a small white box," my mother said. "It looked like it was just made out of fresh-cut wood. He looked like an angel laying there, his eyes closed, his body so still. He was such a quiet baby anyway, never cried all that much, slept well. I watched them nail shut his coffin and walked behind him to the cemetery, Anthony by my side."

My mother was twenty-four years old and, in less than a year's time, had lost both a husband and a son. She and Anthony were both dressed in black and had rosary beads wrapped around their hands, crucifix hanging down. Anthony would wear black for the next three years, while my mother would know no other color until the day she married my father.

The sun was in full zenith, its rays bouncing off the curved edges of the tombstones, as my mother watched two men lower her infant son into his grave, thick ropes wedged underneath the bottom of the coffin. Widows surrounded the open hole, some of them crying, some tossing in red roses and bouquets of flowers, others silently mumbling prayer. All of them familiar with the sight of death.

"We had all buried so many people," my mother said. "All of us. In such a short span of time. Husbands, daughters, sons, fathers. There wasn't a woman living in that town who wasn't wearing black for someone. It was too much. Too much death. Too much destruction. There was nothing else for me to do. It was time to go back home. Back to Ischia."

One week after she buried her son, my mother began packing up, preparing for the move from Salerno to Ischia. She boxed as many of her belongings as she could and sent them on ahead, content to travel with only one full valise in hand and her son in tow.

She went about town tearfully bidding farewell to the people with whom she had shared so many life and death moments. They had all been warm friends to her, welcoming her and making her transition from island girl to town woman as smooth as possible.

"We had been through so much together," my mother said. "A few good times and, thanks to the war, far too many bad ones. No matter what, the people of Salerno were always ready and willing to lend a hand, regardless of the need or their own problems. I can't say my memories of those years are happy ones. They're not. But those people I will always remember. What we did together and what they did for me, I can never forget."

My mother's sister Anna came up from Ischia to help prepare for her return to the island. She brought with her enough food for a week and slept next to my mother during her last nights at home.

"She was very quiet those last few days," Anna told me. "Stayed to herself, lost in thought. Trying to make sense of everything that had happened. You have to understand something. The people of Ischia don't trust life away from their island. They don't like to look beyond the sea. They think you'll only find trouble there. It sounds silly and superstitious, but not to those who believe it, and your mother's one of them. Twice in her life she's ventured beyond the sea. And both times she's known only death and misery. For your mother, life beyond the sea has been measured only in pain."

XIII

During their first five years of marriage, my father and Grace were separated on three occasions. Each time, my father would clear out the apartment he shared with his wife and either settle in a small furnished room somewhere in Hell's Kitchen or move back into his mother's apartment. During those separations, while Grace lived in nearby hotels or with members of her own family, my father would always be on the neighborhood prowl.

"We knew when he and Grace had split," one of my father's oldest friends, Tony, said. "He'd start comin' around again, his head down, kinda mopey. No matter what you hear, he loved that girl, was crazy about her. His problem was he was a jealous guy, very jealous."

The separations never lasted longer than four months at a time. In those months, my father would make every effort to see his wife.

"They'd shack up for a coupla days," another old friend said.

"And when he left, he'd leave her money. Because of that, his mother started sayin' the girl was a tramp, a trollop, a whore. I got news for you. She wasn't any of those things. She was his wife and he gave her money to help out with their kid. It's that fuckin' simple. Tell you the truth, Mario's biggest fuckin' mistake was not takin' his wife and kid and gettin' the hell outta Hell's Kitchen. They woulda been fine if only he had done that."

My father always worked steadily during the months he and Grace were apart, down at the docks, hauling cargo off ships anchored in the well of Pier 64. On any given week, my father, with overtime, earned as much as $120 take-home. He would kick half his pay back to his mother, peel off twenty dollars for pocket money and save the rest, to be used to buy new furniture or as down payment on rent whenever he and Grace were reunited.

"He used to be a dapper guy," Tony said. "Always bought himself sharp hats, nice slacks. When he had it, took good care of the wife and kid, too. Good-hearted guy. His downfall was his temper. I mean, he'd hit you on the spin of a dime. People were afraid of him because of that, and where we lived was a pretty rough neighborhood. They called our block, West 67th Street, San Juan Hill for one fuckin' reason or another. Lots of guys there were good with their hands. But none were better than Mario. You always had to be on your toes when you were out with him. He'd hit you anytime, for whatever the reason. Nobody wanted any part of him, especially when he had his horns twisted."

It was late October 1946, and my father wanted his wife back. They were in the middle of their second separation in less than a year, and he was tired of the whole difficult situation. He had grown weary of his mother's constant carping, annoyed with all the neighborhood talk that centered on him and his wife, and had had his fill of the turmoil and unsteadiness that marked his day-to-day life.

Above all else, he missed being with his wife and his now five-year-old daughter. My father was twenty-nine years old, with no career and a bleak vision of his own future.

"He was startin' to panic," a friend from those years said. "Gettin' scared. Couldn't blame him, really. It was like he was cornered. He wanted everything to work out the right way. But there were too many people jabbin' at his sides. His family, some of his friends, people he worked with, they all seemed to nag at him. And he was the kinda guy open to that, who let that kinda shit get to him. Anybody else they either cut it off or block it out. Not Mario. He took it to heart and he let it eat at him. Too much. It turned out to be too much for the guy to handle."

Grace had left Phyllis with her family and moved out of the West 64th Street apartment she shared with my father. She took a small room at the Mayfair, a third-rate hotel at the time, on West 49th Street between Broadway and Eighth Avenue. She needed to be alone, to be away from the constant fights with my father, the regular beatings at his hand, the overdue bills they faced and the malicious gossip spread by the neighborhood.

Grace had also had enough of my father's persistent but always broken promises. In his phone calls to her or at the end of many pillow-talk visits, my father would always tell Grace how well things were going to turn out. He would talk with purpose about the nice apartment they would live in and the good job he would land. He would swear to her that he would no longer gamble. For Grace, they were all empty words, heard too many times before.

So she hid out in her cramped hotel room, brooding, angry and dreading my father's next visit. The steady snide talk around the neighborhood was that most days she didn't lack for company.

"That kid was innocent," my father's friend Tony said. "Maybe too innocent. The only crime she was guilty of was wanting to have a good time. You know, eat at a nice place, go to a hot club and dance, that sort of thing. Hell, she was only twenty-four years old. Who do you know *doesn't* want a good time at that age?"

My father had missed three straight days of work and owed twelve dollars he didn't have to a street-corner bookie. The short leash he kept on his temper was close to severing, helped along by what he had heard earlier that morning, across a cup of coffee in an empty West Side diner, from one of Grace's few friends.

"Leave her be, Mario," the friend said, dabbing her cigarette against the side of a saucer. "She doesn't want any part of you. She's afraid."

"Afraid of what?" my father said, trying to ignore the smoke winding its way toward his face. "I'm her husband. What's there to be scared of?"

"Give it time," the woman said. "That's all I'm askin'. Give the girl some time."

"You didn't answer my question," my father said. "What's she afraid of?"

"You, Mario," the woman said. "She's afraid of *you*. Who else would she be afraid of?"

"That's bullshit," my father said. "I love her. You hear what I'm tellin' you? I love her."

"I know you do, honey," the woman said, resting her hand across a set of my father's knuckles. "I know. But you know how you can get sometimes. When you get a little angry."

"Yeah, so?" my father said. "I got a lot of shit goin' on. So what? So I get angry. Nothin' special."

"She loves you, Mario," the woman said. "Maybe even more than you love her. But when you get the way you do, it scares her. It scares me and I don't have to live with you. I've seen it, though. Too many times. You get angry enough to kill."

"Is that what she thinks?" my father said. "I'm gonna kill her? Is that what this bullshit is all about?"

"Nobody thinks that, Mario," the woman said. "Believe me. It's just that if you calmed down a little, it would go a long ways toward settlin' things. That's all."

"That ain't easy," my father said, pulling two singles from his shirt pocket and dropping them on the Formica next to his untouched cup of coffee. "Not with all the shit I gotta listen to. Believe you me, it ain't easy."

He left the booth and the woman, who was nervously lighting another cigarette, and walked out into the stiff autumn air toward his mother's house, both hands inside his trouser pockets, head down against the wind.

"I needed my head clear," my father later told me. "My mother's seemed as good a place as any. I hated the way things were turnin' out. My wife in a hotel. My kid somewhere with her aunt. Me floppin' down in a furnished room. It all sucked. I had to fix it. Make it right. Knew I could. If they left me alone, if everybody left me and Grace the fuck alone, we could make it right."

My father sat at his mother's kitchen table, elbows spread out, eating his third hefty bowl of lentil soup and sausage. As he ate, washing down the soup with long swallows from a cold bottle of ginger ale, his mother, by his side, cried and cursed the woman his son had chosen to marry.

The room was almost dark, lit only by two low-watt bulbs hanging from a ceiling cord. My father popped the last piece of a spicy sausage into his mouth and reached over, past the napkin tray, to the far end of the table for a loaf of Italian bread. His mother, across the table, sitting close to the warmth of the stove, stood up, eager to get her son another helping of lentil soup.

"That's it, Ma," my father said. "I'm good. No more."

"You sure?" his mother said.

"Yeah," my father said. "Save it. I'll be by for more. Maybe tomorrow."

"I save," his mother said.

"Cold or hot," my father said. "Don't mean shit. I'll eat it any way you got it."

My father left his mother's apartment and went to visit a divorced woman he had been seeing for three weeks. He spent three hours with the woman, made love to her twice and left ten dollars folded in two on the inside flap of her purse.

"Get yourself something for the next time," my father said to the woman, in her bed, half asleep.

"Like what?" the woman said.

"How the fuck do I know?" my father said. "Something pretty."

"When can I see you again?" the woman said, watching my father dress.

"Anytime you want, baby," my father said. "Anytime you want. All I got is time."

My father was back in his furnished room before midnight. He stripped off the long-sleeved brown sport shirt he wore and fell onto his small bed, his feet hanging off the mattress edge. He was tired, his upper body sore and aching, but had difficulty falling asleep. He tossed and turned throughout the long night, moving back and forth from the hardness of the bed to the coolness of the floor, seeking out a comfort zone.

"I wasn't feeling good that night," my father said. "I can't put my finger on it, something wasn't right. Don't know. Maybe I was nervous about going to see my wife. Maybe I was afraid of what would happen."

My father got up at dawn and made his way to the bathroom down the hall. He shaved his face with a dull razor, nicking himself on the right side of his chin. In place of after-shave or cologne, he splashed alcohol on the wound and dabbed at it with a few shreds of toilet tissue. He ran cold water on both his hands, then rubbed them over the top of his thinning brown hair. He didn't brush his teeth.

Back in his room, my father put on a blue nylon shirt with a frayed collar and a pair of charcoal-colored slacks, stuffing his wallet inside his rear pocket. He looped a brown belt around his pants' waist and put on a pair of black shoes, a half-size too small for his feet.

He wasn't carrying a weapon.

My father left his room at eight-thirty A.M., convinced his day would end with his wife safe and happy by his side.

Book Three

THE DEAD DON'T DIE. THEY LOOK ON AND HELP.

—D. H. Lawrence

I

My father knocked twice on the hotel room door. No answer. He knocked again, harder, and heard his wife's sleepy voice.

"Who's there?" she said.

"It's me, baby," my father said. "Mario."

"Jesus."

"Please, baby," my father pleaded. "C'mon, please. Let me in. We gotta talk."

He waited in silence for a few long moments, his hands back in his pockets, his temper running high, his face flushed red. He bit down on his lower lip as his eyes scanned the empty hallway.

"C'mon, Grace," he said. "Stop fuckin' around and let me in."

He couldn't wait any longer. My father put his right shoulder to the door and beefed it open with a forceful push. The knob lock snapped, and the dark wooden door slowly swung in. My father walked into the room and looked at his wife, standing there in a white silk slip, barefoot, her hair tangled just above her eyes.

"I don't want you here, Mario," she said.

My father walked closer to her, his palms wet and his mouth dry.

"I don't want you," she said again. "Not anywhere. Not anymore. I want you out, Mario. Out of my life."

"Why?" my father said. "Tell me, why?"

"Just go, Mario," Grace pleaded. "Just leave me alone."

"I love you, baby," my father said. "Don't you understand? I love you and I need you. Please don't leave me. You can't do that. You just can't."

"I'm in love, too, Mario," Grace said. "Only it's not with you."

"Another guy, you mean?" my father said. "You're with another guy?"

"Leave it alone," Grace said. "Just go."

"Who is it?" My father's voice was grim, cold. "Tell me, Grace. Who's the fuckin' rat?"

"Stop it," Grace said, her voice rising, colored with anger. "Stop it. Don't go gettin' yourself crazy."

My father grabbed Grace by the top of her shoulders and tossed her on top of the unmade bed in the center of the small room. He leaned his right knee on the mattress, looking down on his wife.

"You can't leave me," my father told her. "You understand? You *can't.*"

He put his other knee on the bed, hovering over the twenty-four-year-old woman, who lay still, quiet, making no attempt to get up.

"I'm your guy," my father said. "Your only guy. Me. Nobody else. I mean it. *Nobody* else."

Grace lifted her head and shoulders from the bed, shifting her weight from one side to the other.

"Stay where you are," my father told her. "Let's get this bullshit settled out once and for all."

"It is settled, Mario," Grace said. "We're over, you and me. There's nothing else to talk about."

"You ain't gonna do this," my father shouted. "You ain't gonna break up what we got."

"There's nothing to save, Mario! We ain't got nothing together, you and me. It broke apart a long time ago. We just been acting like there's something. But there's nothing. *Nothing.*"

My father leaned closer to his wife, pressing his weight against her upper body, their faces inches apart.

"You ain't leavin' me," my father insisted, in a near whisper. "I won't let you."

"I've already left you," Grace said sadly. "A long time ago."

"Tell me his name," my father said, giving in to his temper. "Tell me his fuckin' name. Tell me, you bitch, before I break your fuckin' jaw."

"Get off me," Grace said. "You're hurting me."

"I want his name," my father said, slapping his wife hard across the face. "His name. Give it to me."

Grace pushed against her husband's weight, one hand, nails out, reaching up to scratch my father on his right arm, the other streaking across his left cheek, drawing blood. She kicked at his back with her legs and bare feet. She cried out, with a loud yelp.

My father reached over his wife, across a half-length of the bed, and grabbed a soft feather pillow, its white covering yellowed and soiled. He hesitated as he saw the frightened look in his wife's eyes.

He felt her struggle.

He heard her screams.

My father held the pillow out wide with both his hands and pushed it down on his wife's face, muffling her now anguished pleas for help.

He increased the pressure, his arms hanging straight down, the muscles in his back, forearms and shoulders tense and rigid. His wife was kicking at him with only one leg now, her arms still by her side. Drops of sweat slipped down my father's forehead and across the bridge of his nose. He was biting down hard on the upper part of his lip, a trickle of blood forming at the center. His eyes were glazed and wet with tears.

"I knew what I was doin' as I was doin' it," my father said. "I just couldn't stop. I really wanted to lift that pillow from her face, kiss her, tell her I was sorry. But I couldn't. And I didn't. Not until it was too late. Not until she stopped moving and I was sure she wouldn't scream at me no more. You know, I didn't see her there. I didn't see her in my mind. All I saw was a guy. A guy with his arms around her, takin' her on the town somewhere, takin' her to bed. That's what I saw in those last, crazy minutes."

My father wiped his brow with the sleeve of his shirt and looked around the room, trying hard to ignore Grace's still body. His wife's head hung to one side, her arms and legs weightless and limp, her mouth half-open, her tongue curled near the edge of her lower lip.

She had been dead for less than a minute.

"I was so fuckin' scared," he told me later. "I've never been so scared in my whole life. I didn't wanna kill her, you know. Shit, I didn't think I even could. But I did. I fucked up again. Big time."

My father found Grace's open purse resting against a lamp by a two-drawer table next to the bed. He rifled through its contents and emptied them, keys and loose change mostly, into his trouser pockets. He went into the walk-in closet and pulled out the two dresses—one blue, the other white with red ribbons around the neck and sleeves—that his wife kept there. He held them up against the streams of sunlight drifting in from the window in back of him, staring at them, his hands shaking, crying over what he had done.

He ripped the labels off both dresses and tossed them in a heap into the corner of the closet. He threw the pillows from the bed to the floor, drew the curtains and covered his wife's legs with the edge of the bedspread.

My father took one final look at his dead wife and opened the door to leave, placing the DO NOT DISTURB sign on the outside of the knob. He gently closed the door behind him and walked down the two flights of stairs to the lobby.

"I was shakin' like a leaf," my father said. "My whole body. I felt cold and dizzy. And I couldn't stop sweatin'. I had the dry heaves, tried to throw up and couldn't. I couldn't stand lookin' at her. I tried not to think she was dead. Even shook her a few times, hopin' she would wake up. She looked so beautiful layin' there, so peaceful, calm. I don't think I ever loved anybody as much as I loved Grace. Not even your mother. She was everything to me."

The hotel manager was sitting in the lobby, three paragraphs deep into a Dick Young baseball article about a trade the Brooklyn Dodgers were rumored to be making. He creased the paper in half and looked up when he saw my father.

"Hey, buddy," my father said, walking toward the manager, three dollar bills crumpled inside his right hand. "Do me a big favor, would ya?"

"Depends," the manager, a young man in a plaid shirt buttoned straight to the collar, said. "What is it?"

"I don't want my wife bothered," my father said, handing the manager the three dollars and the key to the room. "She had kind of a rough night. Didn't get much sleep."

"I'll tell the cleaning lady to skip her room," the manager said. "Until tomorrow."

"I appreciate it," my father said.

"You want me to look in on her?" the manager asked. "See if she's doin' okay?"

"No," my father said. "Just let her sleep it off. She'll be fine."

My father turned left out of the hotel entrance, heading uptown, back to Hell's Kitchen. He knew he needed a plan and a solid alibi, and was having a hard time coming up with either. The hotel room was registered in his name, and he and Grace had stayed there together often enough to be known and recognized as a couple. The manager had even seen my father and Grace leave together late on Sunday morning, heading to her family's apartment for an afternoon dinner. The two of them had come back that night to the hotel and were seen by the desk clerk on duty.

"Everybody at the hotel knew us," my father said later. "They knew we were married and they knew that we were havin' our problems. I used to go there sometimes on my own or with another broad for a night or two. You know, just to relax."

Early on Monday morning, my father and Grace had both checked out of the Mayfair, walking out together and heading their separate ways. But my father had returned later that afternoon, just before five P.M., and registered the same room back in his name.

"We both needed to think," he said. "Figure out our next move. She didn't wanna stay with her family and, tell you the truth, I didn't want her to, either. So I told her I'd come back to the hotel and get her a room. I don't know what the hell I told the cops when they caught me. I was havin' a hard time keeping my stories straight. Papers were gettin' it wrong, too. Didn't really matter. There was only one part of my story anybody really gave a shit about. That was that she was dead and that I killed her. The rest was bullshit, all of it. Tabloid talk."

My father confessed to the murder of his wife, Grace, on the evening of Thursday, October 31, 1946.

In part of an oral statement given to then Manhattan assistant district attorney James Yeargin, my father, in a fashion dramatic enough to feed the tabloids, said, "Maybe I am a rat. But no other rat will ever get her."

Also in the statement, my father quoted Grace as saying, "I'm young, Mario. I want to enjoy life. I'm in love. Really in love this time. With another man."

It was then, my father said, fueled by passion and jealousy and out of sheer frustration, that he killed his wife with a pillow.

"Gee," my father said to Yeargin. "She was only twenty-four years old and I'm only twenty-nine. What's gonna happen now?"

Hell's Kitchen, which had never been a neighborhood to shy away from violence, was stunned into silence by my father's actions.

"It was horrible," my father's sister Mary said. "I was just a little girl back then, going to school. On the street, they called us a family of murderers. There were always fingers pointed at us, whispers behind our backs. It was just an awful time."

My father was remanded to the Tombs, a cold and dark stone construction in lower Manhattan. He was put in a cell next to an accused armed robber and down the wing from a man who had raped and killed a teenage girl. There was no toilet paper in my father's cell, and the floor under him felt sticky from dried urine. The smell of old vomit seemed strong enough to touch.

"That place was a shithole," my father said. "There was a damn good reason it was called the Tombs. The smell and the noise drove me crazy. That's the thing about prison nobody ever tells you. The noise. It's all the time, like runnin' water. Steady. Not high. Not low. But steady. If you didn't kill somebody before you got in the Tombs, you sure as shit felt like killin' somebody before you got out. That's why dyin' has never scared me. I've been dead. I've been in the Tombs."

II

My father's crime was considered one of passion, not intent, and so he was spared the death penalty. With the help of his family, he hired one of the most expensive criminal attorneys in the state. For a fee rumored to be in the neighborhood of $25,000, a cunning defense of my father's actions was established. His wife, it would be argued, had brought my father to the brink of madness by conducting numerous adulterous affairs, many of them with alleged members of organized crime.

The idea was to paint a portrait of Grace as a woman who preferred a good time to the strain of maintaining a home and raising a family. My father, meanwhile, would be described as a hard-working man who only wanted what was best for his wife and daughter and who did everything within his power to keep his family intact.

The judge assigned to my father's trial was stern, insisting silence and proper decorum be the overriding rules of his courtroom. According to family gossip and neighborhood speculation, bribes were doled out.

One key defense witness gave verbal evidence placing Grace in the arms of willing strangers. A handful of others took the stand and testified to the strength of my father's character, the love he had for his wife, the pride he took in having a family to call his own.

"I didn't go to the trial," said Tony, a close family friend. "Didn't want to. But I followed it. We all did. Nobody was surprised at the lawyer Mario got for himself. The old lady came through, you know what I mean? This guy had major connections. He could get things done. We all hung around the candy store, the one near St. Matthew's Church, and talked about it. Nobody was angry at Mario, nothing like that. We were just saddened by it. We knew something bad was bound to happen between them. Especially the way things were going. Had to happen."

Throughout the three-week trial, my father sat straight up in the defendant's chair, hands folded, eyes focused on the drama swirling around him. He shaved every morning, wore a clean shirt every day and always made an effort to make eye contact with the various members of his family in attendance.

Not once during the course of the trial did my father ask to see his child, the little girl whose mother he had killed.

"I missed her," my father said. "You bet your ass, I missed her. She was my kid. But I was ashamed of what I had done. I was so fuckin' ashamed. I couldn't look at her. What could I have told that kid? That I was sorry? That I was gonna bring her mother back to her? There was nothin' left to say. Nothin' to do but leave that kid alone. And that's what I fuckin' did. Like it or not, that's what I did."

When the jury foreman came in and announced the guilty verdict, my father hung his head and kept his hands, one on top of the other, behind him.

Second-degree manslaughter.

Five to fifteen years in prison.

His mother screamed and punched at her legs in anger. The older sister cried quietly. His lawyer patted him gently on the back. Two court officers surrounded my father, handcuffed him and led him away.

"I'm sorry," one of the officers said to my father. "I would have done the same thing myself. You got yourself a raw deal."

"Yeah," my father said. "I know I did."

"You'll do easy time," the officer said. "You'll see."

"You think?" my father said.

"I know," the guard said. "A guy's wife fuckin' around on him. Every guy in the hole has the same problem. They'll leave you be."

"I'm not lookin' for any trouble," my father said.

"Then you won't get any," the guard said. "And the time'll pass. It always does. Nobody can kill time like a bird in for a stretch."

III

My father watched the four-man handball game, his hands in his jacket pockets, his back against a cement wall, in the low end of the exercise yard at the Comstock Correctional Facility in upstate New York. He was three months into his prison sentence and was still considered fresh fish by many of the seasoned cons.

One of the men in the game, muscular and middle-aged, wanted out, tired from the thirty-minute set.

"You want in?" he asked my father, wiping his face and neck with a hand towel.

"Sure," my father said. "Wouldn't mind."

"Go to it," the man said, walking away.

My father took off his heavy denim jacket and laid it on the ground. He rolled up the sleeves of his blue cotton shirt and bent down to tighten the laces on his black work shoes.

"Forget about playin'," one of the remaining three convicts in the game said. "We don't need a fourth guy."

"Why not?" my father said, standing up, looking over at the bald man, stripped to the waist, an Oriental dragon tattooed down the side of his right arm. "You can't play with three. Rules say you need four."

The bald man walked past my father and toward a small group of convicts standing in a semicircle, watching the game. He tapped one of them on the shoulder.

"C'mon, Frankie," the bald man said. "Play a couple of hands."

The bald man turned and came back to my father, bouncing the hard black ball against the cracked cement.

"Happy?" he said to my father. "We're followin' the rules. Now, why don't you take yourself somewhere else. Make the rest of us happy."

"You got a beef with me?" my father said. "If you do, let's hear it."

"I got no beef," the bald man said. "I'm just a particular guy."

"Oh, yeah," my father said. "What about?"

"Simple things," the bald man said. "I don't play or stay with a wife-killer. Any problem with that?"

My father clenched his hands into fists and looked around the yard, staring at the men who had stopped their game, waiting for his response to the courtyard challenge.

"No," my father said. "I got no problem with that."

"Didn't think you would," the bald man said. "Seeing as how none of us are wearin' skirts."

My father rolled his sleeves back down and tossed his denim jacket over his right shoulder. He took one final look at the men around him and left, slowly making his way to the far end of the yard.

My father was in the top bunk of his cell, hands folded behind his head, eyes staring at the ceiling.

"You got no choice, buddy," his cellmate, also in for murder, said to my father. "You gotta stick the cocksucker."

"I gotta get him alone," my father said. "Him and me. Then, we settle it."

"A fight ain't gonna end it," the cellmate said. "This ain't the street. He's gonna keep comin' at you. Maybe alone. Maybe not. You only get one chance at him. Don't waste it. Make it count."

"Where?" my father said.

"The shower," the cellmate said. "Best place. Takes the guards a while to get in there. By the time they do, damage is done."

"You know him at all?" my father said. "He a hard guy or what?"

"He's been in here three years," the cellmate said. "Got about another three, maybe four, to go."

"What'd he do?" my father said. "Kill somebody?"

"Two guys," the cellmate said. "During a robbery. Something went wrong. I don't know. Never got the whole story."

"He connected to anybody?" my father said.

"Nobody I ever heard of," the cellmate said. "He's got his crew in here. Three or four guys who watch each other's ass. But nothin' on the outside."

"What about them?" my father said.

"He goes down, they stay away," the cellmate said. "On one condition."

"What?" my father said.

"You do it right," the cellmate said. "You do this right and nobody'll ever fuck with you again, not so long as you're in here."

"It's like no place else in the world," my father said. "The joint's got its own set of rules, its own way of life. The chief rule is respect. Property. Person. Same difference. It's the only thing you got. Somebody fucks with your respect, you gotta do something about it. You got no choice to do otherwise. Not if you wanna do easy time and stay a man. What the hell else you gonna do? Call a cop? Not there. Not in my time."

My father wrapped a towel around his waist and walked into the shower room, the area hot and steamy from the running water. There were four other men in the room, each in various stages of scrubdown. The bald man was at the far end, soaping his chest and arms under the shower head closest to an overweight guard on a stool.

My father stood before an empty valve and turned on the water. He unhitched his towel and hung it on a hook to his left. He reached for the soap, rubbed both hands on the bar and spread the suds across the front parts of his arms and legs. He nodded to the man on his right, who was quietly shampooing his hair.

On the other side of the shower, my father's cellmate, pushing a rickety cart filled with books and magazines, stopped in front of the guard.

"Anything good?" the guard asked.

"Same old shit," the cellmate said. "You guys must be holdin' out on us. There's gotta be better stuff than this on the outside."

"What, you expect me to know?" the guard said. "I'm in this shithole every day. Same as you."

"Your pay's better," the cellmate said. "So I hear."

"Not by much," the guard said, waving the cellmate and his cart forward.

My father found the shank in the far left corner of the shower room, inches from his feet, its point resting against a loose tile. He picked it up and palmed it in his right hand. He turned off the water and grabbed for his towel, patting dry his face and eyes. My father then hung the towel around the hand holding the shank.

"Look who it is," the bald man said to my father's back, walking past him, out of the shower. "I guess even a wife-killer needs to wash."

My father looked at him and smiled.

"Fuck you smilin' at, wife-killer?" the bald man said. "You sweet on me, that it? Mouthful of cock, that what you lookin' to get for yourself?"

My father shrugged his shoulders and held the smile, his grip around the hidden shank firm.

"That why you killed your wife?" the bald man said. "She didn't have a cock? That it?"

My father moved closer to the bald man, careful not to slip on the wet tiles. The three other cons stayed under their showers, turning the water pressure on as high as it would go, the steam and heat partially blocking the guard's view of the room.

"Well, I got a cock, if that's what you want," the bald man said, running a hand between his legs. "Big one. Fit inside you real nice."

My father was inches from the bald man, still smiling, looking in his eyes and at his chest, taking deep breaths with his mouth half-open.

"Don't scream," my father said to the bald man.

"Why should I scream?" the bald man said. "You ain't gonna bite me, are ya'?"

"No," my father said. "I ain't gonna bite. Don't worry about that."

"Get to it then," the bald man said, with a wink over at the three men. "I never had a wife-killer suck me off."

My father dropped the towel and raised the shank. He caught the bald man just below the neck line, moved the blade in deep and pushed it down. Blood shot out, spraying my father's face and upper body. The bald man's hands held my father's arm, his eyes were flushed wide, and a low moan came from his mouth. Thick streams of blood flowed down his chest as he began to sink down to his knees.

None of the other convicts made a move except to watch.

None spoke.

One of them laughed.

My father stood over the bald man, his hand still on the shank. He put a knee to the left side of the bald man's chest and yanked the shank out, holding it flat against his side, point side down.

"Die now, fuck," he said to the bald man. "Die now."

My father turned around, grabbed his towel from the wet floor and walked out of the shower room, the shank hidden. The three cons turned off their water, held their towels to their bodies and followed him out.

The bald man was spread out, head down, on the tile floor. His eyes were half-open, blood gurgled out of his mouth, and his legs were curled back behind him. His chest wound pulsed and bled heavily. The inch-deep pool of water around him was colored a light red as it ran down toward the center drain.

The bald man, his face still, his upper body twitching, the last remnants of his life spilling out onto a slippery floor, never heard the overweight guard get up from his stool and blow the alarm whistle.

IV

My father stared at the prison cell around him. It was Christmas Eve, 1949, and he missed his family, his friends, his neighborhood. He lowered his head against an iron bar and thought of the food he couldn't eat, the music he couldn't hear, the women he couldn't love.

"Don't get me wrong," my father said. "I didn't mind being in the joint. Most times I actually liked it. Didn't miss the outside all that much. Except on holidays. Christ, how I hated fuckin' holidays in that place. Everybody tries to treat it as just another day. But you know. Unless you're fuckin' brain dead, you know."

My father settled in at Comstock, landing a steady job in the prison kitchen, cooking and preparing meals. He exercised for an hour each day, kept his face and arms constantly tanned and drank joint gin from a small tin cup whenever he longed to be around a woman.

"You know what I liked about prison?" my father said. "There were no worries. You kept your nose clean, didn't fuck with anybody, did your job, did your time, things were fine. You didn't have to worry about payin' any bills, makin' your boss happy, buyin' clothes, none of that shit. In a way, I felt freer inside than I ever did on the outside."

He thrived on the quiet routine of prison life. He enjoyed the lack of responsibility that allowed him to care for no one other than himself. He answered to no authority other than the duty guards and the main cell-block convicts.

"We called the joint 'college,' " my father said. "It was like school to us. You learned what you wanted to learn. Some guys learned how to be better crooks. That wasn't for me. I didn't wanna go down that block. Instead, I worked in the kitchen and learned how to be a butcher. Thought it was something I could make use of when I got out. You know, maybe make some money from it."

V

"C'mon, will you please," my father said to one of the convicts standing around him. "How can you say that? How can you say Robinson's better than La Motta? How the fuck can you say that?"

" 'Cause it's true," said the convict, tall and thin, with slicked-back black hair and a cigarette in the side of his mouth. "Kicks his ass everytime they fight."

"He's got the cuffs on," my father said. "That's why he loses."

"What cuffs?" the convict said. "The Boys, you mean?"

"Yeah," my father said. "They tell you to lose, you lose. But that don't make the other guy a better fighter."

"What about Pep?" asked another convict, older, huskier, also with a lit cigarette in his mouth. "You like him?"

"Willie Pep is better than pussy," the first convict said.

"Let me think on that one," my father said, smiling. "I mean, he's good. I just don't know if he's *that* good."

"There ain't nothin' that good," a third convict, his head against the yard wall, his face up to the warm sun, said. "At least not where I'm from."

"Let's not talk about what we ain't got," the second convict said, stomping out the butt end of his cigarette with the heel of a work boot.

"That don't leave us much, Bobby," the first convict said. "Smokes and time. That's about it."

"And food," my father said. "That steak we had last night wasn't half-bad."

"That wasn't steak, Mario," the second convict said.

"Yeah, it was," my father said. "I ought to know. I cooked the fuckin' thing."

"No, not steak," the second convict said. "Linoleum. That's what it was. Linoleum."

The four convicts stood their ground, enjoying the laugh. All of them, with the exception of my father, flicked match tips and lit up fresh cigarettes.

"You like that kitchen?" Bobby asked my father. "It's workin' out?"

"I do," my father told him. "It's quiet in there, you know. Do my work. Eat whenever I want. Prepare the food. Shit like that. It ain't bad. Kills the time, anyway."

"Prepare the food," the first convict said, winking at the others. "Mario here thinks he's a fuckin' chef."

"I'm the only fuckin' chef you guys got," my father said. "No use bitchin' about it. That ain't gonna change. Not until I'm out."

"You gonna use it?" Bobby said. "On the outside."

"I want to," my father said. "You know, work in a nice place. But I don't know. I don't know what it's gonna be like out there for a guy like me."

"You'll get what you can get," the first convict said. "At first. Then, if you got any luck, people around you forget. Let you go about your business."

"Unless you gonna go pro," Bobby said. "Then you can land a job in no time."

"Not me," my father said. "I had my fill. Don't ever wanna come back here. I'm gonna go out and stay out."

"Whatta you sayin', Mario?" Bobby asked. "You don't like us?"

"I don't like you *that* much," my father said. "You wanna see me, you see me in New York City."

"Maybe these guys will," Bobby said, nodding toward the other convicts. "Not me. I'm doin' natural. The only thing I'll see when I get outta here is dirt. From the inside of a cheap coffin."

My father stood there quietly and blew warm air into his hands, cupped together by his face.

The nights at Comstock were always the roughest for my father. The noises from the cells around him were constant, low groans from the sick, muffled screams from the raped, streams of whispers from the conspiring. My father never fell asleep until the slanted light from the first sign of dawn made its way to his bunk. Then, when he did, finally, sleep, it was an uneasy rest, filled with visions of his crime.

"I never had nightmares," my father said. "Nothin' like that. I just would see things I did all the time. When I closed my eyes I would always see Grace. Sometimes she'd be dancin' or sometimes she'd be standin' alone in front of a crowded bar or maybe a restaurant. And no matter what we were doin', laughin' maybe, talkin', whatever the fuck it was, it would always lead back to the hotel. Back to the Mayfair. With me there, holdin' a pillow over her face."

There were no televisions at Comstock. Radios were often smuggled in, the music enjoyed under the covers of blankets and darkness. Checkers, poker and gin were the preferred indoor games, while touch football, two-bounce handball, boxing and boccie tournaments ruled the outdoor yards. The hot currencies were cigarettes, skin magazines, wristwatches and after-shave lotion, which was often boiled down and included in the prison hootch mix.

"They were hard guys in that place," my father said. "Tough, knock-around guys. They were pros, for the most part. Most of them were around my age, some older. They weren't scared of shit, not even dyin'. During one of my first weeks there, a guy I knew from the Kitchen got the electric chair. When they hit him with the juice all the lights in the place went on and off, on and off a coupla times. They say he screamed like a woman and spit up enough blood to choke on. But he was a tough guy. He stood up. He never gave in to the Bulls."

VI

My father stood to the left of the center ring, his feet firmly planted, his taped and bandaged hands working a cut pattern on the speed bag. He was wearing black gym shorts and a white T-shirt, wet through on the back and front with sweat. A white bath towel hung from his neck, and his white woolen sweat socks were bunched up around the top edges of his black ring shoes.

"You fight much on the outside?" asked a guard, watching my father's workout. "In the ring, I mean, not the streets."

"A coupla bouts," my father said, still slamming the speed bag. "Nothin' big. Whiskey bouts mostly."

"Three rounders?" the guard said. "That what you mean?"

"That's right," my father said. "Winner keeps the purse."

"You ever get to keep the purse?" the guard said.

"Every time," my father said, slowing his pace on the bag. "Every fuckin' time."

"You miss it at all?"

"What, fightin'?"

"Yeah, fighting."

"I miss a lot of things," my father said. "Why you askin' all this?"

"We're looking for somebody to take on our champ," the guard said. "Not some fat bird with a hard punch. Somebody good. Or at least, somebody who looks good. Guy like you. Interested?"

"Why should I be?" my father said. "What do I get?"

"Nothing," the guard said. "No special privileges. No better food. No better place to sleep. None of that shit."

"Don't sound good, does it?" my father said.

"It's only worth it to someone who likes to fight," the guard said. "I think you're one of those guys."

"Yeah?" my father said. "What makes you think that?"

"I seen you in here. Seen you pound away at the bags. You handle yourself pretty good. Why'd you stop fighting?"

"I got a tin ear," my father said. "Didn't wanna be deaf on top of everything else."

"Think about it," the guard said. "Next time I see you around, let me know."

My father nodded at the guard, watching him as he walked away. He bent down and picked up a jump rope near his feet. He looked across the gym floor at a full-length mirror, checking his body for proper form, and then started his jumps.

He winked at himself in the mirror and smiled.

My father sat on the wooden stool in his corner of the makeshift ring, taking deep breaths, letting a corner man rub Vaseline on his face and chest.

"Go easy with that shit," my father said. "I don't like too much on me."

"Makes the punches slip," the corner man said. "Won't hurt as much."

"Worry about yourself," my father told him.

"Need anything else?" the corner man asked. "Sponge, water, anything?"

My father shook his head. "I'm good." He looked around the crowded yard, at the dozen cons raising fists in his direction.

"Kick some ass, Horse," one of them yelled up at him. "Bring him down, baby. Make him pay. Time to pay."

My father filled his mouth from the water bottle and spit half of it back into the empty bucket by his feet, on the outside of the lower ring rope.

"Lot ridin' on this one," the corner man said.

"Like what?" my father said.

"Lot of cig bets laid down between the boys and the Bulls," the corner man said. "Boys'll smoke for free for a year, you pull this one off."

"Where is this fuck?" my father said, looking over at the empty corner on the other side of the ring. "What the fuck's he waitin' for?"

"He's the champ," the corner man said. "Gotta make an entrance."

"Champ, my ass," my father said. "He's a fuckin' Bull. That's all. Just a fuckin' Bull."

The guard was big, four inches taller than my father and twenty-five pounds heavier. He was older, with a great deal more ring experience, well over a hundred bouts. He was a former Marine Corps light-heavyweight champion, and had been a guard for seven years, boxing for them for a little under four. He had fought twelve convicts prior to my father and beaten them all. Five had required hospitalization.

"He was bulky," my father said. "Big arms and thick legs. He had a wide stomach, a little too much beer maybe. That seemed to be his only weakness. I never laid eyes on the guy until he came in the ring, musta worked in some other part of the prison. He was a cocky-lookin' bastard. Waved at me when he got in the ring. Even had some kinda half-ass belt on around his waist. The other guards didn't think I had much of a chance. Everybody in the joint called me Horse, you know, and in the weeks before the fight they all kept sayin' how the Horse was gonna get his ass whipped. I didn't say shit one way or the other. I mean, fuck, for all I knew they were right."

My father and the guard stood in the center of the ring, receiving their instructions from a short referee in sweatpants. The bout was scheduled for six rounds, and the three-knockdown rule was waived. The fight could not be stopped on a cut and a ring second could not throw in a white towel. Only the ref could bring a halt to the action.

"It was set to prison rules," my father's cellmate remembered.

"That usually works to a con's advantage. But not this time. Everything seemed to lean toward Horse's opponent. The guy had better gloves, had more time to train and looked like he had the ref workin' his side of the room. Horse knew goin' in that he had to put the guy out if he was gonna get his hand raised. He was a little nervous about it all. Not scared. Just nervous."

My father and the guard circled each other in the first minute of the fight, each flicking out a few jabs, bobbing and bending in dancelike rhythms. The guard landed the first punch, a hard hook just above my father's right temple. He followed with a body blow that landed on my father's chest.

"Nice shots," my father said. "Both of them. It answered the first question I had about the guy. Now I knew the fuck could hit."

My father landed two short jabs against the guard's right shoulder and a left to his exposed midsection. The guard took both punches well and countered with three of his own. An overhand left, landing on my father's jaw, did the most damage, sending him straight back against the middle of the ring ropes. Two short rights, both glancing off the top of my father's head, brought an end to the first round.

In his corner, my father took some salt in the nose and cold water across the face. A corner man dropped some ice inside my father's trunks and wiped his chest with a damp towel.

"We got him right where we want him, Horse," the corner man said to my father.

"Yeah?" my father said. "Where's that?"

"How the fuck am I supposed to know?" the corner man said, smiling. "It just sounds like something I'm supposed to say to you."

"Rinse off my mouthpiece, would ya?" my father said. "And keep an eye on that fuck's corner. Make sure they don't put anything in his gloves."

"Don't worry about any of that shit," the corner man said. "We got a guy on that. From the get-go."

My father broke the two middle knuckles of his right hand early in the second round and split his lower lip just before the bell. In between, he took three hard below-the-belt punches, each causing him to clutch the guard and strain for breath. The ref ignored each illegal blow.

"You lookin' for your balls?" the guard said to my father as they held above a neutral corner, after another low punch found its mark. "They're up against the wall."

My father pushed the guard away and whipped off a double left-and-right combination, head to heart and back again. The power behind the blows buckled the guard's knees.

"I'm gonna kill you before this is over," my father said to the guard through his mouthpiece. "You're dead."

At the bell, rung by a bald con with a thick brown moustache, the guard brushed against my father's shoulder, holding his right elbow with the thumb of one glove.

"Forget it, scumbag," the guard said to my father. "They'll carry you out of this fuckin' place with a sheet."

My father yanked his arm away from the guard's grip. When he did, the convicts clapped, whistled and stomped their boots in approval.

"Those fuckin' low blows," my father said, sitting in his corner, letting his seconds rub his chest and arms. "The ref ain't doin' shit about it."

"And he ain't gonna do shit about it," the corner man said to my father. "He's with them."

"His gloves are greased, too," my father said. "Makin' my eyes burn."

"Guards ain't never lost one of these fights," the corner man said. "They don't wanna lose this one, neither."

"I can beat this prick," my father said. "On the square."

"That's just it, Horse," the corner man said. "It ain't on the square. We stepped into it."

"I ain't tankin' it," my father said. "I don't give a fuck what the deal is."

"Let's go, kid," the corner man said. "Bell's about to go. Watch yourself in there."

The guard landed another series of low blows early in the third round. The pain they caused forced my father to fight from a crouch position.

"C'mon, tough guy," the guard said. "Come to me. Come get some more."

The guard hit my father with two rabbit punches and a vicious uppercut that sent him reeling against the corner ropes. There, the guard continued his assault, working the lower parts of my father's stomach and kidneys. A head butt opened a cut just over my father's right eye, a thin river of blood starting to flow down his face.

My father spit his mouthpiece out of the ring toward a guard sitting in the second row as the bell rang ending the third round.

"Why don't you take a fuckin' seat for yourself," my father said to the ref on the way back to his corner. "All the good you're doin'."

"Fuck you, loser," the referee said. "Just fight the fight."

"Count on it," my father said.

My father tried taking a deep breath, the corner man holding the ridges of his trunks away from his stomach.

"I can't," my father said. "Hurts too much."

"Let it go, Horse," the corner man said. "There's nothin' to prove. Not to these pricks."

"And what, quit?" my father said.

"Why not?" the corner man said. "You did what you could. You toss the towel and get the fuck outta here."

"No," my father shouted. "Hear me? No. This bullshit ends now. This round."

"Another one of those low blows'll fuck you up real good," the corner man said. "It ain't worth it."

"Yeah it is," my father said. "I can't have that prick walk around the rest of his life thinkin' he kicked my ass."

"Cons never change," the corner man said, pouring a sponge full of water over my father's head. "Okay, Horse. You wanna do this, do it. Knock this fuck out. And maybe we get outta here before they leave us both for dead."

My father and the guard moved to center ring to touch gloves for the start of round four. As they did, my father, with both feet planted down solid, right leg ahead of left, backed his body up slightly and threw a straight and solid overhand right that found its intended target, the base of the guard's unprotected jaw.

"I knew he couldn't take a punch," my father said. "Most big guys can't. The blow made his eyes glassy and wobbled his legs. He was in queer heaven and I went after him. The ref tried to step in between us, give his guy time to shake it off. I pushed that little bastard outta my way. The cocksucker was mine now. All mine."

My father shot two more rights to the guard's head. A hard left landed just under the man's heart. The guard went sprawling toward the ring ropes, and every con in the yard went silent, standing on their feet and on top of their chairs watching my father do what many of them had never seen a con do.

"I hooked him twice more under the heart," my father said. "That was it for him on the air. I hit him with four straight rights and then a left above the eye. He was headin' down, but I shouldered him. Kept him up. I wasn't finished yet. Fuckin' ref was jumping all over my back, tryin' to get me off. He couldn't do it. Him and ten other guys couldn't do it."

The guard's face was washed in blood, his arms and chest red with welts, his head and shoulders hanging over the top rope strand. My father, his body crouched, his legs bent, his feet flat, landed one unanswered blow after another, his eyes never shifting from their mark.

The bell rang, ending the fourth round, but my father kept landing, throwing punches until his arms grew weary. The guard crumpled under the attack, his lifeless legs giving way, his arms down flat by his side, both his eyes wet, bloody and fluttering.

My father threw a final punch, grazing the top of the guard's head, and then stepped back, watching his opponent drop to the ring floor.

My father stood in the center of the ring, wiping his face with the edges of his glove. The corner man jumped through the ropes, rushed up to my father and put his arms around him, slapping at his back with both hands. The cons whistled and applauded, all chanting "Horse" as one loud, unrehearsed chorus.

The guards stood facing the cons, hands wrapped around batons, staring straight ahead, in silence.

"Champion, my ass," my father said, taking one final look at the fallen guard as he was being helped to a stool in his corner. "Champion, my fuckin' ass."

VII

My father was asleep in his cell bunk. The warmth of the early winter sun was snaking its way up the cold walls. He slept naked, a thin white sheet and a brown woolen blanket spread out over his body, the top of his head exposed. He was snoring, breathing through his open mouth, his nose still clogged from the punches he took in the fight.

The four guards, brown batons in hand, marched down the cellblock corridor, walking two abreast. The sound of their shoes on the cement floor echoed throughout the silent wing. They stopped in front of my father's cell. One of the guards, middle-aged and muscular, banged his baton against the iron bars.

"Carcaterra," he said. "Shake it off. Let's go. Somebody to see you."

My father looked up from the edge of his blanket, saw the four guards and tossed the covers aside.

"Who?" my father asked, rubbing his eyes, trying to ignore the cold air.

"Fuck do I know," the guard said. "Put something on and let's go."

"Right now?" my father said.

"Right now," the guard insisted. "Move it."

They walked down the hall, my father in between the four guards. He had put on gray pants, a gray shirt, and a pair of black work shoes, no socks. My father kept both his hands inside his pants pockets.

"Early for visitors," he said to one of the guards.

"Maybe it ain't a visitor," the guard who woke him said.

"Who, the warden?" my father said.

"Walk more and talk less," the guard said. "You'll find out soon enough."

They went through three sets of gates and down two short flights of stairs. They made a wide right turn down a darkened hall and stood facing a thick wooden door, double-locked from the inside.

"This is it," one of the guards said to my father.

He knocked on the door twice, using the base of his baton instead of his knuckles. The lock clicked twice and the door swung open. A fifth guard stood holding the knob, a wide smile on his face.

"C'mon in, Horse," the guard said. "Been waitin' for you, buddy."

"What is this?" my father asked suspiciously.

"Get the fuck in there," one of the guards said, shoving my father into the room.

The four guards followed my father inside, the last one once again double-locking the door.

There was one chair in the room, hard-backed and wooden.

"Sit down, prick," one of the guards said. "Make yourself comfortable."

My father sat down and looked at the five guards around him.

"Whatta you pricks want?" he demanded.

"You gotta learn, lover boy," one of the guards said. "You fuck with one of us, you fuck with all of us."

"Who you mean?" my father said, scratching at the back of his neck. "That asshole champ of yours. That who?"

The lead guard side-armed his baton across the top of my father's head, breaking skin and drawing blood.

"Respect, lover boy," the guard said. "You're a couple of quarts low on respect. But we'll fix that. Don't worry about a thing. Just leave it to us."

"It's always gonna take five of you fuckin' bastards," my father said, "to take on one of me."

"His hands," a short, stocky guard said to the one who had swung the baton. "Don't forget about his fuckin' hands."

"Not forgettin' shit," the guard said. "We're goin' soup to nuts on this prick."

*   *   *

Two guards dragged my father back to his cell, each holding him under one arm. His head was down, the back of his shirt was thick with blood, his legs lifeless and still. His hands were swollen and he wore no shoes.

The guards walked my father into his cell and dropped him to the hard concrete floor, brushing against the bottom of his legs as they moved past.

"Your roomie's back," one of the guards said to my father's cellmate. "Go easy on him. He had a rough morning. Slippin' down all over the fuckin' place."

My father held the cold towel across his face, blood still oozing down from his forehead. His hands were puffy, his knuckles broken, his eyes closed and crusty. Both his upper and lower lips were split open.

"You gotta see the doc," my father's cellmate said to him. "And soon."

"Later," my father said, in a barely audible whisper.

"We're gonna nail the cocksuckers did this," the cellmate said. "I swear to you, Horse, we gonna nail their fuckin' asses to the bars."

"Let it go," my father said, talking slow, tossing the cold towel to the floor next to his bunk. "Leave it be."

"Fuck them," the cellmate said. "Why should we let these pricks walk away from this?"

" 'Cause it's over," my father said. "I had enough."

"You gonna need stitches on some of this shit," the cellmate said, looking over my father's wounds. "Maybe even casts for your hands."

"Help me up," my father said.

"Where you wanna go?" the cellmate said.

"No place," my father said. "Just wanna sit up."

"This is the worst one I've seen, Horse," the cellmate said. "And I've seen these pricks work over lots of cons."

"Feels like the worst," my father said, leaning his back against the cold cell wall, his feet, cracked and tinged with dried blood, hanging over the bunk.

"You gotta get back at these guys," the cellmate said. "Straight business. Can't let 'em walk. Not from this."

"I'm only gonna do one thing," my father said.

"Yeah," the cellmate said, "what?"

"Time," my father said. "My time. Now till the end. That's all. Just my time. Nothin' else."

VIII

The word in Hell's Kitchen was that my father would soon be paroled and back out on the West Side streets. Few, if any, of the people who knew him were excited at the prospect of such a return.

"Everybody dummies up their feelings in the Kitchen," my father's old friend Tony said. "That's just the way it is there. But you can tell what people think. That's not hard. And with Mario, people wanted to forget the murder, especially forget it happened right under their noses. Nobody on the street was looking forward to his coming back. I mean, what do you say to a guy who's been sent away for murdering his wife?"

During his years in prison, my father's daughter, Phyllis, was sent away to live with a favorite aunt, a sister of her mother. Grace's family never encouraged any talk about my father, content enough to raise the sad and shy girl in a loving atmosphere.

"We didn't hear much about her," Tony said. "We knew she was well, going to school, things like that. It was hard not to feel for the kid. Her mother dead for no reason. Her father in jail for murder. Not an easy way to grow. I never knew how you could do that to a kid. I liked Mario and all, but you don't do that to your kid, leave her like that, make her grow up with all those awful memories. There are at least a hundred other ways to handle problems like he had. Hundreds."

My father had made it very clear, in messages from prison through both family and friends, that his intention was to return to Hell's Kitchen, find an apartment and begin his life again. It was the

241

neighborhood he knew and felt comfortable in, a tough place with a history of understanding and tolerance for acts of violence. Especially if the crime was one of passion. Such an act, in such a sealed world, was seen, especially among the men, as the most acceptable form of murder.

"Nobody was gonna give me shit about what I done," my father said. "Not there. Not the Kitchen. It would be safe for me. Don't get me wrong. I was still nervous about it. Hell's Kitchen is one of those neighborhoods with a long memory. You never knew if some guy's nose was gonna be outta joint over what happened. But I would rather be where people knew me, whether they liked me or not, than in some strange place where nobody knew who I was. Or gave a fuck about it."

IX

My father let both his arms dangle through the opening in his cell bars. He had a lit oregano joint in his mouth and a cup of prison hootch next to his polished right boot. His face was relaxed, unlined, free of concern or worry.

It was New Year's Eve, 1952, and the cons of Comstock were preparing for a celebration.

"It was party time," my father said. "More so for me than for a lot of the other guys. It was gonna be my last year in college and I was startin' to count the days. At the same time, I wasn't in that much of a rush to get out. It's hard to explain. I had built a good life in the joint. Yeah, I had a few problems. But I had a helluva lot more problems on the outside. Comstock just seemed safer to me in most ways. There were never any surprises. I always hated surprises."

The lead guards made the call for lights out. Convicts shifted to their bunks, wrapping themselves in cold sheets and warm blankets.

The overhead lights dimmed, and the cell block eased its way into night.

"Guys would spend weeks gettin' ready for New Year's Eve," my father said. "A night like that is a big deal in the joint. Especially among lifers. In their thinkin', it was one more year they stuck it to the state. We didn't do anythin' that special. Just booze and dope made on the inside and anything good that could be smuggled from the outside. Shit like that. It was more about what you could get away with than anything else."

The guards were gone, their attention diverted toward their own planned celebration. Two convicts, in a cell down the hall from my father, banged spoon handles against the edges of their bunks. The fresh batch of hooch, made from potato skins, rubbing alcohol and anything else that could be boiled down, was hidden behind a loose cinderblock in a cell to my father's left, under the watchful eye of a lifer other cons called the Rabbi.

"He was a guy found religion in the joint," my father said. "Nice guy. Didn't bother anybody. Always walkin' around blessin' people. Even performed his own service on Saturdays. I never asked what he did got him life. That's a question you never ask. Never. Don't care who you are or what you done. Somebody tells you, okay. But, askin's out. Some cases, could even get you killed."

My father flipped a line of rope through the bottom bars and along the floor, slinking it toward the cell next to him, to his left. A convict's hand reached out from the other end. The convict held the rope, slowly wrapping it around the middle of a jelly jar half-filled with jailhouse whiskey.

Once that was done, my father dragged the jar back toward his cell. He brought it over to the side of his bunk where his cellmate waited, two empty cups in his hands.

"Every cell had a rope," my father said. "And a place to throw it to. Didn't take long for everybody to get their hootch. A half hour, maybe longer. Half a jelly jar was plenty enough to get any two guys drunk, no matter how strong your taste for hard stuff. Put that in you along with a coupla fat oregano joints and it's highway time. Takes about three days before you know where the fuck you are. I only did that kind of shit a coupla days a year, like New Year's Eve, maybe my birthday, like that. There were some guys in the joint did it every fuckin' night. Don't know how they managed it. Maybe it was just another way of them doin' time."

The prison hootch stung my father's throat, already raw from smoke from the oregano joint. My father coughed, burying his face on top of a pillow and wiping tears from his eyes. He lifted his head and took another hit from the cup.

"How's it feel?" his cellmate said. "Your last year in here."

"No different," my father said. "Still got a few months left. Not like I'm gonna walk outta here in the morning."

"A few months is nothin'," the cellmate said. "Not after you did years."

"Maybe," my father said. "It's still time, either way you cut it."

The cellmate reached down for the jelly jar and poured my father and himself three more fingers of hootch.

"What's the first thing you gonna do?" the cellmate said. "You hit the streets."

"Pay for a broad," my father said. "Get that done and outta the way from the get-go."

"Do her for me, too," the cellmate said, clinking his cup against the one my father held. "Coupla times."

"Count on it," my father said.

"What about your kid?" the cellmate said.

"What about her?" my father said.

"You gonna try and connect?" the cellmate said.

"I don't know," my father said. "Don't know what that deal is. For all I know, she thinks I'm dead. Maybe that's the best way."

"It's a tough play," the cellmate said.

"Might be better to leave it alone," my father said. "Start fresh. Clean. Get a job. Keep my head down and stay outta trouble."

"Only way," the cellmate said, pulling on a fresh oregano joint and then handing it to my father. "Don't wanna end up back here. For damn sure."

"Bet your ass," my father said. "Be clean and stay clean."

"Meet somebody," the cellmate said. "Get a brand-new family in no time."

"You mean get married?" my father asked, surprised.

"Why not?" the cellmate said. "Still legal, ain't it?"

"Been married," my father said, taking a full drag from the herb weed. "Got me no place but here. Ain't for me. Maybe other guys. But not for me."

My father put his empty cup under his pillow and passed the last half of the joint to his cellmate. He jumped up onto his bunk and slid under the sheet and blanket, dizzy from the whiskey and dope.

"I'm done, buddy," he said. "Calling it a night."

"You sure?" the cellmate said, holding up the empty jelly jar. "I could get us a coupla more rounds."

"Not me," my father said. "I'm shit-faced enough the way it is."

"Sleep it off, Horse," the cellmate said. "I'll still be here when you wake up."

"Happy New Year," my father said, burying his head under the covers.

"You, too," the cellmate said, putting a match to a joint.

At midnight, while my father slept, a half-dozen convicts twirled prison-made party favors. A handful of others whistled and slammed cups and spoons against the bars and walls of their cells.

All welcoming in a new year.

X

My father won his parole and walked out of Comstock a free man in the spring of 1953. He had spent nearly six years behind bars, including an eleven-month stint at the Tombs. The prison parole board deemed my father a model convict and judged him an unlikely repeat offender.

He walked out of jail the same way he walked in, wearing the same jacket and hat he had had on the day he murdered his wife.

Before he was cut loose, my father was handed $47.42 by a prison official, payment for work done during the course of his sentence.

"It felt good to get out," he told me. "Real good. Get a chance to breathe real air, not those prison clouds. No more livin' tight, guys right on top of you, watchin' your every move. That first day out was one of my best days ever. Meant more than any other day of my life. Had everything in front of me, you know. Was startin' out with a clean plate. All my fuck-ups were behind me. In the past. The future was mine. Belonged to nobody else but me."

Book Four

THE PAST IS NOT A PACKAGE ONE CAN LAY AWAY.

—Emily Dickinson

I

It was mid-September, 1969. I sat on a wooden chair in the back room of my high school library, searching through rolls of microfilm for any details about my father's crime. I scrolled past the pages of every late-1946 edition of *The New York Times*, looking for his name. It was warm in the room, so I stood up to remove my blue jacket, my eyes never leaving the dark green monitor in front of me. I folded the jacket at the waist and tossed it on a chair to my left. I rolled up the sleeves of my white shirt, stopping at the elbow, and freed the top button.

Then I saw it.

The item that proved my mother did not lie.

It was on page three of the newspaper's Metropolitan section, dated November 1, 1946, buried in a lower right-hand slot, with a short headline that summarized its contents.

For the next hour I studied and stared at the following item:

HEARING ON STRANGLING SET

The mystery of the strangling of Mrs. Grace Carcaterra, 24 years old, last Monday in a room at the Mayfair Hotel on West Forty-ninth Street appeared to have been solved yesterday in the Homicide Court. Her husband, Mario, 29, a part-time chef, of 112 West Sixty-fourth Street, was said to have admitted he strangled her with a pillow in a rage because she told him she was in love with another man. Carcaterra was remanded to the Tombs by Magistrate Abner C. Surpless to await a hearing Nov. 14.

I took a copy of the page from the Xerox machine, folded it in four, and shoved it into the back pocket of my blue slacks. I rolled down the sleeves of my shirt and grabbed my jacket from the table.

"Did you find what you were looking for?" the librarian asked, watching me as I gathered my books.

"Yes," I said. "I'm afraid I did."

I had been back from Italy just under three weeks and was doing all I could to avoid my father. I stayed at school late, logging longer hours in the gym and the library. I also found an after-school job, three evenings a week and half a morning on Saturday, in an East Bronx dry cleaner, working for an old man with a severe lung condition.

"It's the fumes from cleaning the clothes," he told me. "All these years. All these clothes. All these fumes. It adds up. Trust me."

"Ever think of retiring?" I said.

"And do what?" he said. "Live with you? This is my business. My job. What I do."

"How long you been here?" I said.

"Since the area was all Jewish," he said.

"When was that?"

"Nineteen fifty-one," he said. "After that, the Italians and the Irish started coming in. That was okay. Still safe. But now, the blacks are coming in. That's not so good."

"Why not?"

"Getting robbed three times in one year reason enough for you?"

he said. "Who knows how many times I get held up this year. Maybe even get shot a couple of times."

"They take clothes?" I asked. "Or just money?"

"Money," he said. "They have the clothes. It's the money they don't have."

"How much they take?"

"Doesn't matter how much," he said. "What matters is they took. It takes the pleasure out of a business. I'm glad I have to put up with it for only a few more years."

"Why's that?" I said.

"My time's about up," he said. "I'll be dead soon enough. Then they can steal the whole building for all I care."

I stood next to him, watching his shaky and vein-riddled old hands count out money from the register, the last step before shutting the store for the night.

"I love listening to you," I said.

"Really?" he said, not looking up from his count. "Why? Why would a young man like yourself like to listen to an old man like me?"

"Because you cheer me up," I said.

"Come back tomorrow," he said, looking up, a half smile on his face. "I'll tell you about the time they came after me. With a knife."

"Did you almost die?" I said.

"You bet," he said.

"I'll be here," I said. "Early."

II

During the cab ride home from the airport, I had sat in the backseat next to my father. My mother was up front, trying hard to fall asleep, already having voiced her concern about the excessive speed of the cab.

"It's good to have you back, One-punch," my father said, slapping a hand across my knee. "I missed you."

"Thanks," I said.

"How'd you like it?" he said. "Over there I mean."

"Loved it," I said. "Didn't want to come back."

"So I hear," he said. "Maybe, next big score I make, we all move there. That work for you?"

"Maybe," I said. "Let's wait for the score first."

"What's that fuckin' mean?" he said. "It ain't gonna happen—that what you sayin'?"

"Nothing, Dad," I said, slumping down farther in my seat and shutting my eyes. "I didn't mean anything by it. I'm just tired from the trip. That's all."

"Sleep then," my father said. "We'll talk later. We got plenty of time for it."

"That we do," I said.

"We'll sit down together," my father said. "Figure out where you fit in."

"Fit in to what?" I said, opening my eyes and looking over at him.

"My new business," my father said, gripping my arm. "I can't wait to tell ya about it. I'm makin' you my full partner."

"What do you mean?" I said. "Partner in what?"

"Tell you later," my father said. "When you're not so tired."

"Is this another can't-miss deal?" I said. "Another sure thing?"

"Where the fuck is that from?" my father said.

"Nothin'," I said. "Forget it. It's nothing."

"Nothin' my fuckin' ass," my father said, raising his voice in anger. "You get off that plane with a fuckin' chip on your shoulder? 'Cause if you did we stop this cab right here, right now, and turn her back. Hear me? Put you back on that plane. You and the cold-hearted bitch up front."

"It's nothin'," I said. "I didn't mean anything by it. Honest."

"All right," my father said. "Get some sleep. We'll cut our deal later."

"Okay," I said, once again closing my eyes.

"This is the one," my father said, turning his head toward the passing traffic. "I just know it. This is the one's gonna make us all rich. Make us all fuckin' rich. You'll see. You'll all see."

As I got older, the attention my father focused on his get-rich schemes and elaborate con games dramatically increased. He would stay on a job just long enough to bring his next plan to fruition. During the weeks and months it would take to bring the scam to life, my father seldom missed a day's work, and spent his free afternoons staring out our living room window, mapping out his thoughts, a pen and note-pad always nearby.

At times, the scams he hatched were simple ones, nothing more complicated than borrowing money from coworkers without any intentions of a payback. My father would then dump the take from what he called "friendly loans" inside a local OTB office or with a candy store bookie, always looking to double his score on the legs of a fast horse running a slow track.

Other times the schemes were elaborate ones, thought out, well focused and well executed.

Once, over a six-month period of time, my father conned eight thousand dollars from my half-brother's wife, and never paid it back.

Across the months of one particularly grueling summer, my father duped seven of his own cousins out of a total of $17,400, promising each a full pension in the meat packer's union in return for their investments.

As always, the money from these hauls was used to bet on horses and buy presents for people my father felt he needed to impress.

"He knew which buttons to push," my half-brother's wife, Clara, said. "With me, he worked on the idea that no one liked him or trusted him, that all he needed was a chance. By lending him all that money, I gave him a chance to prove everyone wrong. He would say whatever he had to say to get whatever it was he wanted. He was smart in that way. Very smart."

The money my father would con, borrow and sometimes steal was never brought into any of the places my mother and I lived. It was spent elsewhere, on other people, living in other places, in conditions far superior to our own.

My father took care of friends and corrupt union officials in need of appliances or loans. He willingly came to the aid of family members strapped for food and cash. It never mattered to him how he got the money that fed his largess. The bigger the scam, the happier he seemed. His life was one large revolving con game, played against anyone who happened to cross his path.

He also knew that when the scam ended and the strangers came calling, my mother would be there to dig him out of the trouble he had created, the kind of gullible partner to answer any con man's dreams.

"I made do with the money he earned when he worked," my mother said. "I would set aside as much as I could from what he gave me off the weekly paychecks. Put it in a savings account. He made a good salary when he worked, and I was able to deposit as much as fifty, sometimes sixty, dollars a week. That was enough to cover us in the months he didn't work."

Our first home away from Hell's Kitchen was a dank and tiny three-room basement apartment at 4327 Boyd Avenue in the northeast Bronx. The floors were cement hard, each room cold and narrow. The building, a three-story private house with a large garden, was owned by a retired man who walked with a limp and always had a lit pipe in his mouth.

The apartment was low enough that, from each open window, we could see the legs of passersby as they walked; we could touch the concrete sidewalks with our hands.

"It was a horrible place for anyone to live in," my half-brother, Anthony, said. "I hated to come for Sunday visits. It would break my heart seeing my mother in such a place. People would walk their dogs past the kitchen window or toss cigarettes or garbage as they passed by. But your father loved it there. You would look at him sitting in this tiny living room, barely big enough to hold a couch and a TV, big smile always on his face. You'd think he was on a throne in the middle of some large palace."

The tension between me and my father grew in the years after I was told about his murderous past. He sensed something was wrong, felt my coldness toward him grow by the day, but he said nothing.

I was eager not to confront him, to avoid tossing my knowledge about his crime back into his face. I needed time, both to sort out what I knew about the murder and to find out everything I could about that day and the moments that led up to it.

I just hadn't a clue as to how to go about it.

III

"Go get the car," my father said. "I wanna go see my sister."

"What for?" I said. "We were just there last week."

"Whatta you, my parole officer?" my father said. "Just go get the fuckin' car. I need some air."

"We're low on gas," I said. "And I'm low on money to get gas."

"Don't worry about it," my father said. "I got a few bucks. We'll make it. Now, c'mon. Enough with the bullshit. Let's hit the road."

It was my first car, a green and rusty four-door Toyota Corolla, paid for with portions of a $1,500 North Side Savings Bank loan, taken out a week past my sixteenth birthday. My mother had argued against both the loan and the purchase, but my father insisted on the need for a family car.

"Be nice to have," my father said to her. "We don't need nobody if we wanna go out."

"We don't go anywhere," my mother replied.

"That's because we ain't got a fuckin' car," my father said. "Plentya places we could go if we have a car."

"We don't need to take out a loan," my mother said. "We don't need any more bills."

255

"Fuck the bills," my father said. "What, am I askin' you to go out and lug meat? Am I? No. Don't worry yourself about any of the bills. That's my department."

"We get calls every day," my mother said. "People want their money. What am I supposed to tell them—you're out buying a family car?"

My father jumped up from the kitchen chair he was sitting in, kicking it back behind him with his right foot. He grabbed my mother by the front of her open house apron and pushed her down to the floor, the side of her head hitting the base of the stove.

"You don't tell them shit," my father said. " 'Cause you don't *know* shit. Understand me, you fuckin' bitch? You know why they call? I'll tell you why. It's those fuckin' friends of yours, the ones you're always yappin' away with. They open their fuckin' mouths to anybody. They don't give a shit."

"What friends?" my mother said, crying. "I don't have any friends. They're all afraid to be seen with me."

My father kicked my mother twice in the chest and once across the back. He picked up a glass, half-filled with ice water, from the table and threw it down at her, watching as it shattered on the cement floor, shards landing across her face and neck.

"You don't talk to anybody," my father said. "You hear me? I don't give a fuck if the Pope himself rings the fuckin' doorbell. Nobody you talk to. I'll kill ya, I get a call I ain't supposed to get."

My father walked past my mother and into the bedroom several feet away. He came out wearing a zippered windbreaker and a hat.

"I gotta go out," my father said. "Get your ass off the floor and get me some money. Twenty dollars'd be good. Thirty'd be better. I got business to take care of. Wasted enough fuckin' time hangin' around here."

I veered the car left onto the Grand Central Parkway, still uneasy behind the wheel, uncomfortable with the feel of speed. The radio was tuned in to an AM rock 'n' roll station. My father sat to my right, both hands jammed inside his jacket pocket, his hat on his lap, staring out the window.

I felt uneasy around my father, especially in my teenage years, his presence a visible reminder of a murder I needed to know more about. Any conversation we had in that time was driven forward by either anger or sheer necessity, both of us keenly aware we were in the early rounds of a battle that didn't hold much promise for winner or loser.

"You decide yet?" my father said, suddenly enough to startle me.

"Decide what?" I said.

"What you gonna do?" he said. "You know, after you finish school."

"You mean what kind of work?" I said.

"Yeah," he said. "What you want to be? A doctor, a lawyer, a banker, what?"

"A writer," I said. "On a newspaper."

"A writer?" he said. "Where the fuck you get that?"

"I don't know," I said. "You asked me what kind of work I wanted to do. Well, that's what I want to do."

"Business," my father said. "That's what you should do. That's where the money's at. You want my opinion, this writing crap is horseshit. A waste of fuckin' time."

"I didn't ask for your opinion," I said. "And I don't want it."

"You used to want it," my father said. "There was a time my opinion was the only fuckin' thing you *did* want. Now you could give a fuck. You don't need the old man. You just need his money."

"Money?" I said. "What money?"

"What money?" my father said, lifting himself up higher in the car seat. "You ungrateful little prick, who you think's paying for that fancy school you go to every fuckin' day?"

"Save that one," I said, slowing the car as traffic ahead of me built up. "You want to tell your family you pay for my school that's okay by me. Brag all you want. Just don't do it in front of me."

"Who you think pays for it, wise guy?" my father said. "Who? Your grandmother in Italy? You believe that shit your mother feeds you. Do you?"

"No, Dad," I said. "You pay for it. You just use Grandma Maria's money to do it."

My father pulled a hand from inside his jacket pocket and slapped me across the side of my face, knuckles side up and curled into a half-fist.

"Fuck you, prick," my father said. "You hear me? Fuck you. Don't tell anybody you're my son. You understand? Don't tell anybody you're my fuckin' son."

"Don't worry, Dad," I said. "I never do."

IV

In 1973, I was eighteen years old and a college student, and still no closer to understanding the truth about my father than I was on that day on the beach in Ischia.

My obsession with my father's crime had continued to grow and was being reflected more and more in my everyday existence. His murder impacted on nearly everything I did, from the books I read, to the movies I saw, to the places I visited. The vision of my father, a pillow in both hands, his wife struggling under his weight, never once left me through all that time.

I was a nervous young man during those years, unsure of what my father's actions meant to me, afraid of ever finding out the truth behind them.

I was afraid that my father was a stone killer who would do to me and my mother what he had done to his first wife. I feared the secrets he had kept from me, and dreaded how the revelation of those secrets would follow me for the rest of my life. I convinced myself that my father would find a way to kill again and that I could not escape being there when he did.

I didn't socialize much in or out of high school, preferring, for the most part, my own company and counsel. I never confided in anyone, never had friends see where I lived, choosing to spend the major portions of any free time I had away from the Bronx, a safe distance from my father.

What I knew about my father shaped and affected a number of distinct changes in my personality. I was no longer talkative, my gears switched to a quiet and often sullen stance. I also fed and nurtured the private feeling that one day someone close would die by my hand.

"It was a strange thing to see," Anthony's wife, Clara, told me later. "You would be over for an afternoon visit, sitting on the couch, watching a movie, relaxed, happy. Then you would go blank, an empty look on your face, as if you saw something or felt something you didn't want to see or didn't want to feel. Nothing was ever said. It was just a look. A very lonely look."

At the same time, I lived with the fear that people would find out about my parents, the debts they had and the manner in which they lived their lives. I didn't want anyone to know about the beatings my mother still received, or the angry calls that came to us in the middle of the night armed with threats, or even about the stolen desk my father gave me one year as a Christmas gift.

There was no one I trusted enough to confide in, no one to turn to for advice or help. My mother was pained enough over the turns of her life; discussing them would only sadden her further. She saw herself as a prisoner, a woman without options, trapped in a marriage whose failure was evident and whose end could well lead to her death.

I passed through the hours of each and every day convinced that news of my father's crime would leak out and everyone, from stranger to neighbor, would know the dark secret kept in my heart.

My biggest fear, however, and the one that kept me awake most nights, dreading the night in my Bronx apartment as much as my father had dreaded it in his prison cell, was that he would kill again. Stuff a pillow over my mother's face, ending her life in the same way he had closed Grace's eyes for the final time.

My relationship with my father collapsed as this internal trauma played itself out in both my life and my mind. The silent weight wedged between us was too much for either one to handle. He knew I had been asking questions about him, making calls, writing letters, trying to get some truth out of relatives, friends, enemies, looking for anyone willing to give up information about his early years.

My father never said a word to me about any of it, smart enough to sense I no longer trusted him or liked being around him.

"It was tough for me," my father later remembered. "I had already lost one kid, my daughter. Now I was losing my son. Except this time, I couldn't figure out what the hell it was I'd done. First, I thought it was the loans, the money we owed out. Then I figured it was the fightin' I was doin' with the old lady. But I'd owed out money and been fightin' her since you were in diapers. There was nothin' new there. Nothin' that would make you hate me. And believe you me, you hated me. Hated my fuckin' guts. There were days when I was sure you'd kill me if you had half a chance. You had that look in your eye. It's a look I know. Trust me, kid. That's one look I know."

V

I was sitting in the kitchen of my aunt Mary's Long Island home. My father's youngest sister was a small, intense woman whose company I sought when the craziness at home became too much to bear. I loved her and trusted her more than I did any other member of my father's family.

Aunt Mary handed me a platter filled with scrambled eggs, strips of crisp bacon and two pieces of white toast, buttered and sliced. She poured us both a cup of coffee and sat down across the table from me.

"You want ketchup for those eggs?" she said.

"No," I said. "I'm good."

"More bacon?" she asked. "I made plenty."

"No thanks," I said. "This is more than enough. Really."

Aunt Mary dropped a spoonful of sugar into her coffee and stirred the mix, smiling as she did.

"You said you wanted to talk about something?" she said. "Now's a good time. Everybody's still asleep."

I chewed my eggs, looking past my aunt's shoulder at the tree-clustered backyard behind her, the warmth of the early Sunday morning sun cutting through the windows.

"It's about my father," I said. "I want to talk to you about my father."

"What's wrong?" she asked, putting her cup down. "Is he sick?"

"No. He's not sick."

"He in trouble?"

"He's always in trouble," I said. "I'm sort of used to that by now."

My aunt reached across the small table and put one of her hands on top of mine. Her eyes were warm and caring, her handsome face lined with concern.

"What is it?" she said. "Tell me."

"I know about his wife," I said. "I know what he did to her."

"I figured you would find out," she said. "Some day. It was only a question of when."

She stood up and walked over to the stove, one hand out, reaching for the pot of coffee. Her head was down, her shoulders slumped.

"How'd you find out?" she said, coming back and pouring us both a fresh cup.

"My mother told me," I said. "A few years back."

"I wish she hadn't," Aunt Mary said, wiping tears from both her eyes with the palm of one hand. "You'd have been better off not knowing."

"Too late for that," I said. "Now I need to know as much as I can."

"Why?" she said. "What good will it do you?"

"I don't know," I said. "I don't have enough answers to know anything yet."

"What do you want to know?" she said, blowing her nose into a tissue, her eyes still moist. "How much more is there?"

"You tell me," I said.

"There isn't much I can tell you," she said. "It was a sad and ugly time for us that happened long ago. We've all tried so hard to forget. I wish you would, too."

"Aunt Mary," I said. "Believe me. I wish I could forget. I wish I could get it out of my head. But I can't. I've tried and I just can't."

"Then learn to live with it," Aunt Mary said. "It's your only other choice."

"That's not going to be easy," I said.

"It's not supposed to be easy," she said. "But it can be done."

"You can live with it?" I said.

"Yes," she said. "I do. It's the only way. You'll find that out as you get older."

"What if I can't?" I said.

"That's a question only you can answer," Aunt Mary said. "Nobody else. Only you."

She pushed her chair back, finished the last of her coffee and stood up.

"I have to get ready for church," she said. "You coming along?"

"Think it'll help?" I asked, a smile on my face.

"It won't hurt," Aunt Mary said.

She stopped and kissed me on the cheek and forehead before heading to her upstairs bedroom to change clothes in time for the twelve o'clock Mass.

VI

The second hard slap across my mother's face woke me. I tossed aside the covers and jumped to the floor. My father was standing to my left, one leg braced against my open sofa bed, one hand holding my mother by the hair. His face was flushed red and his free hand was ready to strike again. He turned away from my mother to look at me.

"Get back in bed," he said. "You're not in this."

"Let her go," I said, surprisingly calm. "Just let her go."

"Get back in that bed," he said. "Get the fuck back in that bed. Now."

"Listen to him," my mother said to me in a shaky voice. "Please. Do what he wants."

"You feel like hittin' somebody?" I said. "Then hit *me*. Let her go. And hit *me*."

My father shoved my mother against the wall nearest the kitchen, the back of her head dislodging the phone from its cradle.

"C'mon, punk," my father said, turning to me, punching his chest with his right fist. "I'm here. You want a piece a me, I'm here."

My father cornered me between the sofa bed and the TV set, both my arms wedged by my side. The first punch he threw grazed the top of my head. The second, a left hook coming off planted feet, landed just under my heart.

"I've taken all the shit I'm gonna take," my father said. "From you and her."

My father landed a right hand against my shoulder and then another flush to my jaw. The force of both blows buckled my legs and blurred my vision. I grabbed the side of the television and held myself up, feeling my father's warm breath coming down on me.

"Stop it," my mother screamed behind him. "Stop it. He's your son. He's your son."

My father turned away from me and stalked his way toward my mother, his body coiled and controlled, his fists closed and ready, his breathing nasal, heavy. He swung a punch at my mother, the fist hitting her chest, landing just above her right breast. He followed with a short kick to her lower back, sending her down to the floor moaning in pain.

I stood behind my father, just over his right shoulder. I looked at my mother on the ground by his feet and him towering over her, ready to hit again if she dared to move.

I closed my right hand into a fist and edged myself away from the bed. I looked down at my hands and feet and took in a deep breath, feeling the thin line of sweat making its way down the small of my back.

Then, for the first time in my life, I hit my father, three knuckles landing just above his right eye.

He turned his head and body to face me, surprised more than hurt by the punch.

"Not many sons hit their own father," he said, touching at his eye with an open hand. "Not many I know anyway."

"Don't ever hit her again," I said in a nervous voice. "Ever again."

"And what if I do?" my father said smiling. "What? You gonna kill me? That it? That where you wanna take this? Kill the old man so you and her can make off with my money."

"It's over," I said. "You feel like hittin' somebody, hit a man, not a woman."

"That you?" my father said. "A man. Is that what you are now? A fuckin' man?"

"Get out of here," I said. "Go where you gotta go. Just leave. We've had enough. Everybody's had enough."

"You're dead to me," my father said. "You hear? Dead. You piece of shit. Dead. Anybody asks, I don't got a son. He died a long time ago."

"I wish I could say the same," I said. "About my father."

"Say it," he said. "I give a fuck."

"I don't have to say it," I said. "Just feel it."

"You and me don't talk," he said. "Ever again. Look the other way when you see me. I'll do the same when I see you. You and me ain't father and son. We're strangers."

He turned away from me and stepped over my mother, heading for the door out of the apartment.

"Happy now, bitch?" he said to my mother before he left. "You got what you wanted. Took you a long time, but you finally got what the fuck you wanted."

He stared at me and then at my mother for a few more seconds, put a fedora over the top of his head and slammed the glass-framed door shut behind him.

I held my stance until I no longer heard his footsteps on the sidewalk outside.

VII

It was the night of my twentieth birthday, and my mother had bought a small Italian cake to celebrate. We sat alone, the two of us, sipping espresso in the kitchen at Boyd Avenue, a table lamp our only light.

I watched as she cut a thick slice of cake and dropped it on a dessert plate that was chipped on two sides. Her hands shook, the joints below the knuckles puffy. She looked much older than she was, the years of debts and abuse taking a cold, physical toll.

"Sorry I couldn't get you a present," she said, handing me the plate. "It's been a bad week."

"It's okay," I said. "I got what I need."

"How's the cake?" she said. "They made it fresh today. I was there when it came out of the oven."

"It's great," I said between mouthfuls. "Thanks."

"It's not too sweet?" she asked. "Sometimes they make it too sweet."

"No, Mom," I said. "Really. It's great. Thanks for getting it."

"Let me get you some more coffee," she said, grabbing my cup and reaching for the pot and a refill. When she finished, she pushed the cup back toward my end of the table.

"Drink it while it's hot," she said. "It helps keep your heart going."

"You sound just like Grandma," I said. "Except you don't put pieces of chocolate in the coffee."

"It's because we don't have any," my mother said.

"I miss her," I said. "Miss everybody over there."

"So do I," she said. "More each day that passes."

"But you won't go back," I said. "I can't understand that."

"What's so hard to understand," my mother said. "My family is here. Not there."

"Family?" I said. "What family? Tony? He's married. Me? I can take care of myself. Who else? Him? You're stayin' here because of him?"

"He's my husband," my mother said. "It's my place to be where he is."

"That's crazy," I said. "You sound like some woman from another time. Another place."

"I am," my mother said. "I know how people think today. One marriage after another, what's the difference. Half the time, they don't even bother to get married. That's okay for them. But not for me. I feel different about these things."

"Mom, listen to me," I said. "He beats you whenever he feels like it. He owes money to everybody he knows. He keeps us living in this dump. What's the point? What the hell's the point?"

"It's the bed I made for myself," my mother said. "And the one I'll keep until I die. Or he dies."

"Or kills you," I said. "Is that what you want? Is that what we've been waiting for all these years?"

"No, it's not," my mother said.

"Then what is it?" I said. "Why can't we just pack up and leave?"

"What would you do there?" my mother said. "How would you live? This is your country. You belong here. Your life is going to be here. Your future."

"I'll work for Uncle Mario," I said. "I'll drive a bus. A cab. Anything. I don't care, Mom. I really don't care."

"Yes you do," my mother said. "Not now, maybe. But as you get older. You will care then."

"So we're stuck," I said. "You know he'll never stop. Never stop. You know why he won't? The real reason? Because he knows that as long as you and me are here, there'll be somebody to bail him out. Somebody to pay his debts. Christ, we send money every month to people we don't even know. Haven't ever met."

"Maybe," she said. "Maybe one day he'll see what he's doing to you. And to me."

"Like he gives a shit," I said. "He only cares about food in his belly and money in his pocket. Other people's money."

"Then don't be like him," she said. "Ever."

"*Be* like him?" I said. "I don't even want to be near him, let alone like him. You can forget that one."

"Do you want some more coffee?" my mother said, looking sad and old. "Another piece of cake?"

"No, thanks," I said, pushing my way from the table. "I'm going for a walk. I need some air. You want anything while I'm out?"

"No," my mother said. "I don't need anything. Not today."

I left her there, her head bowed, a cup of espresso before her, sitting at the kitchen table, alone. She waved a weak goodbye and pulled a set of rosary beads out of the front pocket of the torn apron she wore every day.

As I closed the door, my mother began to pray.

VIII

Not all our days together were dark ones. There were enough happy times, spread out unevenly through the years, to occasionally give rise to hope, a glimmer that the ugliness of our lives might finally be placed behind us.

My parents fought one another on a fairly regular basis, the echoes of their yells, screams and slaps heard throughout the hallways of any building we ever lived in. But they also laughed with one another, often at a pace as fast and as furious as their fighting.

My mother and father had a horrible marriage and a difficult friendship. Yet their relationship was a complete one, if to no other set of eyes but their own.

"Marriage is supposed to be hard," my mother said. "I don't know where people get the idea it's supposed to be easy. A woman once told me marriage was like a constant pain in the side. In time, you learn to live with the pain. I had a difficult time with your father. But we stayed together. It's what people like us do. There was a lot of hurt, a lot of anger, and that pain in the side was sometimes impossible to bear. But we stayed together. We did what we were supposed to do."

The three of us sat side by side, my mother settled in at the far right end of the couch, next to a brown coffee table that held a cracked lamp, sipping from a cup of Lipton tea with milk and sugar. My father sat on the left, a cold mug of seltzer and ice lightly balanced on one bare knee. I sat in the middle, staring at our nineteen-inch Zenith black-and-white television, a Christopher Columbus flower boat positioned over the middle of the screen, flanked by three framed pictures of my nieces and nephew.

Two Bronx neighbors, Louie and Ada, a painter and his wife, sat across from us, a full bowl of pretzels crunched between them. All waiting for the start of *The Perry Como Christmas Special*, with guest star Claudine Longet.

A Perry Como special was a twice-a-year ritual in our home, and the only time my parents warmly welcomed guests. The South Philadelphia barber turned singer had a near cult following among Italian-Americans, and none were more fanatical in their devotion to him than my mother.

She saw Como as the complete and ideal man, a gifted singer, religious and deeply devoted to his wife and family. My father watched the specials only out of habit, even though he was as teary-eyed as my mother whenever Como hit those "Ave Maria" high notes.

I watched because I was told to.

"You want to be a good man," my mother said. "Be like Perry. Copy him. Don't be like his friend."

"Who's his friend?" I said.

"Dean Martin," my mother said, taking another sip from her tea. "That bum. I don't watch his show anymore. Not since he left Jeannie."

"Who's Jeannie?" I said.

"His wife," my mother said. "He left her and the kids."

"For another woman," Ada said. "A younger one."

"It's just as well," my father said. "I never cared for him. Can't sing for shit."

Como appeared on screen, surrounded by well-lit trees and fake falling snow, the sounds of an off-camera chorus filling our tiny living room. He was wearing a cream-colored sweater and slacks, his white hair and gentle face perfectly suited to the mood around him. The first song, sung softly but with passion, was "Silver Bells."

"He looks so young," Ada said in Italian. "He never gets old."

"He leads a good life," my mother said, looking over at my father. "He loves his wife."

"How do you know he loves his wife?" I said.

"I know," my mother said.

"I know, too," Ada said.

"Must be true then," I said.

Claudine Longet came on to sing something in French. Her hair was in the flipped-up Alberto VO5 fashion of the day, her dress short and tight, her voice an Alvin and the Chipmunks squeak.

"She's not a bad actress, this kid," my father said.

"She's blind," Louie said.

"She's not blind," my mother said. "She played a blind girl on *Combat*."

"Oh," Louie said. "I thought she was blind."

"Vic Morrow saved her," my father said. "From the Germans."

"I can't watch that show," Ada said. "Vic Morrow looks like my brother Dominick, God rest his soul."

Como was back on screen, his arm around the shoulders of a smiling little boy, no older than ten, dressed in a button-down shirt and black bow tie.

"That must be his grandson," my mother said. "Looks just like him."

"How many kids does he have?" my father said.

"Five, I think," Ada said. "Maybe six."

"And they all love him," my mother said, looking directly at me. "A good man is always loved."

During the commercials Louie and my father talked horses, Ada and my mother talked numbers.

"I had such a dream last night," Ada said. "Dark clouds all around me. Heavy rain and fog. I think it means Louie is going to die this month."

"That's the death number," my mother said. "One hundred and sixteen. You should play it. You'll win.'

"That way you'll have money," my father said. "To pay for Louie's funeral."

"I had a dream about my father last night," my mother said.

"What did he do?" Ada said.

"I was washing clothes by the sink," my mother said. "And he came up to me and told me to play one hundred and five."

"Your father told you to bet on a number?" I said. "Why would he do that?"

"He wants to give us money," my father said.

"Do me a favor?" my mother said to me. "Get up early tomorrow. Go to the candy store. Put two dollars on one hundred and five. But get there before he opens for business."

"Why?" I said.

"First one there always wins," my mother said.

"Candy store opens at six," I said. "That's crazy."

"Do what your mother tells you," my father said. "You lazy bastard."

Ten minutes before the end of the hour-long special, Perry Como began to sing "Ave Maria." Everyone sat silently, listening to their favorite singer and their favorite song. Louie put out his cigarette and stopped munching pretzels. My father put down his seltzer glass. My mother emptied her tea cup. Ada rolled her gum from her mouth and put it in an ashtray.

Halfway through the song, they were all sitting there crying openly, each reaching for tissues to dab softly at the corners of their eyes.

"So beautiful," my mother said. "Just so beautiful."

"It's a gift," Ada said. "From heaven."

"Like an angel," my mother said. "He sings like an angel."

"An angel from heaven," Ada said.

My father gave me a hard tap on the shoulder. I turned to look at him, saw the tears welled in his eyes, his cheeks flushed red, a tissue wrapped around the knuckles of his right hand.

"Don't forget," he said to me.

"Forget what?" I said.

"To lay down that bet tomorrow morning," he said. "I don't wanna get fucked outta that money."

"Song really got through to you," I said.

"Don't forget, smartass," he said. "Just don't forget."

IX

I was staring at a $1,200 Macy's bill when the phone rang. I picked it up on the third ring. It was my father's voice, cracked and scared, at the other end.

"What is it?" I said.

"You gotta come get me," he said. "Come get me now. Before I kill myself."

"Six thousand," I said. "A guy was here yesterday morning asking me for six thousand dollars. Said it was all he had and he gave it to you. Trusted you with it."

"Somebody stole it," my father said. "I swear on my mother's grave, somebody stole it."

"Where are you?" I said. "Where you calling from?"

"Downtown," my father said. "The Empire Hotel. I'm lookin' out the window of my room. On the ninth floor. I'm gonna throw myself out. I swear to God, kid. I'm goin' out. I got no other choice."

"You want me to stop you?" I said. "That it?"

"Gonna kill myself before they come and kill me," he said.

"Who's going to kill you this time?" I asked wearily.

"The guys that took the money," my father said. "They gonna come back. Finish me off."

"Dad, why'd you call?" I said.

"Let me talk to Mom," my father said. "I wanna say goodbye to my baby before I go."

"She's not here," I said. "She and Ada went to church. Probably throwin' a few prayers your way."

We stayed silent for a few moments, aware only of each other's breathing, coming in short whiffs across the telephone lines.

"Hey, One-punch," my father finally said, in a low voice colored sad. "You still there?"

"Yeah," I said. "I'm still here."

"Do me a favor, then, would ya?" he said.

"What?"

"Come get me," my father said. "Please, One-punch. Come get me outta here."

"Give me an hour," I said.

I laid the phone back in its cradle, put on a denim jacket and went outside, locking the apartment door behind me. A neighbor was washing his new car, sponging down the hood and side doors with soapy water from a bucket by his feet, the car radio blasting out Bobby Darin and "Mack the Knife."

Across the way, another neighbor listened to a Puccini opera from a cassette in a boom box on her porch as she quietly trimmed the tips of her hedges. A white miniature poodle followed her as she made her cuts.

271

I waved to both of them, started up my car and headed for Manhattan.

To bring my father home.

My relationship with my father had evolved in the years since I found out about his crime. As we got older, our roles seemed to reverse. He seemed more dependent on me, emotionally and financially, and I less so on him. He was wary of me now, especially since our first physical confrontation. He avoided arguments with me, not out of any fear of what might happen, but because he just didn't want to hear words of hate aimed in his direction. He felt my dislike for him and it hurt. I knew it did, but I did nothing to change it.

"Your hatred helped to kill me," he said to me toward the end, when he was dying in his hospital bed. "I can beat cancer. Easy. But I can't beat a son who hates me. No father ever can."

The debts my father accumulated were getting harder and harder to pay off, but we always found a way. My mother was the most dependable bail-out, coming up with ready cash from the two rental apartments she had inherited from Grandma Maria. I pitched in with table money from my *Daily News* salary. In a pinch, my father would borrow from a Household Finance line of credit or would pay off his loans with credit-card-bought appliances—washing machines and heavy-duty dryers in cold weather, air conditioners and dishwashers in hot.

Each new debt locked us deeper into the life my father seemed to prefer. Plans could never be made and holidays were always dreaded; the apartments we lived in were cramped and poor, and our furniture was old and torn. Money for clothes and expenses was always difficult to find, since everything we had always found its way into the hands and pockets of strangers.

"We must have bought twenty washing machines from Macy's," my mother said. "God only knows how many air conditioners and dishwashers. Your father loved paying off his debts with appliances. Those people at Macy's must have thought we lived in a mansion. Little did they know where those machines were going."

X

I stood before a concrete counter on the eleventh floor of 100 Centre Street, in lower Manhattan, filling out a short form requesting the transcripts of my father's trial.

"Jesus Christ," the court clerk, overweight and bald, said, holding the form closer to his eyes. "This is from 1946. That stuff's in the subbasement. I don't even know if my guys can find it. Wait here. Hold on. Let me check the books. See if it's even in there."

I watched him walk slowly behind a long row of dirty brown ledgers, the back flap of his uniform shirt hanging over his belt loops.

"Here it is," he said, his voice buried under a pile of ledgers. "Carcaterra, Mario. Manslaughter two. Five-to-fifteen. That the one?"

"Yes, it is," I said, trying to ignore the cold sweat on my back and forehead. "That's the one."

The clerk put the ledger bearing my father's name back in its slot. He walked around the row of documents, making his way back to me.

"You know this guy?" the clerk asked, handing me another form to fill out.

"Yes," I said. "I know him."

The clerk looked at me, watched as I filled out the questions on the form and nodded.

"Like I was tellin' you, don't know if these transcripts can be found," he said. "I mean, that's what? 'Forty-six? That's takin' it back pretty far."

"What are the chances?" I asked. "That you'll find them?"

"We'll do our best," the clerk said. "Call me in about two weeks. I should know something by then."

To this day, the transcripts of my father's trial have never been found.

Piecing together a complete account of my father's bloody past was slow, unforgiving work, and it became increasingly difficult to ignore the overall effect it was having on my life.

By now, I was in my early twenties, a college graduate working as a copyboy for the New York *Daily News*, still living at home, afraid to leave my mother alone with my father at night. I had no intentions of getting married and just the thought of having children made me freeze.

"Annie's kid, the druggist, is getting married," my mother said to me one morning, pouring us both hot cups of tea. "He's younger than you."

"Some guys are born married," I said. "He's one of them."

"You can't stay single forever," my mother said. "You can't live alone."

"Do you like being married?" I said to my mother. "Do you like the life you have here?"

"No," she said, sipping her tea.

"Then why do you want me to get into it?" I said. "Why is it so important to you?"

"It's important to any mother," she said. "To see her son settle down and raise a family."

"I don't want a family," I said. "Not now. Maybe not ever."

"Why?" she said. "Because of your father? Because of what he did?"

"That's right," I said. "Because of my father and because of what he did."

"That has nothing to do with you," my mother said. "Why would you even think something like that?"

"I don't want to talk about this anymore," I said, getting up, reaching for my jacket. "I'm glad Annie's son is getting married. I'm happy for him. Tell him that for me when you see him."

"I wish it were you," my mother said sadly.

"It's not, Mom," I said. "Get used to it."

"I could find you someone to marry," my mother said. "If that's your problem."

"Okay, Mom," I said with a smile. "Go ahead. Knock yourself out. Find me a wife."

"Does she have to be beautiful?" my mother said, walking to the kitchen sink, both empty cups in her hand. "Don't expect me to find someone out of a magazine."

"No, Mom," I said. "Ugly. Make sure she's very ugly. And fat. Don't forget fat."

"I'll ask," my mother said, laughing. "Can't promise you any-thing."

"Do your best," I said, opening the apartment door. "I'm countin' on you. Don't let me down."

"She'll have teeth," my mother said.

"What more can I ask for?" I said.

I passed my father on my way out of the building.

He had gone out to get a quart of milk and the morning papers, and to lay down six dollars in bets on a Saratoga daily double. We gently brushed shoulders with each other by the lobby door.

Neither one of us spoke.

XI

I spent the major parts of my days, outside of work, talking to as many people as I could find who knew anything at all about my father.

The stiffest resistance came from the relatives on my father's side.

"This family's been dragged through mud once before," one uncle told me when I asked about the murder. "I don't want to ever see it dragged down again. Especially by a punk like you. Besides, why the hell *should* you know? Why the hell should you know anything?"

But I kept asking, hopeful that someone would break and confide in me enough to tell the whole truth.

"What are you out to prove?" my father's brother-in-law asked. "That he *didn't* do it? Is that what this is all about? If it is, you can forget it. Let it drop and get on with the rest of your life."

Occasionally, the denials went beyond the expected stonewalling and grew more ominous.

"What do you think your father will do to you when he finds out that you know?" a cousin warned. "And what do you think he'll do to your mother when he finds out she was the one who told you?"

Through it all, despite my growing frustration and some occasional lapses, I continued to look for the missing pieces to the puzzle. I needed answers to a lot of questions, and there was really only one place to find them. So, three afternoons a week, I went back to the comfort of Hell's Kitchen.

Back to the place that knew the truth.

There, sitting on torn stools in dark bars that smelled of spilled Irish whiskey, I talked to dozens of men and women who had known my father.

I drank with a woman who'd had a weekend affair with him while he was married to Grace, and another who slept with him during the years he was with my mother. I talked to an old lady who had testified at his trial, and had dinner with a cellmate from prison.

I talked to friends who still thought he was innocent and enemies who thought he had killed more than once. I met people who had cried at Grace's funeral and others who claimed they knew her to be a flirt. I sat across from cops who had walked a Kitchen beat and had busted my father, as well as lawyers who had tried to help him beat a murder rap.

I had coffee with women who were still owed money by my father and men who said he had bailed them out of financial jams. I ate with guys my father had trained with at the gym and women he had taken dancing. I met a priest who heard his confession and a nun who saw him hit his wife in front of a movie theater.

I stayed away from the people who wanted money to talk, avoided talking to more than one person at a time and made it a habit never to let anyone see me taking notes. The process took time and patience, but gradually I would win their trust and their belief that I would do nothing that would betray them.

I sat in the back booth of a Tenth Avenue bar, watching the old man's fingers grip the edge of an unfiltered cigarette. I filled the two shot glasses at our table from a bottle of Wild Turkey and nodded as the old man lifted his glass toward me in a shriveled gesture of salute.

"Okay with you if I get a glass of milk with this?" the old man asked. "Helps wash it down."

I signaled for a waiter, who ambled over and took the order, scrawling it on a flipped-open pad.

"How about you?" he said to me. "Want one, too?"

"No," I said. "I'm okay with what I got."

"You just gonna drink?" the waiter said. "Or you want me to bring menus?"

"In a while," I said. "We'll nurse what we got for a bit."

The waiter shrugged his shoulders, turned his back to us and walked away.

"I don't like your father," the old man said, looking directly at me and helping himself to another splash of Turkey. "You ought to know that upfront. Didn't like him back when. Don't think I would much care for him now."

"How well did you know him?" I said, both of us ignoring the return of the waiter with the glass of milk.

"Well enough to know he was all trouble," the old man said. "Quick to hit. Quick to borrow money."

"You work down the docks?" I said. "That how you met?"

"I worked," the old man said. "Worked those holes every day up till my legs went. Your father showed up. There's a big difference."

"You know his wife?" I said. "The first one? Grace."

"Knew both his wives," the old man said. "The one he killed and your mother, the widow, the one he brought over from the other side."

I leaned across the table, closer to the old man, waited as he lit another cigarette, watched as he scratched at the stubble spread across his thin cheeks.

"How well you know her?" I said. "Grace."

"He tried to kill her before, you know that, right?" the old man said, smoke dripping out both his nostrils. "Anybody ever bother to tell you that?"

"No," I said. "No one."

"Almost beat her to death that first time," the old man said. "Beat her with punches. He was ugly with his hands. Especially around women. Some guys're like that. They like slappin' 'em around."

"How do you know this?" I said. "Who told you?"

"Just know, that's all," the old man said. "Neighborhoods talk. Alls you gotta do is listen."

"Ever see them together?" I said. "My father and his wife."

"Lots of times," the old man said. "They were both dancers, hitting different clubs around the neighborhood. Your father would go anywhere for a good time. His wife, too."

"You ever lend him money?" I said, watching as the waiter walked past our table. "He ever ask you?"

"He asked all the time," the old man said, shifting the milk glass to his right, behind his shot glass. "He asked everybody all the time. That's how he lived. But no, I never lent him a nickel. I'm one of the lucky ones. One of the few you ever gonna meet didn't get ripped off by your father."

The old man reached for a fresh cigarette from a crushed pack, his gnarled hands streaked with veins, his fingernails chewed to the quick. He lit the cigarette and kept it in his mouth, swallowing the loose smoke.

"You hungry?" I asked. "Want some lunch?"

"This *is* lunch," the old man said, pointing to the drinks and smokes laid out on the table. "I keep it light. May not be good for you, but it's what I like."

I drank my shot glass empty, the warm rush in my chest causing my eyes to cloud with tears. I wiped at my lips with the back of my hand and sat with my shoulders against the ridges of the wooden booth.

"Anything else you wanna know?" the old man said. "Anything else I can tell you, just let me know."

"Whatever you can remember." I said. "About my father."

"What are you lookin' for?"

"The truth."

"Truth about what?"

"Everything."

"Let me give you some advice," the old man said. "Free of charge."

"Okay."

"You'll never find what you're lookin' for," the old man said.

"Why's that?" I said.

"It's easier for people to lie," the old man said. "Or not bother to talk at all. Truth's a tough thing to face. Especially for men like your father. Men like me. And neighborhoods like the Kitchen. Place was built on lies. Ain't gonna change just because you come around askin' questions."

"What's that mean to me?" I said. "I'm supposed to act like I don't know what happened? Turn my back on it?"

"Not what I'm sayin'," the old man said. "Ask all the questions you want. Ask anybody. Anybody who'll talk. Just don't walk through this like some innocent baby. Keep your eyes popped wide. Your father did it. He killed his wife. That's a cold fact. Don't ever think otherwise."

"I believe that," I said. "I'm just tryin' to figure out why."

" 'Why' you can only get from him," the old man said. "He's the one can answer that. If it's bothering you all that much, go ahead and ask him. You come this far with it. What's he gonna do? Kill you?"

XII

Eight years had passed since I had learned about Grace's murder. Eight years of playing it back in my head, digging up the details, running down the small leads that had developed.

Eight years of steeling myself to ask my father the questions I felt needed answers.

It was another hot summer morning, and my parents were in the living room, in the heat of yet another argument, this one over a $1,500 credit card bill for three household appliances we didn't own. We didn't have next month's rent, let alone a loose $1,500.

"Why?" my mother said, pounding a fist against her own chest. "Why do you keep doing this to us?"

"Will you relax?" my father said. "Take it easy. Don't go gettin' all excited."

"We don't have it," my mother said. "And we're not paying it. You want to be a big shot. Go ahead. But we're not paying it. Not anymore."

"Will you listen to this crazy bitch?" my father said, slapping a hand against the side of his knee. "Like she gets up in the middle of the fuckin' night, rides the trains and goes to work. Like she's the one bustin' her hump every fuckin' day."

"Who did you buy these things for?" my mother said. "Who are you trying to impress this time?"

"None of your fuckin' business," my father said. "I do what I gotta do. I take care of my end. You take care of yours."

"How are you going to pay for it?" my mother said. "How? You haven't got two nickels to rub together. How are you going to pay off fifteen hundred dollars?"

"I'll take care of it," my father said. "It's of no concern to you. It's business. *My* business. Now, stay the fuck out of it."

It should have ended there. My mother should have walked away, silent, avoiding any further damage.

But she didn't.

Instead, she kept at him, complaining, in a voice loud enough to carry, about his debts, his gambling habits, his loans and his family.

My father poured himself a glass of seltzer, still looking at my mother, listening to her yell. He drank the glass empty and set it back down on the kitchen table. He picked up the spray seltzer bottle, his fingers wrapped around its neck and threw the bottle at my mother.

It shattered just above my mother's head, glass and water falling down all around her. She put both hands across her mouth and muffled a loud scream.

"Stay the fuck out of my business," my father said to her on his way out of the apartment. "It's the last time I'm gonna tell you. Next time, it's your funeral."

I was sitting in my car, engine running, waiting for my father.

The apartment windows were open wide, allowing me to hear every bit of the argument between my parents. Their fights were lasting longer, moving closer to dangerous borders, to a place where my mother could be seriously hurt.

I looked up and saw my father making his way toward the car, his jacket open, his hat held in one hand, his face beet red, a newspaper doubled up under his arm.

He opened the car door on the passenger side, got in and shut it with a quick tug.

"Hit the road," he said to me. "I wanna get there before dark."

"Hold tight," I said, getting out, leaving the engine in idle and the radio on low. "I'll be right back. Don't steal the car."

I ran into the apartment and saw my mother where my father had left her, seltzer still dripping down her face, her back to the wall, small pieces of glass by her feet.

She looked scared and shocked, the eyes behind her glasses shimmering with tears, her extended arms trembling.

"Get out," my mother said to me. "Get out and take him with you."

"You okay?" I said, reaching for a kitchen hand towel. "He hit you?"

"Go," she said, her voice loaded with terror. "Just go. Don't worry about me."

"You sure?" I said.

"Get in your car and go away," my mother said. "Get him as far from me as you can."

"I'll call you later," I said. "Check in on you."

"Don't bother," my mother said. "I'll be fine."

"I'm sorry, Mom," I said, turning from her, walking out of the kitchen and back to my car.

"I'm sorry, too," she said to no one, her body sagging, her tears flowing. "I'm sorry, too."

We inched along in heavy traffic on the Long Island Expressway, my car radiator about ready to surrender to the heat, the gas gauge teasing empty.

My father sat up front next to me, felt-tip pen poised, studying the newspaper's racing sheet.

I braked in front of a Dodge Dart, looked over at my father and knew our moment had arrived.

"Do you ever plan to tell me about it?" I said, holding down my anger and apprehension, trying to keep my voice calm.

My father put down his pen.

"Tell you about what?" he said.

"About your wife?" I said. "About Grace Carcaterra."

My father reached over and cuffed me across the face with the back of his hand. The quick blow pushed my head back and reddened my cheek.

"Don't ever say her name," my father said. "You hear me, punk? Don't you ever say her name."

"How did it feel, Dad?" I said. "How did it feel when you had that pillow down on her face? Come on, tell me. How did it feel?"

"You're a bum," my father said, his hands shaking, his eyes glassy. "You're always gonna be nothin' but a bum. And you're nothin' to me. Nothin' to nobody. You hear me? Nothin'."

He reached across and hit me again, harder this time, landing just below my right eye.

"A punk," he said. "A soft mama's-boy punk. That's what you are. That's all you are."

My father's two fists were clenched, his teeth biting into his lower lip, the rage welling up inside him. I saw how simple it would be for him to take a life, and I knew how easily he would be able to do it again.

"Maybe," I said. "Maybe I am. But I'm not a murderer. I'm definitely not that."

XIII

My father unwrapped a twenty-two-steak side of beef, spreading brown butcher paper across the length of the kitchen table. He picked up a twelve-inch carving knife with his right hand and an iron sharpener with his left, took two steps back and rubbed the sharp edge of one against the round surface of the other.

He dropped the sharpener back on the table, moved closer to the meat and began his cuts.

I sat in the living room, halfway through a paperback thriller; a radio tuned to an Italian station played softly to my right. My mother sat across from me, a handful of folders and shoe boxes stuffed with papers and booklets opened around her.

I watched her leaf through a couple of old passbook savings accounts, a number of holes punched across each page, and then toss them to the floor.

"All that money," she said. "Gone to waste."

"How much?" I said, looking at the four empty books by her feet. "All together."

"Eighty thousand dollars," my mother said, shaking her head, still sifting through the boxes. "At least."

"That's a house," I said.

"That's *two* houses," she said.

I laid the book on the couch pillow to my left, cover side up, and walked closer to my mother, looking over her shoulder, a half-dozen collection-department notices and late-payment slips balled up in one of her hands.

"What are you looking for?" I said.

"The bank book," my mother said. "It's missing."

"So what?" I said. "What's that mean? We're out another five dollars."

My mother dropped the notices and bills back into a shoe box and looked up at me.

"There's twelve thousand dollars in it," my mother said. "I was using it to pay off some of the bills."

"Twelve thousand?" I said. "Where'd we get that kind of money?"

"Here and there," my mother said. "Italy mostly. What little he gave me, you gave me. Saved as much as I could."

"When's the last time you saw it?" I asked.

"Last week," my mother said. "I took it to the bank and made a thirty-five-dollar deposit."

"You keep something with that much money in a shoe box?" I said. "You couldn't think of a better place?"

"It's the only place I thought would be safe," my mother said. "Your father never looks through these things."

"Was it a joint account?" I said.

"Yes," my mother said.

"Then, there's really only one place left to look," I said.

"He's not going to tell you anything," my mother said.

"Stay here," I said. "Don't come in there. I don't care what you hear. Stay here."

"Be careful," my mother said.

My father had finished cutting the steaks and was packing them into groups of three, double wrapping each set. He had his back to me and was whistling an old Glenn Miller tune as he worked.

We had not talked to one another since that day in the car eight months earlier.

We both knew I had crossed a line, walked into an arena my father never wanted me to enter. Now, like it or not, we both had to live with it.

We ate our meals at different times, ignored each other while under the same roof and, if we could avoid it, never went out together.

It was the way we wanted it.

"Where is it?" I asked him, his back still to me.

He ignored the question, wrapping and taping another package of steaks and tossing it into the open freezer.

"Where is it, Dad?" I said in a louder tone. "Where's the money?"

"The dead don't talk, scumbag," my father said without looking at me. "And you're dead."

"The money, Dad," I said. "What happened to it?"

My father loaded the last of the steaks into the freezer, rolled the loose brown paper into a bunch and threw it into the garbage.

He brushed past me without speaking, making his way to the sink.

"What'd you do with the fucking money, Dad?" I said. "Who'd you have to buy off this time?"

My father poured Ivory dish soap onto his hands and held them under the hot spray of the water, scrubbing away the dried fat and blood from his palms and his fingernails.

"Another great business deal," I said. "Is that it? Another million-dollar brainstorm?"

My father clutched at a small handful of paper towels and patted dry his hands. He continued to whistle the same song, his gaze never reaching my eye level.

"Answer me," I said. "You fucking bum, answer me. This one time, look at me and answer me."

My father grabbed the knife from the kitchen table, his knuckles white from the pressure of their grip. His face was ash white, his body crouched, his legs balanced and planted.

"Who the fuck you callin' a bum?" my father said. "Who? You fuckin' piece of shit. You better 'n me? Is that it? Is that what you think?"

My father moved closer to me, the knife in his hand held out at his side, at an angle.

"Wouldn't you rather have a pillow?" I said. "More your style."

"You're gonna die today, scumbag," my father told me. "I've had enough of your shit. Today, we gonna end this bullshit once and for all."

"Then do it," I said. "Use the knife. I'm as sick of this shit as you are. I'd rather be dead than look at your fucking face ever again."

"All I done for you," he said. "This is how you thank me."

"Yeah, Dad," I said. "All you done for me."

"I broke my ass for you," my father said. "And her."

He pointed the tip of the knife over my shoulder, behind me, where my mother was standing against a far wall.

"Both of you should drop dead the way you treat me," my father said. "I swear to God, you should both drop dead."

"We can't die, Dad," I said. "We haven't finished paying off all your debts yet."

"Don't worry about me, scumbag," my father said. "I pay what I owe."

"You haven't paid shit," I said. "You don't have a job and you don't have a chance. How you going to pay back the twelve thousand dollars? Or the fifteen hundred dollars to Sears? Or the eight thousand you still owe Tony? How you going to do that?"

"My business," my father said. "My way."

"And how you going to pay back all that you did to Mom?" I said. "How do you pay back the years you've taken?"

My father stared at me, his eyes as filled with hatred as I had ever seen them. He lowered the knife, easing the grip, leaning his body closer to the table.

"And how you going to pay back the life you took?" I said. "What's that going to take? What's that one worth? When's it come in even?"

My father dropped the knife from his hand and came at me, reaching out with both his arms extended. He caught me around the waist and threw me against a white two-drawer cabinet. The force of our weight knocked over a two-slice toaster and sent two white serving plates to the floor.

He brought me down to my knees, landing a series of hard punches on my forehead and the right side of my jaw. He kicked aside a kitchen table and shoved my mother off the back of his shoulders as she tried to separate us.

"I'm the one who made you, prick," my father said. "And I'm gonna be the one to take you out."

He held my shirt with one hand and hit me with the other, each blow finding flesh. My mother scratched at my father's neck and back and kicked at his legs, all to no avail.

"Get away from me, bitch," my father screamed at her. "Before I kill you, too, tonight."

I was on the ground, my father above me, the blows coming in steady numbers. He started kicking at me, forceful shots to the chest and groin.

I fell to my side and saw the knife.

My father ignored me for a moment, his anger now directed toward my mother, his wrath aimed at her.

"The both of you," my father said. "They gonna bury the both of you tonight. The bitch and the prick in one fuckin' grave."

I grabbed the knife with my right hand and used my knuckles and the butt end to help me to my knees.

My father was slapping my mother, pushing her head against the side of the refrigerator. An empty pig-faced cookie jar shook, toppled and crashed to the ground.

"Turn around," I said to my father.

My father looked at me over his shoulder, a madman's smile spread across his face.

"Now you got it," he said to me, letting go of my mother's hair.

"Come on, One-punch. Stick me. Stick me right in the fuckin' chest. Let's go. Don't wait. Do it."

I swallowed hard, my mouth dry, my upper body numb. I bled from the lips and nose and my eyes felt swollen, making it hard to focus. I saw my mother on the kitchen floor, on her hands and knees, spitting blood from her mouth.

"C'mon, One-punch," my father said. "Stand up for yourself. Be like your old man. I killed. So can you."

I took a step toward him, the knife at my side, wiping at thin streams of blood with the back of one hand. Outside, I heard loud knocking on our front door.

"That's it," my father said. "Get even. That's what you want? Here's your chance. Won't take much. One shove. Fast. In and out. You can do it. I know you can."

We stared at each other for the longest time, both of us breathing hard, our bodies covered in sweat. Our hands were clenched.

One of mine was still wrapped around a knife.

"What's it gonna be, One-punch?" my father said. "I ain't got all fuckin' day."

I tossed the knife back to the floor.

"You're not worth it," I said.

"I know," my father said.

He put a hand towel under the cold water faucet, wadded it up and tossed it to me.

"Clean yourself up," he said. "You got blood all over your face."

He lifted my mother to her feet and helped her onto a chair. He then bent down, picked up the knife and held it in his hand for a few seconds. He turned around and threw it into the kitchen sink.

"I can't stay here anymore," I said to both my parents. "I just can't."

"Then don't," my father said. "Don't worry about us. We'll be fine."

I bent down and kissed my mother on the cheek and walked by my father, nodding at him as I passed.

"Hey, One-punch," my father said. "You were right about one thing."

"What?" I said, turning back to him, one arm inside the sleeve of a denim jacket.

"You'll never be a murderer," my father said. "Never. It ain't in ya. Now you can rest easy. You're not gonna be like your father. Fuck what everybody else may tell ya. You and me. We know the truth."

I nodded and walked out of the apartment and far away from the only life I had ever known.

XIV

In the summer of 1980 I fell in love with an editor at the *Daily News*. The idea of marriage suddenly surfaced as a possibility. But so did leaving my mother totally in my father's hands.

I had kept a distance between myself and both my parents in the months since that final fight with my father. I called my mother each day, sent her money every paycheck and slept over a few nights each week. I needed time away from both of them, the weight of their constant battles too much for me to continue to carry, the physical and verbal abuse too steady for anyone's sanity.

I felt removed from the lives of the people around me, a stranger to their memories of shared experiences. It was as if I had lived the bulk of my time in a vacuum, so locked into the confines of my world and its struggles that everything else seemed alien to me.

Many of my new friends came out of schools and places I had never heard of or seen; practically all of them were open and free with their feelings, while I remained closed and suspicious with mine. I felt apart, afraid people would know about me, find out all the things that I had kept hidden.

Find out there was a bloodstain in my family.

The restaurant was small, four tables crowded around an old wood bar, and smelled of grease and burnt meat. Cigarette smoke fouled the air. Three of the tables were empty, lit votive candles at their center, cane chairs folded up against the edges. An older couple, one sipping scotch, the other rye, filled the fourth.

We sat on the far left, my back to the redbrick wall, facing the outside door. Susan sat across from me, her legs crossed under the table, her hands folded in front of her, strands of brown curly hair partially obscuring one of her eyes.

I lit her cigarette and listened while she ordered a glass of red wine from a bored waiter.

"How about you?" she said. "You want anything to drink?"

"Seltzer," I said, looking at the waiter.

"Club soda," he said.

I nodded and he walked away.

"You like this place?" I asked.

"It's quiet," she nodded. "We don't have to shout when we talk. And their burgers aren't bad. At least not that bad."

"And they take plastic and their glasses don't stick to the tables," I said. "What more could you ask?"

I looked at her, watched as she sipped her wine and dragged on her cigarette, her hands soft, her face unlined, her nails flattened down by daily pounding on the computer keyboard she edited stories on.

We had known each other eight months. In that span of time Susan had vaulted past being a boss and a trusted friend to the point where we were seriously thinking marriage.

"What is it you wanted to tell me?" she asked, pouring ketchup on her cheeseburger and across her french fries.

"My father wants to meet you," I said, doing the same to mine. "Wants to have lunch."

"Okay," she said. "When?"

"Whenever," I said. "Believe me, he's free. But only if you want to meet him. If you say no, it won't be a big deal."

"Why should I say no?" she said, taking a bite from the burger. "It's only lunch. And he's your father. I'll call him if you want."

"That's okay," I said. "I'll set it up."

"You coming?" she asked. "Or does he want to meet me alone?"

"No," I said. "I'll be with you. Don't worry about that. I'll be with you."

"I'm not worried," Susan said.

"I know," I said. "I am. I'm very worried about it."

When I first told my mother about Susan and our plans, she reacted as expected. She panicked, telling me I wasn't ready for marriage and that the woman I had chosen wasn't the right one for me.

"You're too young," my mother said. "You have no experience in these things. And she has too much."

"You don't know anything about her," I said. "Haven't even met her yet."

"I don't have to meet her," my mother said. "I know what she is and I know what she wants."

"I'm going to do this, Mom," I said. "Doesn't matter if you like it or not."

"It's the wrong move," my mother said.

"It's my move," I said. "If it's wrong, I'll live with it. But this one move, I make."

My father sat on the couch across from us, listening, his head turned toward an open window.

"I want to meet her," he said, without moving his head. "Sit down with her."

"Why?" I said.

"You want this to happen?" he said to me. "You want this to go down smooth? Let me handle it. Leave it to me, One-punch. I know this game. I'll know if this broad's on the level or out for a ride. Trust me, I'll know it."

My father stood up, walked past me, limping on one arthritic knee, and patted my shoulder.

"I'll clear it with the old lady," he said. "Don't worry. Let me handle it."

My father met us at the Oyster Bar at the bottom level of Grand Central Station. He wore a three-button short-sleeve blue sport shirt and was still bleeding from a shaving nick on the lower end of his cheek. He sat to my right, facing Susan, a smile on his face, a glass of seltzer in one hand. He ordered a dozen cold clams and a large bowl of hot chowder, and munched on sea crackers while he waited.

"My son lied to me," my father said to Susan. "Big time."

"Lied about what?" Susan said, buttering the corner of a hard roll.

"About you," my father said, sipping his seltzer.

"What about me?" Susan said.

"He told me you were cute," my father said. "You're not cute. You're beautiful."

"Oh," Susan said, a rise of red coming to her face. "Thank you."

"No," my father said. "No bullshit. You're a knockout. Who knew? I always figured he'd end up with some geeky broad with bad teeth. Not somebody like you."

"Thank you again," Susan said.

"I hope you don't mind the way I talk, honey," my father said. "It's the only way I know."

"I don't mind," Susan said. "I'm used to it from the paper."

"Good," my father said. "It'll make this easier."

The restaurant was crowded, the small tables bunched close to each other. Businessmen in dark suits flanked us on all sides, their small talk drowned out by the noise from glass against bottle and fork against plate.

My father moved back in his seat, watching as the waiter laid a mixed platter of cherrystones and littlenecks in front of him. He poured Tabasco sauce and squeezed lemon juice over every one and began to eat.

"So, fill me in," my father said, his mouth filled with clams and crackers. "What's the attraction? What do you see in this guy?"

"Lots of things," Susan said.

"You love him?" my father asked.

"Very much," Susan said.

"Good," my father said. "That's all that counts. The rest is all bullshit. Me and my old lady, we're closin' in on thirty years. Yeah, we had ups and downs. I'll let him tell you about those. They don't matter. So long as we still love each other. That's the only fuckin' thing. That's all you need. You got that, you got everything. Am I right?"

My father talked for the next forty-five minutes, straight through the cheesecake dessert and the short walk out of Grand Central. He did his all to charm Susan and win her to his side. He told her stories

291

about his life, about his days as a fighter and his years as a butcher.

He called Susan "sweetheart" and "baby," pointed out how good the two of us looked together and how much happiness we each deserved. He promised to straighten things out with my mother, make her come around to a more modern way of thought.

He told Susan how he had courted my mother and married her over strong objections from family on both sides. He told her he would die if forced to go through life without my mother.

I sat through it all, nursing two drinks and picking at my food, my words at a minimum, audience to one of my father's best performances.

Outside, under a red light at the corner of 42nd Street and Third Avenue, my father hugged Susan, kissed her on both cheeks, and welcomed her to our family. He then dug both hands into his pants pockets and headed off for the IRT subway, back to the Bronx.

Susan and I walked back to the newspaper, one of her arms under mine, her head resting on my shoulder.

"I really envy you," Susan said.

"You do?" I said. "Why?"

"You're lucky," she said. "You grew up surrounded by so much love, so much attention. Not many people have that, have what you had."

"No," I said. "You're right. Not many people do."

My father walked into the apartment and slammed the door shut behind him. My mother was sitting by the kitchen radio, halfway through her daily rosary, listening to an Italian religious program.

She stood when she saw my father.

"Well," my mother said. "What's she like?"

My father crossed over to my mother and slapped her twice across the face.

"She's a fuckin' bitch," my father said. "Just like you are."

He punched my mother twice in the mouth and pulled her hair, bouncing the back of her head against the alcove wall.

"You forced him outta here," my father said. "You fuckin' bitch. You forced that kid outta here. And now he's gonna go and marry some tramp."

He threw my mother to the floor and kicked her twice in the side, just below the rib cage.

"I oughta kill ya for what you did to him," my father said. "You bitch. You fuckin' no-good bitch."

My father lifted my mother's arm and bit down on her hand, bending back three of her fingers. He reached over and grabbed for a red wine bottle that was resting near the rusty base of the stove. He picked up the bottle and brought it down hard against my mother's spine.

It shattered after the third hit.

"His life's over," my father said to her. "And it's your fault. Your fault, bitch. Nobody else. You."

My father walked away from my mother and went into the living room. He sat down on the couch and put both hands across his face and began to cry.

"Fuckin' bitch," he said. "Fuckin' no-good bitch. Cost me my boy."

I sat at the wooden dining table in the middle of Susan's East Side studio apartment. I sipped a glass of red wine and looked out at the picture window view of 14th Street and lower Manhattan. Over the two stereo speakers, Guy Clark softly sang about "A Coat from the Cold."

Susan came in from the kitchen, a plate covered with sliced London broil and vegetables in each hand. She placed one in front of me and sat on the opposite end of the round table, adding salt to her dinner.

"You okay?" she said.

"I'm good," I said. "I just have something to tell you and don't really know how."

"About us?" Susan said, resting her fork against the side of her plate.

"It involves us," I said.

"Say it then," Susan said. "It's the best way."

"It's about my father, too," I said.

"He didn't like me," Susan said. "Is that it?"

"No, honey," I said. "He liked you. Wouldn't matter to me even if he didn't."

"What is it, Lorenzo?" Susan said.

I refilled both our wine glasses and took a long gulp from mine. Outside, three fire engines honked their way past traffic, heading toward the Alphabet City tenements.

"My father was married once before," I said, looking right at Susan. "Back in the forties. Her name was Grace."

"And?" Susan said.

"And she died," I said.

"How?" Susan said.

"My father killed her," I said.

I watched Susan cover her mouth with one hand, her eyes opened wide, her other hand holding the edge of the table.

"Killed her how?" Susan said.

"With a pillow," I said. "In a hotel room on the West Side. He went to jail for it. When he got out, he went to Italy and married my mother."

"Did she know?" Susan said. "What he had done."

"I don't know," I said. "It's been hard finding out what anybody knew. I've been trying. Haven't had that much luck. So far."

"How long have you known?" Susan said.

"I was fourteen," I said. "My mother told me. On a beach."

We sat in silence for a few moments, a nervous tension spread across the table between us.

"I wish I didn't have to tell you," I said.

"Why did you?" she said.

"Because I love you," I said. "And if you marry me you should know."

"What makes you think I'll marry you?" Susan said.

"Thought it would be a good idea," I said. "Unless you got other plans."

"You haven't asked me," she said.

"Been waiting for a good time," I said. "A lot's been going on."

"This a good time?" Susan said.

"Good as any," I said.

"Well," Susan said, a smile across her face. "I'm waiting."

I reached for her hand and squeezed her fingers.

"Do you want to get married?" I said.

"Yes," Susan said.

"Wait," I said. "Let me ask this. Do you want to get married to me?"

"Yes," Susan said.

That night, I told her everything. From my obsession with my father's crime to my apprehension about having children, the street noises outside the apartment our only distraction.

I knew as I told her that Susan and I would be together for as long as we both wanted.

We had both found our safe place.

Six months to the day, on May 16, 1981, Susan and I were married on a cloudy afternoon outside a friend's house in Pound Ridge in Westchester County. There were seventy-five people in attendance.

My mother and father chose not to come.

XV

The next years were lived at a distance.

I saw very little of my parents, focusing the bulk of my attention on my own life and family. I still sent my mother money, called occasionally and sent gifts at Christmas and on her birthday. But the cord between us had finally been severed, and we both knew it.

I never asked about my father, nor did I speak to him during my first years away from home. Nonetheless, my mother filled me in on his latest schemes and scams, his cons getting smaller in scope as he got on in age. The debts were still heavy, but appeared more manageable than before.

"He was running scared," said Frankie, who helped plan some of my father's scams. "He knew you weren't around to bail him out. He cooled it down. He thought small. He worked a price range he could pay off himself if he had to. He wasn't the same guy without you around. He always talked about you. The stuff you wrote for the papers, things like that. He always used to carry articles of yours in his pocket, pulled them out whether we asked or not. His mind was on you. Not on the con."

He was also sick.

Early in 1984, after months of nagging pain and long, uncomfortable nights, my father walked into an East Bronx hospital and had himself checked out.

Three days later, following a number of blood tests and X rays, a young resident told my father that traces of cancer had been found near the base of his spine.

"I don't believe you," my father said to him. "I don't trust you and I don't believe you."

"The tests don't lie," the doctor said. "It's in an early stage and we may be able to help if you let us."

"I'm outta here," my father said. "Hear me, kid. You're not gonna use me or any part of me to earn your pay. Understand? If I got what you say I got, I'll live with it. Long as I can. We understand each other?"

"I understand," the doctor said. "But I should warn you. I think you're making a mistake by not treating the problem."

"It's my problem ain't it?" my father said.

"Yes, sir," the doctor said. "It is your problem."

"Okay then, doc," my father said. "Help me get the hell outta here."

"Is there anyone in your family I should call?" the doctor said. "Someone who could take you home?"

"There's just me, doc," my father said. "Nobody else. You're lookin' at the only fuckin' family I got. I don't need anybody. Never did. Never will."

"I'll finish the forms," the doctor said. "You can probably go home after lunch."

"You don't mind, doc," my father said, "I'm gonna go home before lunch. I've seen the food here."

"You'll be passing up the soup of the day," the doctor said with a smile. "Cream of spinach."

"If I eat any of that shit, I'll be more than passin' up," my father said. "I'll be passin' out."

"Wouldn't be the first time," the doctor said.

"It would for me," my father said. "Toss me my pants, would ya', doc? It's time to hit the road."

Thirty minutes later, my father was out of the hospital and back on the streets of the Bronx.

My father's cancer did not slow down the physical and verbal battles he continued to have with my mother. They fought daily, for the slightest, and often silliest, reasons. Each fight would, as always, end with a slap or a punch or a kick. My parents had lived this way for more than three decades, and there seemed to be no end in sight.

"Mom changed after you left," Anthony said. "She closed up even more, was quieter, sullen. She was always angry. Her life had become everyone else's fault. Yours. Mine. My wife's. Your wife's. Anyone she could point a finger at, for whatever the reason. You couldn't blame her for being angry. We had both left, gone our way. She was left with him. Just the two of them. Like a couple of punch-drunk fighters. Reliving the past every chance they could."

My father would still disappear for weeks at a clip, leaving unannounced and showing up in much the same way. Each time he took off, the money he and my mother had managed to save left with him, replaced upon his return by a large bill from Macy's and a due loan from the Household Finance Corporation.

Then the fights, as vicious as ever, would pick up where they had left off.

In the summer of 1986, my parents were short of money and tired of living in what had become a crime-filled neighborhood. They decided to move out of the Bronx and return to Ischia, taking over a one-bedroom apartment my mother had inherited from Grandma Maria.

"I didn't want to go back with him," my mother said. "But what other choice did I have? His cancer was spreading a little more each day. He was always in pain. Some days he couldn't walk at all. Other days he walked with a cane. And every day he asked for you."

I could not bring myself to speak to my father, my hatred fueled further by the long spans of silence that had gone by. I felt a balance

297

of sadness and relief when news of my parents' plans reached me. I knew that once she was in Italy, my mother would be safer, surrounded by her own family. My father would still hit her, though not quite as often. He would still borrow money from strangers, though not in large sums. He would still tell lies, but to people who knew he never spoke the truth.

Their life didn't matter to me anymore. I now had my own family, my own children and my own difficulties. I viewed my mother and father's constant squabbling as petty and turned my attention from them on far too many occasions.

My parents had become easy to ignore.

XVI

I had just gone to bed, resting my head against the pillow, my wife curled by my side, when the phone rang. I picked it up on the second ring and heard my mother's voice shouting at me from the other end.

"Come get him," she said. "I need you to come get him. I can't care for him anymore."

"Mom, calm down," I said. "Call a doctor. Take him to a hospital, if he's that bad."

"He wants to die in America," she said. "He wants you to come get him."

"I don't care where he wants to die," I said. "Let him die anywhere. Why should I care? After all the hurt he's caused, why should I care? Why should *you* care?"

"He's your father," my mother said. "And he's my husband."

"Mom, it's late," I said, checking the clock by the night table. "Get some sleep. I'll talk to you later. After you've calmed down."

"Come and get him," she said. "Come get your father now."

* * *

My father was paralyzed from the waist down, had lost control of his bowels and suffered from sporadic bouts of dementia. The doctors caring for him in Italy told my mother he only had weeks to live.

My mother's phone calls continued, growing more desperate and pleading with each one.

"How can you be so cold?" she said in the middle of one call. "How can you not care about him?"

"I feel nothing for him," I said. "He beat it out of me a long time ago. I'm through running every time he snaps his fingers."

"Don't you want to see him before he dies?" my mother said. "Say goodbye to him."

"I already said goodbye," I said. "Years ago. So did he. No point in repeating it."

"You're filled with hate," my mother said. "I didn't raise you that way."

"Yes you did," I said.

"Too much hate," my mother said, crying as she hung up the phone. "Too much."

It took my mother's sister and my favorite aunt, Anna, to bring me back to Italy.

Back to my father.

"You're right," she said to me in the middle of another late-night conversation. "He's caused us all a great deal of pain. But that part's over now. No one has suffered more than your mother, yet she cares for him every day. Washes him like a baby, feeds him, rubs his back and legs when he can't sleep. It's no longer a question of forgiveness. It's now a question of humanity. That's all."

XVII

"You want anything?" I said to my father, as the Alitalia 747 left Rome's Leonardo da Vinci Airport. "Something to drink? A pillow?"

My father shook his head and remained silent for the first third of the flight back to New York. He had lost a lot of weight. His strong arms were now shriveled, skin sagging at the sides. He was in steady pain and had great difficulty with his breathing.

He stared out the window, watching soft white clouds mix with a clear blue skyline, his hands folded in front of him, his skin with a waxy shine to it. His shoelaces were undone, his blue shirt opened to the waist and his diaper soiled.

He turned away from the window and looked over at me, patting me on the arm.

"I know you hate me," he said, more a whisper than a full voice. "I don't blame you."

"Thanks," I said.

"You always wanted to know about me," he said. "Askin' questions you shouldn't have been askin', no matter what. Why? What were you lookin' to find out?"

"The truth," I said.

"About what?" he said. "About the murder?"

"I know about the murder," I said. "What I don't know is how you feel about it. How you can live with it."

"You can live with anything," my father said. "If you have to."

"You never think about it?" I said.

"No."

"Why not?"

"What would thinkin' about it prove?" my father said. "Would it bring her back? Would it?"

"Would you want that?" I said. "Would you want her back?"

My father took a deep breath, a rattle coming from his chest, the sagging muscles quivering from the effort.

"Yeah," he said. "I would. I loved that girl."

He turned his face back toward the window.

"I loved her," he said away from me. "You may not believe that, but I don't care if you do or not. I loved her."

"What went wrong?"

My father shrugged, pain etched on his face.

"I screwed up," he said. "What's the surprise? I screwed up everything. I listened to my mother. I listened to people from the neighborhood and I got a little crazy. There was never another man. If there was, I didn't know about it. She was a good girl. She was a good girl and I killed her."

He looked down at his lifeless body, the legs numb, the arms trembling.

"I guess I'm payin' for it now," my father said. "That must make you happy. That must make a lot of people happy."

XVIII

My father lingered in a tenth-floor bed at St. Luke's–Roosevelt Hospital Center in Manhattan, less than a mile from the hotel where he had killed his first wife.

In the middle of summer, three weeks into his stay, my father refused spinal surgery, which would have given him a 70 percent chance of regaining full use of his legs, though it would not have slowed the cancer.

He was afraid of the knife.

"Don't let 'em cut me, One-punch," my father said. "No matter what. I wanna die whole."

"They won't cut you," I said.

"Promise me," my father said. "Promise me, One-punch. Promise me you won't let them put a knife on me."

"I promise," I said. "Don't worry."

"That's my boy," he said. "That's my One-punch."

I visited him every other day, bringing fresh fruit and the morning papers. I would stay for an hour, wipe his brow, pour him water, joke with his nurses and listen as he talked about his life.

As expected, the truth was usually buried under a rubble of lies.

We talked about his days as a boxer and his nights spent in jail. We talked about his father and the beatings he received at his hands and how hard the old man worked the docks. We talked about my mother and the grief he had caused.

"You remember when she had that operation?" he said in a voice clogged with phlegm. "The one for breast cancer?"

"She almost died," I said.

"That was my fault," he said. "One of the doctors asked me if she fell or had some kinda accident. I knew what he was gettin' at. I punched her on the spot they operated. Musta hit her harder than I thought. It healed on the outside. Never on the inside."

We talked about the people he had taken money from, working men and women who couldn't sit for the loss. We talked about his time on the piers and at the 14th Street meat market, lugging hindquarters of beef off the backs of freezer trucks. We talked about lost hopes and dreams, cons and scams, Marciano and Killebrew, Sinatra and Krupa, Chick Webb and Sugar Ray Robinson, cancer and death.

Most of all, we talked about the long minutes spent in the Mayfair Hotel in a small back room on a brisk late October day in 1946.

"She was hung over," my father said, chewing on a slice of grapefruit, the juice dripping down the flat of his chin and onto his caved-in chest. "Didn't take that much to get her drunk. She was angry, a look of disgust in her eyes. Your mother gives me the same look. Said she was tired of me not workin'. You know, the usual crap. I asked for one more chance. Then . . . well, you know the rest."

"You think you would get away with it?" I said.

"I didn't think anything," my father said.

"What do you think now?" I said.

"I think you should leave," my father said. "And let me get some sleep."

*   *   *

On November 1, 1988, my father was transferred to a nursing home in the Bronx, a five-story building that was a ten-minute walk from Yankee Stadium.

My mother had, by this time, arrived from Italy, and joined in caring for her dying husband.

I watched them in their moments together, laughing, holding hands, kissing, a couple very much in love. They whispered and teased one another, my mother feeding him, wiping his mouth, drying sweat from his head and arms with a cool cloth.

"All the nurses wanna take me home," my father said to my mother, winking at me. "That okay with you?"

"They can have you," my mother said. "And you can have them."

"I got your permission?" he said.

"I'll put it in writing," my mother said. "Why should they have to go through life without you?"

"I'm gonna miss you, baby," my father said.

"I'll call," my mother said. "Maybe visit."

"I'm afraid to die," my father said. "I don't know what it's gonna be like."

"No one knows," my mother said. "And everyone's afraid."

"I don't wanna die, baby," my father said. "I don't wanna leave you."

"Then don't," my mother said. "Stay strong. Eat what they give you and rest. Get plenty of rest."

"I'm gonna get plenty of that," my father said. "Sooner or later."

"Do you need anything?" my mother said. "I'll bring it next time I come. I put some new pajamas and socks in the bureau."

"Tell the nurses," he said. "They dress me."

"I will," my mother said, grabbing hold of one of my father's cold hands. "Anything else?"

"Yeah," my father said, his throat dry, his lips cut and flaked. "There is."

"What?" my mother said.

"I'm sorry, baby," my father said.

"About what?" my mother said.

Lorenzo Carcaterra

"Everything," my father said. "Every fuckin' thing I ever did wrong. I'm sorry."

"There's nothing to be sorry about," my mother said, kissing the cold hand. "Nothing at all."

It rained the next morning.

I stood in a corner of the drab room, over a covered heater, staring out the window at the traffic streaming by the Grand Concourse. Across the way, in the entryway of a brick prewar building, three Puerto Ricans in baseball jackets pitched pennies and drank beer, a radio blaring salsa at their feet.

Behind me, my mother rubbed my father's bony legs with a damp towel, scrubbing off dead skin and dirt. She whistled softly as she moved the white hand rag up and around my father's still thighs.

"Hey, baby," my father said. "Do me a favor, okay?"

"What?" my mother said, looking up, cutting off her whistle. "Am I hurting you?"

"No," he said. "Feels great. But take a break. Go outside. Rest awhile. I wanna talk to the kid."

My mother looked over at me and then turned back to my father. She nodded, tossed the towel into a bathroom sink, dried her hands and closed the door as she left.

My father and I stared at each other. The room was dark and smelled like an old dog. I could hear nurses outside talking and laughing in loud voices.

My father pulled one hand from under the thin white sheet and brown blanket and patted it against the bed.

"Come over here, One-punch," my father said. "I wanna ask you somethin'."

"Go ahead and ask," I said. "I can hear you."

"C'mere," my father said. "Don't worry. I ain't gonna hit you."

I walked the five feet to the bed and sat down, his eyes never once leaving mine. The skin on his face looked fake, drawn thin and tight around cheekbones and jaw. His mouth was half-open and his breath smelled of death.

"Do you love me?" he said.

I continued to stare at him.

"What?" I said.

"Do you love me?" he said, trying hard to swallow.

"You never made it easy," I said.

"Fuck easy," my father said. "My life's over and I wanna know if you love me."

"No," I said.

My father dropped his head back against the propped-up pillows, his fists clenched, his eyes filled with an old familiar rage.

"Get your mother in here," my father said. "And you get the hell outta my sight."

It was the last time I would see my father alive.

XIX

At 7:08 A.M., Tuesday, November 8, 1988, my father, Mario Carcaterra, died. He was seventy-one years old.

Three days later, his body was cremated, and a memorial Mass was held on a Sunday afternoon at Blessed Sacrament Church. A Filipino priest served the Mass in Italian, at my mother's request.

A small number of my father's relatives were present, including his two sisters and younger brother. We didn't speak before or after the service.

The next morning, I returned to the quiet of Blessed Sacrament, an old but somehow timeless building on West 71st Street. I knelt before a side altar, slid a ten-dollar bill into an open slot and lit three large votive candles.

One was for my father. A man I never understood. A man I had cursed for so many years. A man I loved more than any other.

The second was for his wife, Grace Carcaterra. The woman he killed. The woman who haunts me.

The third candle was for me, a silent prayer for help in my struggle to live with a bloody heritage. One act, one moment, frozen in time. Alive in my mind's eye. Forever.

That was my father's sentence.

It was now mine.

My mother spent the Thanksgiving holidays with my family and then flew back to Ischia. For the first time in thirty-four years she was at peace with herself and her world.

She wears the widow's black every day and will until her own death, mourning the soul of a man who gave her so many reasons to live with hate.

I spend a great deal of time with my children, Kate, ten, and Nick, six.

They are being raised in a world far different from the one I knew as a child. They see their parents hug and kiss. They hear the occasional fights and arguments common to any marriage, and see them settled with smiles and flowers.

I know that right now I am an infinitely better husband and parent than my father ever was. Yet there are so many things my father taught me that I would like my children to learn.

I want them to see Yankee Stadium under the lights, watch their faces as their favorite players autograph their new baseballs. I want to take them to a boxing match, talk to them about Jimmy Cagney and Humphrey Bogart and sit with them through a freezing football game in late December.

I want to tell them about all the great old fighters and gangsters my father told me about, from Owney Madden's class to the "no quit" in Jake La Motta's heart. I want my kids to know how special Chick Webb was over a set of drums and how magical Benny Goodman could make a clarinet sound.

When my children get older, I will tell them all about their grandfather, both the good and the bad.

I will end each story by telling them how much I loved him and how much, with each passing day, I miss my father.

It used to bother me when people noted how much my son resembles my father. It used to please my wife even less.

There's no denying, however, that Nick has my father's smile, his walk and his charming manner.

One recent night, Nick and Kate fell asleep on my bed. I leaned down and kissed my daughter, moving her brown hair away from her face.

Then I noticed Nick sleeping on his side, his arms flat against his legs, his belly exposed, the top of his butt spilling out of pajama bottoms.

It was exactly the way my father used to sleep.

I kissed my son and gently coaxed him into a more innocent position.

It pays to be careful.

That much I have learned.

Epilogue

YOU HAVE TO DIG DEEP TO BURY YOUR DADDY.

—A Gypsy proverb

Epilogue

My father picked me up out of bed and held me in his arms, my late-night cries waking us both.

"Take it easy, One-punch," my father said. "I got you. Don't worry. Relax. I'm here now."

I wiped tears across the sides of his bare shoulder and wrapped my arms tight around his neck.

"I'm scared, Dad," I said.

"What is it?" my father said. "What scared you?"

"I don't know," I said. "A wolf, I think."

"C'mon, One-punch," my father said. "Let's go in the other room. See if we can grab somethin' to drink. Get away from this fuckin' wolf of yours."

We sat by the kitchen table. I was cradled in my father's lap, one arm still held around his shoulder. We were both holding open bottles of 7UP, my father's nearly empty.

"You keep watchin' those scary movies," my father said, "you gonna keep seein' werewolves in your sleep."

"It wasn't a werewolf," I said. "It was a wolf."

"Same difference," my father said, finishing his soda and resting the empty bottle on the table.

"I like those movies, Dad," I said. "You like 'em, too."

"They're only movies," my father said. "Ain't nothin' about them that's real."

"You told me werewolves were real," I said. "You told me vampires were real, too."

"I was kiddin' around," my father said. "Besides, even if they were real they would never come here."

"Why?" I said.

" 'Cause *I'm* here," my father said. "And no werewolf or vampire's gonna fuck with me. Understand?"

I nodded and sipped my soda.

"What about Frankenstein?" I said.

"What about him?" my father said.

"Could he come here?" I said.

"Fuck Frankenstein," my father said. "He better not show his face, so long as I'm around."

"And anybody else?" I said.

"Anybody else," my father said, rubbing the top of my head. "So don't worry about it, One-punch. You're safe."

I lifted my head toward my father and kissed him on the cheek, his beard rough against my lips.

"Gotta remember something, One-punch," my father said. "Remember and never forget."

"What?" I said.

"I'm here for you," my father said. "It's the only reason I'm here."

"What about Mom?" I asked.

"Her, too," my father said. "But you most of all. You're my guy. My job is to make sure nothin' happens to you. Not tonight. Not ever."

"Is that what dads do?" I said.

"I don't know about other dads," my father said. "I don't give a fuck, either. I only know about this dad. And that's what I do."

My father grabbed the 7UP bottle from my hand and put it on the table next to his empty. He stood up, me still in his arms, and moved to the small bedroom in the rear of the apartment. He put me back

312

in bed and pulled the covers to my chin. He sat down on the bed, close to me, one arm holding me through the blankets.

"You get some sleep, One-punch," my father said. "It's late."

"You going to work?" I said.

"About that time," my father said. "I'll try to be back early. Maybe we'll catch the matches tonight."

"Wrestling?" I said.

"Mom tells me Sammartino's at the Garden," my father said. "We'll eat Chinese after. Sound good to you?"

"Great," I said, a smile across my face. "I'll tell Mom when she wakes up."

"Do that," my father said, getting up from the bed.

He bent over and kissed me on the forehead and cheeks. He rubbed his open hand against the sides of my face and flattened my hair down, away from my eyes.

"I love you, One-punch," my father said.

"I love you, too, Dad," I said.

"I'm never gonna leave you, kid," my father said. "Never. Wherever you go. Whatever you do. I'm there. No matter what. I'll be there. For you. Always. You better never forget. Understand me, One-punch? Never forget."

ABOUT THE AUTHOR

LORENZO CARCATERRA is the managing editor of the CBS
television series *Top Cops*. He is currently working on
his second book.